Analytical Procedure Development by Quality by Design

Analytical Procedure Development by Quality by Design

Galla Rajitha
Ph.D, F.N.E.S.A., FAPAS
Professor,
Institute of Pharmaceutical Technology,
Sri Padmavati Mahila Visvavidyalayam,
Tirupati -517502.

Aggarapu Susmitha
M.Pharm., (Ph.D.)
Associate Professor,
Annamacharya College of Pharmacy,
Rajampet - 516126, A.P.

Gireesh Kumar Eri
M.Pharm., (Ph.D.)
Associate Professor,
Annamacharya College of Pharmacy,
Rajampet - 516126, A.P.

Pharma Med PRESS
An Imprint of BSP Books Pvt. Ltd.

PharmaMed Press
An imprint of BSP Books Pvt. Ltd
4-4-309/316, Giriraj Lane,
Sultan Bazar, Hyderabad - 500 095.

Analytical Procedure Development by Quality by Design
by **Galla Rajitha, Aggarapu Susmitha and Gireesh Kumar Eri**

Disclaimer: The authors and the publishers have taken due care to provide the authentic, reliable and up to date information related to the subject. However, neither the authors nor the publisher shall be responsible for any liability for any damage caused as a result of use of this book. The respective user must check the accuracy from other sources too.

Published by:

PharmaMed Press
An imprint of BSP Books Pvt. Ltd.
4-4-309/316, Giriraj Lane, Sultan Bazar, Hyderabad - 500 095.
Phone: 040-23445688; Fax: 91+40-23445611
e-mail: info@pharmamedpress.com
www.pharmamedpress.com/pharmamedpress.net

ISBN: 978-81-961469-5-5 (Paperback)

Preface

Welcome to the "**Analytical Procedure Development by Quality by Design.**" In the dynamic landscape of analytical chemistry, the development of robust analytical procedures is essential for ensuring the accuracy and reliability of results. This book serves as a comprehensive guide, delving into the intricacies of analytical procedure development and embracing the innovative principles of Quality by Design (QbD).

The journey through this book begins with an exploration of the fundamentals, ranging from classical methods of analysis to the advancements brought about by instrumental techniques. Chapter 1 provides an overview of the analytical procedure development process, introducing various approaches, including the Minimal and Enhanced approaches, to cater to the diverse needs of analytical scientists.

Chapter 2 navigates the reader through the realm of Analytical Quality by Design (AQbD), shedding light on its key components, strategic principles, and the regulatory perspective that shapes its implementation. The workflow of AQbD is dissected, offering insights into its terminology and emphasizing its significance in modern analytical practices.

A pivotal aspect of this book is Chapter 3, dedicated to the Design of Experiments (DoE). Here, readers will gain a comprehensive understanding of the principles, terminology, and basic techniques of DoE. Practical insights into screening designs, optimization designs, and the selection of appropriate DoE tools are provided, making this section a valuable resource for analytical scientists seeking to optimize their experimental approaches.

Chapter 4 merges the principles of QbD with analytical procedure development, offering a detailed roadmap for implementation. From the creation of a knowledge space to the establishment of an Analytical Target Profile (ATP), and from risk assessment to continuous method monitoring, this section guides the reader through every step of the AQbD lifecycle.

The subsequent Chapters, each dedicated to a specific analytical method, illustrate the application of QbD principles in UV-Visible spectrophotometric, HPLC, GC, HPTLC, and bioanalytical method development. Practical examples, ranging from estimating Trospium Chloride to quantitating Fluoxetine in human plasma, provide a hands-on understanding of AQbD application in diverse analytical scenarios.

The book is crafted to cater to the needs of students, researchers, and professionals in the field of analytical chemistry. Whether you are embarking on the journey of analytical procedure development or seeking to enhance your understanding of Quality by Design principles, this book is designed to be a reliable companion.

We extend our gratitude to the contributors whose expertise and insights have enriched this book. It is our sincere hope that this resource proves valuable in advancing your knowledge and proficiency in the fascinating realm of analytical chemistry.

Happy reading and successful analytical endeavors!

Galla Rajitha | Aggarapu Susmitha | Giressh Kumar Eri

Contents

CHAPTER 1

Analytical Procedure Development

1.1 Introduction

Drug analysis serves as the foundation for determining the properties of a product. Often, there is a time gap between a drug's introduction to the market and its inclusion in pharmacopoeias. This delay can occur due to factors such as uncertainties regarding widespread usage, reports of new toxicities, development of patient resistance, and the introduction of superior drugs by competitors. Consequently, standard analytical procedures for these drugs may not be available in pharmacopoeias, necessitating the development of new analytical methods.

The reasons for developing novel analytical methods are as follows:

1. The new drug/drug combination may not be officially recognized in any pharmacopoeias.
2. Adequate analytical procedures for the drug may not be documented in the literature due to patent regulations.
3. Analytical methods may not be available for the drug's formulation excipients.
4. Analytical methods for the drug in combination with other drugs may be lacking.
5. Analytical methods for quantifying the drug in biological fluids may not exist.
6. Existing analytical procedures may require expensive reagents and solvents and involve complex extraction and separation techniques, which can compromise reliability.

An effective analytical approach not only ensures that the drug attains the desired therapeutic quality but also functions as a means to verify purity throughout every phase of the product development process. The diagram presented below (Fig. 1.) offers a comprehensive outline of the process involved in developing an analytical method, highlighting the method goals, analytic goals, validation requirements, and documentation requirements at various stages of drug development.

Drug Development Stage	Goal		Requirements	
	Method	Analysis	Validation	Documentation
Early Development	Effective, reliable	Robustness	Not required#	GDP
Non-Clinical Studies	Rigorous	Validation elements@	Not required$	GDP
Manufacturing (Phase-I & II)	Validated	Precision & Robustness	Required*	Protocols & Reports*
Manufacturing (Phase-III & VI)	Validated	Precision & Robustness	Required	Protocols & Reports

#-unless requested by Client; @-appropriate; $- unless requested by Study director; *-by Phase-II

Fig. 1. Analytical method development process – Goals & Requirements.

ICH Q2 defines the analytical procedure as the way of performing the analysis. Its description should include in detail the steps necessary to perform each analytical test. Analytical procedures or methods are mainly intended to determine the identity, purity, and effectiveness of drug substances or pharmaceutical formulations. A variety of procedures are used for analysis, from simple weighing to advanced techniques using highly specialized instrumentation. Analytical methods are classified into two types: Classical and Instrumental.

1.2 Classical Methods of Analysis

They refer to traditional techniques that have been used for a long time in chemical analysis. These methods rely on various chemical reactions and observations to determine the composition or concentration of analytes in a sample. Some common classical methods include volumetric and gravimetric analysis.

1. **Volumetric Analysis:** Volumetric methods involve measuring the volume of a reagent solution required to react with the analyte.
   These methods are often based on stoichiometric relationships between the analyte and the reagent, allowing for the determination of the analyte's concentration.
2. **Gravimetric Analysis:** This method involves the determination of analyte concentration based on the measurement of mass.
   It often involves the formation of a precipitate, which is then weighed to calculate the analyte's concentration.

1.3 Instrumental Methods of Analysis

They involve the use of advanced instruments and equipment to measure various physical or chemical properties of analytes. These methods offer increased sensitivity, precision, and speed compared to classical methods. Some common instrumental methods include spectroscopy, chromatography and electroanalytical methods.

1. **Spectroscopy:** Spectroscopic methods involve the measurement of the interaction between analytes and electromagnetic radiation. Examples include UV-Vis spectroscopy, infrared spectroscopy (IR), atomic absorption spectroscopy (AAS), and nuclear magnetic resonance spectroscopy (NMR).
2. **Chromatography:** Chromatographic methods separate and analyze analytes based on their distribution between a stationary phase and a mobile phase. Common types of chromatography include gas chromatography (GC), liquid chromatography (LC), and high-performance liquid chromatography (HPLC).
3. **Mass Spectrometry:** Mass spectrometry measures the mass-to-charge ratio of ions produced from analytes. It provides information about the molecular weight, structure, and composition of analytes. Techniques like gas chromatography-mass spectrometry (GC-MS) and liquid chromatography-mass spectrometry (LC-MS) are widely used.
4. **Electrochemical Methods:** Electrochemical techniques measure the electrical properties of analytes. Examples include voltammetry, potentiometry, and coulometry. These methods are often used in the analysis of electroactive species or to study redox reactions.

Instrumental methods offer advantages such as high sensitivity, selectivity, and the ability to analyze complex mixtures. They often require specialized instrumentation and data analysis techniques but provide accurate and precise results.

1.4 Analytical Procedure Development

Along with Validation and transfer, analytical procedure development plays a crucial role in the process of drug development and manufacturing. Its primary objective is to establish the identity, purity, physical properties, and potency of drugs, including their bioavailability and stability. This involves ensuring that the analytical procedures are adequate for assessing drugs, particularly the active pharmaceutical ingredient (API). Analytical procedures are designed to test specific characteristics of substances against predetermined acceptance criteria. Analytical techniques widely include the estimation of physical, chemical, physicochemical, and/or biological parameters of the analyte substance. Therefore, analytical method development entails evaluating and selecting the most precise assay procedures for determining the composition of a drug. When developing a new analytical procedure, the choice of analytical instruments and methodologies should align with the intended purpose and scope of the method. The release of product into the market is decided based on the final quality control results of the finished product accompanied by other data of the batch. Chromatographic methods, including High-performance liquid chromatography (HPLC), Gas chromatography (GC), High-performance thin layer chromatography (HPTLC), and supercritical fluid chromatography (SFC), are extensively recognized for their numerous benefits compared to non-chromatographic approaches. These techniques are versatile, resilient, and demand smaller sample quantities. Through automation, they also mitigate the potential for human errors.

1.5 Approaches to Analytical Procedure Development

The foremost concern of an analytical chemist is to formulate an analytical procedure that precisely fulfills its intended purpose. This procedure's development holds immense significance within the drug development journey. Two distinct approaches, OFAT and AQbD, are employed for crafting these analytical methods. A comparative overview of these approaches' key characteristics is provided in Table 1.1. To avert potential risks or shortcomings, it is vital to implement the Quality by Design (QbD) principles as outlined in the ICH guideline Q8 (R2). Analytical Quality by Design (AQbD) refers to the process of integrating QbD principles into the development of analytical procedures. AQbD assists in establishing a dependable and cost-effective analytical protocol that can be consistently utilized throughout the product's lifecycle to facilitate regulatory adaptability. By embracing AQbD principles, a deeper comprehension of the impact of diverse factors on procedure performance can be achieved.

Table 1.1. OFAT & AQbD Key features.

Approach 1 (OFAT) **ONE FACTOR AT A TIME**	**Approach 2 (AQbD)** **ANALYTICAL QUALITY BY DESIGN**
It relies on the trial-and-error approach, as observed in OFAT studies, where a single parameter is optimized for the desired response, while keeping other variables constant.	It systematically applies scientific knowledge to method implementation, beginning with method quality, linking risk assessment in method selection, considering method parameters and outcomes, and ultimately identifying a robust and cost-effective approach.

contd...

Approach 1 (OFAT) ONE FACTOR AT A TIME	Approach 2 (AQbD) ANALYTICAL QUALITY BY DESIGN
It results in a highly robust method for the instrumental variables employed during the method development phase.	DoE is a component of AQbD, illustrating the interplay among input variables that ultimately influence the method response and outcomes.
A revalidation protocol is necessary whenever there's a method transfer or during the development of an alternative method.	It doesn't necessitate a revalidation protocol post method transfer or during alternative method development.
It carries a high risk of method failure.	It carries a low risk of method failure,
It leads to an escalation in method costs.	It diminishes the necessity and expense of method redevelopment and revalidation.
It is not a favored strategy for method development, as it fails to achieve regulatory flexibility and can lead to undesirable outcomes.	It is a recommended and preferred strategy in method development to achieve regulatory flexibility and mitigate occurrences of Out of Specification (OOS), Out of Trend (OOT), and out-of-control (OOC) results.

1.6 Minimal Approach

In recent times, method failure has become more prevalent, particularly during method transfers and within quality control departments. This trend is thought to stem from the leniency in robust test compliance granted by the ICH Q2 guidelines. In present-day procedures, chromatographic methods are the dominant choice for accurate analytics at all stages of the product life cycle. Common analytical techniques for content uniformity, assay, impurity profiling, and stability-indicating assays rely on HPLC, UPLC, or rapid resolution liquid chromatography (RRLC) methods.

In the context of chromatography, the intricate parameters involved in method development, combined with challenges like low sensitivity, selectivity, and a limited grasp of the relationship between method performance and parameters, have led to the consistent recommendation of revalidation protocols. Conversely, current practices often hinge on the implementation of analytical methods through one-Variable-at-a-time (OVAT) approaches, where only one parameter is optimized while others remain constant. This approach consistently results in a narrow robust behavior of the method concerning the instrumental variables used during the method development phase.

Analytical procedure development should encompass the following essential elements:

- Identification of the specific attributes of the drug substance or drug product that require testing through the analytical procedure.
- Selection of an appropriate analytical procedure technology and the associated instruments or suitable apparatus.
- Execution of comprehensive development studies to assess the performance characteristics of the analytical procedure. This evaluation should cover aspects like specificity, accuracy, and precision across the reportable range, including calibration model, limits at both lower and higher range extremes, and robustness.
- Establishment of a comprehensive analytical procedure description, which includes the analytical procedure control strategy. This encompasses parameter settings and system suitability criteria.

1.7 Enhanced Approach

The current analytical method development strategy, i.e., One-Variable-at-a-Time (OVAT), carries a substantial risk of method failure. It consistently necessitates revalidation protocols post method transfer or when alternative methods are developed, thereby escalating method costs.

In contrast, Analytical Quality by Design (AQbD) employs scientific insights throughout method implementation, commencing with product quality assessment that links risk assessment in method selection. It extends to the correlation between method parameters and expected outcomes, culminating in the identification of a zone for a robust and cost-effective approach. Design of Experiments (DoE) is a component of AQbD, illustrating how input variables interact to impact method responses and results.

At this juncture, adopting the AQbD paradigm as the preferred and recommended strategy for analytical procedure development offers several benefits. These include achieving regulatory flexibility, curbing occurrences of Out of Specification (OOS), Out of Trend (OOT), Out of Control (OOC), and Out of Statistical Control (OOSC) results, attaining a high level of robustness, and fostering cost-effective analytical methods.

The enhanced approach presents a systematic methodology for developing and refining knowledge about an analytical procedure. This approach incorporates additional elements alongside those described in the minimal approach. These elements include:

- Assessing sample properties and anticipated sample variability based on an understanding of the manufacturing process.
- Defining the Analytical Target Profile (ATP).
- Performing risk assessments and leveraging prior knowledge to identify analytical procedure parameters that could influence procedure performance.
- Conducting uni- or multi-variate experiments to explore the ranges and interactions of identified analytical procedure parameters.
- Defining an analytical procedure control strategy founded on a heightened comprehension of the procedure, encompassing appropriate set points and/or ranges for pertinent analytical procedure parameters to meet performance criteria.
- Outlining a lifecycle change management plan with clear definitions and reporting categories for Established Conditions (ECs), Proven Acceptable Ranges (PARs), or Method Operational Design Regions (MODRs) as applicable.
- Employing aspects of the enhanced approach during development can lead to more robust analytical procedures, a deeper grasp of the impact of analytical procedure parameters, and enhanced flexibility for lifecycle management, including broader operating ranges and a more suitable set of ECs and associated reporting categories for changes.

The enhanced approach brings several potential advantages, such as:

- Discerning the essential analytical procedure attributes for procedure performance.
- Utilizing predefined performance characteristics (e.g., within the ATP) linked to Critical Quality Attributes (CQAs) and their acceptance criteria, enabling purpose-oriented protocols for analytical procedure validation and future comparisons between current and new analytical procedures/technologies.
- Enhancing analytical procedure control, resulting in more dependable operation.
- Enabling preventive measures and facilitating ongoing improvement through greater analytical procedure knowledge.
- Reducing the effort required across the analytical procedure lifecycle.

The advantages of QbD in method development can be summarized as

- Increased understanding of method and its control.
- Moving beyond traditional ICH method validation protocols.
- Increased adaptability for analyzing Active Pharmaceutical Ingredients (API), impurities in dosage forms, stability samples, and metabolites in biological samples.
- Diminished variability in analytical attributes to enhance method robustness.
- Maintaining analytical attribute values within pharmacopoeial monograph limits, avoiding Out of Specification (OOS) thresholds.
- Streamlining method transfers to production scale.
- No need for re-validation within Method Operational Design Regions (MODRs).
- Eradicating batch failures, curtailing deviations, and minimizing resource-intensive investigations.

QbD has gained importance in the area of pharmaceutical processes like drug development, formulations, analytical procedure development and biopharmaceuticals. Table 1.2. enlist the differences between traditional method, product QbD and analytical QbD.

Table 1.2. Conventional approach vs product development QbD vs analytical QbD.

Parameter	Traditional	Product QbD	Analytical QbD
Approach	Based on empirical approach	Based on systematic approach	Based on built-in systematic approach
Quality	Quality assurance is achieved through end product testing.	Quality is instilled within the product and process through deliberate design and a scientific approach.	Robustness and reproducibility of the method are established during the method development stage.
FDA Submission	Incorporating solely data for submission.	Submitting with comprehensive product knowledge and process understanding.	Submitting with thorough product knowledge and ensuring through the Analytical Target Profile (ATP).

contd...

Parameter	Traditional	Product QbD	Analytical QbD
Specifications	They are derived from the history of batches.	They are derived from the demands of product performance	They are determined according to method performance against ATP criteria.
Process	The process is locked in and resistant to changes.	A flexible process with defined design space enables ongoing enhancements.	Method adaptability using Method Operational Design Regions (MODR) facilitates continuous improvement.
Targeted Response	Prioritizing reproducibility while disregarding variation.	Prioritizing robustness, which comprehends and manages variation.	Emphasizing a method that is both robust and cost-effective.
Advantage	Limited and simple	It serves as an extended Process Analytical Technology (PAT) tool, eliminating the necessity for end-product testing.	Substituting the requirement for revalidation while minimizing occurrences of OOT and OOS outcomes.

Applications of QbD to analytical methods

QbD can be applied to the various analytical methods such as

- Chromatographic techniques like HPLC, HPTLC, UPLC (For method development, stability-indicating studies, and determination of impurities in pharmaceuticals).
- Hyphenated techniques like LC-MS, GC-MS etc
- Advanced techniques like mass spectrometry, and capillary electrophoresis.
- Karl Fischer titration for determination of moisture content in the samples.
- Vibrational spectroscopy (IR) for identification and quantification of compounds.
- Dissolution studies by Spectroscopy techniques.

***

CHAPTER 2

Analytical Quality by Design (AQbD)

2.1 Introduction

The pharmaceutical industry has introduced the concept of quality by design (QbD) with the aim of improving robust manufacturing processes, enhancing product quality, and achieving "six sigma" manufacturing standards. The process involves a continuous loop of understanding control and capability for ongoing enhancement. "Six sigma" entails a set of methods designed to systematically enhance processes and eliminate defects with statistical precision. Over time, it has become a key aspect of various total quality management (TQM) initiatives. Numerous reports on issues like OOT, OOS, OOC, and OOSC outcomes underscore that the current pharmaceutical system is vulnerable to these challenges. Consequently, the industry is actively seeking new strategies or components to supplement or replace existing elements in the quality and risk management framework. Notably, QbD implementation has been mandated in certain countries, particularly by bodies like the European Medicines Agency (EMA) and other International Conference on Harmonization (ICH) nations. The ICH Q8 (R1) guideline defines QbD as a systematic method that starts with predefined goals, emphasizes comprehension of products and processes, and prioritizes process control and scientific basis along with quality risk management. This signifies that the attributes of product and process performance should be scientifically planned to meet precise objectives, rather than relying solely on performance tests or quality control of released batches.

In the realm of QbD, researchers showcase their comprehensive comprehension of a product throughout its development, scaling-up, and manufacturing stages. The QbD approach mandates in-depth data scrutiny and risk evaluation from the outset of involvement until the product's full commercialization. Developers are tasked with demonstrating to regulatory bodies their ability to foresee the consequences of specific risk elements and to present effective remedies for risk mitigation. QbD serves as evidence to the FDA that the manufacturing process takes reproducibility into account.

Well-defined QbD concepts in ICH guidelines

- Q8 (R1): pharmaceutical development,
- Q9: quality risk management, and
- Q10: pharmaceutical quality system.

2.2 Key Components of Quality by Design

The QbD framework includes three major components: product understanding, process understanding, and control strategy.

Product Understanding → **Process Understanding** → **Control Strategy**

- **Product Understanding:** During this phase, scientists begin to create a target product quality profile detailing the product's desired characteristics. The team gathers data and assesses known factors about all of the drug's components. They also perform risk assessments, with the objective of having solutions prepared to mitigate any risks that may arise.
- **Process Understanding:** Once the team feels confident about the product, the focus shifts to building a thorough understanding of its process. In this phase, scientists design a formulation that meets the target product quality profile. They can begin designing the manufacturing process, which includes identifying parameters and attributes to consistently produce the desired quality. Analytical and process scientists continue focusing on data gathering and risk assessment throughout this phase, ensuring they feel confident in the product and their design process.
- **Control Strategy:** The third aspect of the QbD framework addresses the identification of the various controls which influence product consistency and quality. The process development team leverages risk assessment strategies to understand which variables in the product and process can be changed without affecting the safety and efficacy of the drug.

2.3 Analytical Quality by Design (AQbD)

Adoption of Analytical Quality by Design (AQbD) aids in crafting a resilient and cost-efficient analytical approach that remains pertinent throughout a product's lifecycle. This approach enables flexibility within regulatory confines for analytical methods, granting the ability to modify method parameters within the specified design space, termed as the method operable design region (MODR). The AQbD methodology for analytical methods is relatively unexplored or minimally explored among analytical researchers up to now. In the present landscape, the pharmaceutical sector harbours numerous uncertainties and necessitates extensive dialogues regarding the incorporation of AQbD and its interconnectedness with other facets of pharmaceutical quality frameworks. Several researchers have embraced QbD principles while devising analytical methods.

Translating the QbD philosophy to analytical methods stands as a valid proposition, given the multitude of variables significantly influencing method outcomes. These variables encompass instrument configurations, sample attributes, method parameters, and the selection of calibration models. Since chromatographic techniques dominate the realm of pharmaceutical quality control, the volume of variables implicated in analytical method development mirrors that found in formulation and development protocols for dosage forms. According to the FDA, analytical methods hold a pivotal role in the QbD paradigm. Real-time release testing and non-traditional testing methodologies furnish crucial insights for in-process control and enhancement.

The execution of QbD presents an avenue for regulatory adaptability, albeit contingent on substantial robustness, product excellence, and comprehension of analytical methods. The application of QbD in the analytical realm runs in parallel with the QbD approach for products, as depicted in Table 2.1.

Table 2.1. Product QbD versus analytical QbD.

Stage	Product QbD	Analytical QbD
Stage 1	Define Quality Target Product Profile (QTPP)	Define Analytical Target Profile (ATP)
Stage 2	Critical Quality Attributes	Critical Quality Attributes
Stage 3	Risk assessment	Risk assessment
Stage 4	Design Space	Method Operable Design Region
Stage 5	Control Strategy	Control Strategy
Stage 6	Life Cycle Management	Life Cycle Management

2.4 Terminology of AQbD

Fundamental terminology in AQbD paradigms as per ICH guidelines

Analytical Target Profile (ATP)	It is the Statement defining the objectives of the method employed to drive method selection, coupled with design and development activities. It constitutes the different types of analytical methods of interest as the goal of a QbD exercise. The combination of all performance criteria required to ensure the measurement of a quality attribute is fit for the intended purpose and produces data which can be used within the required confidence.
Critical Method Parameter (CMP)	A method parameter is critical when its variability has an impact on a CAA and therefore should be monitored or controlled to ensure the method produces the desired results.
Critical Analytical Attribute (CAA)	It is a "physical, chemical, biological, or microbiological property or characteristic that must be within an appropriate limit, range, or distribution to have the required product quality". It may cover identification, assay, content uniformity, product deterioration, residual solvents, dissolution, moisture content, microbial limits, and physical properties like colour, shape, and size.
Response	The response of an analytical procedure is its ability (within a given range) to obtain a signal which is effectively related to the concentration (amount) of analyte in the sample by some known mathematical function.
Control Space	Part of the analytical design space, usually employed for setting in-house specifications within the working environment of the company.
Knowledge Space	Defined as"n" dimensional space on the basis of prior knowledge of the "n" number of CAAs and investigated CMPs.
Design Space or Method Operable Design Region (MODR)	Multidimensional part of the analytical knowledge space, enclosed by upper and lower levels of the coded variables, demonstrated to provide assurance of quality. The Multidimensional combination and interaction of method parameters and input variables which has been evaluated and verified as meeting the ATP criteria for an analytical procedure in routine use in a defined environment.
Control Strategy	A planned set of controls, derived from current method understanding, that assures method performance and its quality. The controls can include parameters and attributes related to drug substance and drug product materials and components, facility and equipment operating conditions, in-process controls, finished product specifications, and the associated methods and frequency of monitoring and control.

contd...

Proven Acceptable Range for Analytical Procedures (PAR)	A characterized range of an analytical procedure parameter for which operation within this range, while keeping other parameters constant, will result in an analytical measurement meeting relevant performance criteria.
Risk Management	A systematic process for the assessment, control, communication and review of risks to the quality of the drug (medicinal) product across the product lifecycle.
Calibration Model	A model based on analytical measurements of known samples that relates the input data to a value for the property of interest (i.e., the model output).
Model Validation	The process of determining the suitability of a model by challenging it with independent test data and comparing the results against prespecified criteria. For quantitative models, validation involves confirming the calibration model's performance with an independent dataset. For identification libraries, validation involves analysing samples not represented in the library to demonstrate the discriminative ability of the library model.

2.5 AQbD Strategic Principles

As previously mentioned, Analytical Quality by Design (AQbD) is a methodical strategy for method development that commences with predetermined objectives grounded in sound scientific principles. The incorporation of QbD principles into the development of analytical methods yields a more profound comprehension of the diverse impacts on method performance. Moreover, it simplifies the establishment of a resilient design space encompassing all the method performance targets. Within this design space, flexibility prevails concerning regulations, as modifications within this scope are not deemed changes and thus sidestep the necessity for a regulatory post-approval process. Analytical method development holds significance within the drug development continuum, warranting the implementation of quality principles outlined in ICH guideline Q8 (R2) to mitigate risks and prevent failures.

The application of QbD principles to the creation of analytical methods is recognized as Analytical Quality by Design (AQbD). Similar to the overarching QbD concept, outcomes derived from the AQbD process are presumed to be suitable and consistent, ensuring envisioned performance over the method's lifecycle. The holistic understanding amassed through this approach proves advantageous in delineating the method operable design region (MODR), an intricate multidimensional domain centered on procedure attributes influencing method performance. AQbD serves as a pivotal phase in the control strategy of the pharmaceutical industry's quality system. It encompasses the constraints, features, and associated processes of drugs and their operational milieu. Despite the longstanding existence of Current Good Manufacturing Practice (cGMP) regulations, numerous pharmaceutical companies still grapple with quality control issues. In the course of product development, emphasis on risk management underscores the significance of quality control.

Given the pharmaceutical industry's reliance on robust development processes, the AQbD concept emerges as imperative. It signifies the procedure's quality and resilience throughout its lifecycle. Implementing an advanced approach like AQbD for method development holds the potential to yield outcomes of elevated quality.

Some of the benefits of AQbD Method Development include:

- Data quality improvement.
- Increased success rate of method validation and transfer.
- Reduced need and cost to redevelop and revalidate methods.
- Support for the development of robust methods and performance monitoring.

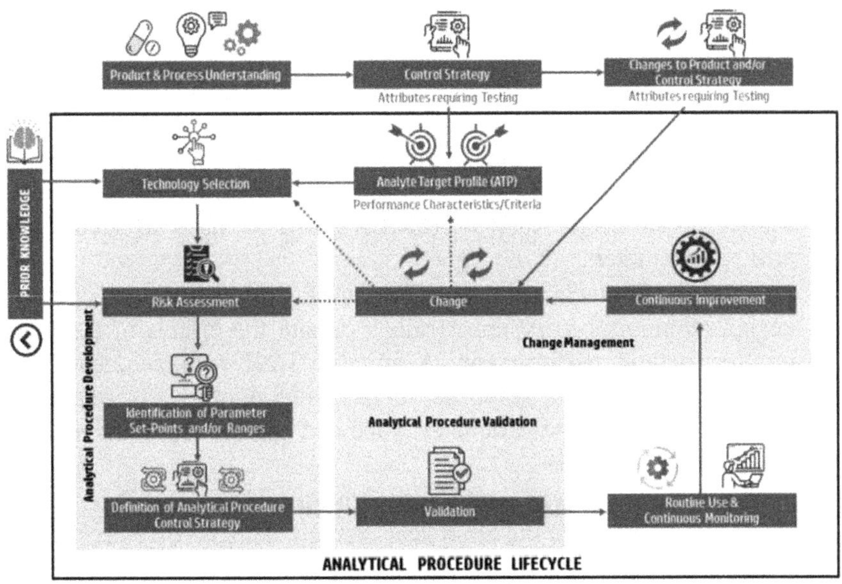

Fig. 2.1. Analytical Procedure Lifecycle.

2.6 Workflow of Analytical Quality by design

Analytical Quality by Design (AQbD) is a systematic approach used in the pharmaceutical industry to ensure the quality and reliability of analytical methods. It involves the application of scientific principles and statistical tools throughout the development and validation of analytical procedures. The general workflow of AQbD is given under.

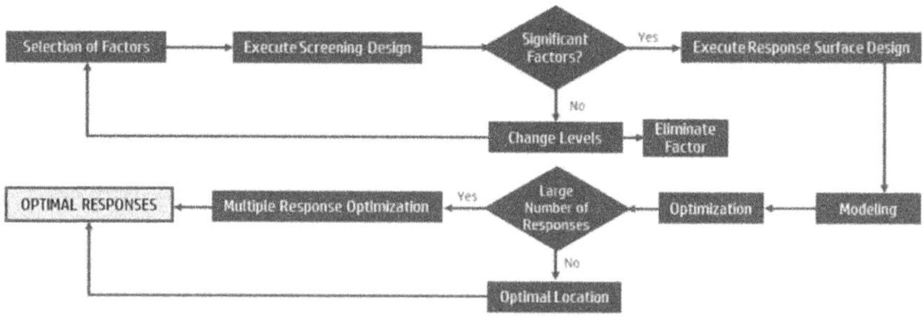

Fig 2.2. Schematic flow chart on how DoE and RSM are applied in Analytical Method Development.

- **Define the Analytical Target Profile (ATP):** The first step is to clearly define the intended purpose of the analytical method and the desired performance characteristics. This includes identifying the critical quality attributes (CQAs) of the method, such as accuracy, precision, selectivity, and robustness.
- **Identify Critical Method Parameters (CMPs):** Determine the factors that can significantly influence the CQAs. These may include instrument settings, sample preparation techniques, chromatographic conditions, and others. A risk assessment approach, such as a Failure Modes and Effects Analysis (FMEA), can be used to identify the critical parameters.
- **Design of Experiments (DoE):** Employ statistical experimental design techniques to systematically evaluate the effects of the CMPs on the method performance. A suitable DoE approach, such as a factorial design or a response surface methodology, is selected to efficiently explore the parameter space and generate a robust model of the method.
- **Method Development and Optimization:** Using the DoE results, develop and optimize the analytical method. This involves conducting experiments based on the designed matrix, collecting data on method performance, and analyzing the results to identify the optimal set of method parameters that meet the desired CQAs.

- **Method Validation:** After the method is optimized, perform a formal validation study to demonstrate its suitability for its intended use. The validation should include parameters such as accuracy, precision, linearity, specificity, robustness, and others, depending on the method's requirements. The validation protocol should be designed based on ICH (International Council for Harmonisation of Technical Requirements for Pharmaceuticals for Human Use) guidelines or other applicable regulatory guidelines.
- **Control Strategy:** Develop a control strategy to ensure the ongoing performance of the method. This may include establishing system suitability criteria, defining acceptance criteria for routine testing, implementing appropriate analytical quality control measures, and monitoring method performance over time.
- **Continuous Improvement and Lifecycle Management:** Implement a system for continuous method improvement and monitoring throughout the lifecycle of the method. This includes periodic evaluation of the method performance, trending analysis of data, and appropriate actions for method maintenance, re-optimization, or potential revalidation if required.

The specific steps and details of the workflow may vary depending on the organization, regulatory requirements, and the complexity of the analytical method being developed. AQbD provides a structured approach to method development, optimization, and control, ensuring that analytical methods are robust, reliable, and fit for their intended purpose.

2.7 Regulatory perspective on AQbD

It emphasizes the importance of AQbD in ensuring the quality, reliability, and robustness of analytical methods in the determination of drug substances and their products. Regulatory agencies, such as the U.S. Food and Drug Administration (USFDA) and the International Council for Harmonization of Technical Requirements for Pharmaceuticals for Human Use (ICH), recognize the importance of AQbD and encourage its implementation as part of a comprehensive quality system.

Through AQbD approach, the regulatory burden is less, because there are greater ranges and restrictions based on product and process understanding," Changes within these ranges and restrictions do not need to be approved in advance". In 2005 USFDA asked participants to submit chemistry, manufacturing, control (CMC) information which demonstrates QbD application as a part of NDA (New drug application). It proposed the importance of the quality of pharmaceutical products by giving Process analytical technology (PAT) as a skeleton or structure for novel or rare pharmaceutical development, manufacturing, and quality assurance. PAT is an important tool for the implementation of AQbD principles. it can be utilized to monitor and control the analytical procedure with appropriate control steps. It can also facilitate the tracking and trending of the procedure to support post-approval continual improvement efforts.

With relevance to pharmaceutical quality systems (ICH Q10), analytical methods are crucial part of the control strategy. Therefore, the execution of QbD in the development of analytical procedure as a control strategy will guarantee the predetermined performance and quality of the method. Implementation of AQbD is predicted to strengthen the concept of "right analytics at the right time" which plays a significant role in procedure development. Thus, this resonance has attracted the pharmaceutical trade to induce the concept of AQbD deliberately.

From a regulatory standpoint, there are some key perspectives on AQbD	
Risk based approach	AQbD aligns with this perspective by identifying and mitigating potential sources of variability and uncertainty that may affect the quality of analytical results. A thorough risk assessment should be conducted to prioritize CAAs and CMPs to ensure that the method's performance is adequately controlled.
Life cycle approach	AQbD promotes a lifecycle approach to analytical methods, spanning from development to routine use and continuous improvement. Regulatory agencies expect a comprehensive understanding of the method's performance over its entire lifecycle, including ongoing monitoring, maintenance, and periodic review of the method's performance. This lifecycle management approach ensures that the method remains fit for purpose and meets the required quality standards.
Design of Experiments (DoE)	AQbD encourages the use of statistical design of experiments to systematically evaluate and optimize method parameters. Regulatory agencies recognize the importance of scientifically robust experimental design and statistical analysis in demonstrating method robustness and reliability. A well-designed DoE study can provide evidence of the method's capability to withstand variations in critical parameters while maintaining the desired performance.

contd...

Analytical Control Strategy (ACS)	The regulatory perspective emphasizes the development of a well-defined ACS as a central element of AQbD. It outlines the controls, specifications, and acceptance criteria for CMPs to ensure the method's consistent performance. Regulatory agencies expect a clear demonstration of the method's capability to meet the predefined specifications, as well as a comprehensive understanding of the impact of changes in critical parameters on the method's performance.
Documentation and Reporting	Regulatory agencies require comprehensive documentation of the AQbD activities, including the rationale for design decisions, risk assessments, experimental designs, and validation protocols and results. Transparent and well-documented reporting of the AQbD studies is crucial for regulatory submissions. The documentation should provide a clear understanding of the method's development, validation, and ongoing performance evaluation.

Specific regulatory requirements may vary across regions and agencies. Manufacturers should familiarize themselves with the specific guidelines and expectations outlined by the regulatory authorities in their respective jurisdictions. However, the overarching goal is to ensure that analytical methods are developed, validated, and maintained in a manner that guarantees accurate and reliable results, and AQbD provides a systematic framework to achieve these objectives.

Specific regulatory requirements in different regions:

- **United States (U.S.) - Food and Drug Administration (FDA):**
  FDA's Guidance for Industry Q2(R1) Validation of Analytical Procedures: This guideline provides recommendations for the validation of analytical methods used in pharmaceutical drug development and manufacturing. It covers parameters such as accuracy, precision, specificity, linearity, range, and robustness.
  Current Good Manufacturing Practices (cGMPs): Under the FDA's cGMP regulations, pharmaceutical manufacturers are required to establish and follow appropriate analytical procedures to ensure the identity, strength, quality, and purity of drug products.
- **European Union (EU) - European Medicines Agency (EMA):**
  EMA's Guideline on Validation of Analytical Procedures: This guideline provides guidance on the validation of analytical methods used in the development and quality control of medicinal products. It covers parameters such as accuracy, precision, specificity, detection limit, quantification limit, linearity, range, and robustness.

contd...

European Pharmacopoeia (Ph. Eur.): The Ph. Eur. provides standards for analytical methods used in the quality control of medicinal products marketed in Europe. It includes general monographs and specific monographs for individual substances or products, specifying the required analytical procedures.

- **International - International Council for Harmonisation (ICH):**
  ICH Q2(R1) Validation of Analytical Procedures: This guideline, developed through international harmonization efforts, provides a globally accepted approach to the validation of analytical methods in the pharmaceutical industry.
  ICH Q8(R2) Pharmaceutical Development: Although not specific to analytical methods, this guideline emphasizes the importance of quality by design (QbD) principles in pharmaceutical development, which includes the application of AQbD principles to analytical methods.
- **Japan - Pharmaceuticals and Medical Devices Agency (PMDA):**
  PMDA's Guideline on Validation of Analytical Procedures: This guideline provides recommendations for the validation of analytical methods used in pharmaceutical drug development and manufacturing in Japan. It covers parameters such as accuracy, precision, specificity, detection limit, quantification limit, linearity, range, and robustness.
- **Canada - Health Canada:**
  Health Canada's Guidance for Industry: Quality (Chemistry and Manufacturing) Guidance - Validation: This guidance document outlines the expectations for validation of analytical methods in the Canadian pharmaceutical industry. It includes parameters such as accuracy, precision, specificity, detection limit, quantification limit, linearity, range, and robustness.
  Canadian Food Inspection Agency (CFIA): The CFIA provides guidelines for analytical methods used in the testing and inspection of food, agricultural products, and veterinary drugs in Canada. These guidelines cover parameters specific to each product category.
- **Australia - Therapeutic Goods Administration (TGA):**
  TGA's Guidance on Validation of Analytical Procedures: This guidance document provides recommendations for the validation of analytical methods used in the Australian pharmaceutical industry. It covers parameters such as accuracy, precision, specificity, detection limit, quantification limit, linearity, range, and robustness.
  Australian Pesticides and Veterinary Medicines Authority (APVMA): The APVMA provides guidelines for analytical methods used in the testing and registration of agricultural and veterinary chemical products in Australia.
- **United Kingdom - Medicines and Healthcare products Regulatory Agency (MHRA):**
  MHRA's Good Manufacturing Practice (GMP) Guidelines: These guidelines

contd...

include requirements for analytical procedures used in the manufacturing and quality control of pharmaceutical products. It emphasizes the need for method validation, verification, and ongoing control of analytical methods.

- **China - National Medical Products Administration (NMPA):** NMPA's Technical Guidelines for the Validation of Analytical Methods: This document provides guidance on the validation of analytical methods used in the development and quality control of pharmaceuticals in China. It covers parameters such as accuracy, precision, specificity, linearity, range, and robustness.
- **Brazil - The Brazilian Health Regulatory Agency (ANVISA):** ANVISA's Resolution RDC 166/2017: This resolution establishes the requirements for analytical methods used in the quality control of pharmaceutical products in Brazil. It includes guidelines for method validation, transfer, and ongoing verification.
- **India - Central Drugs Standard Control Organization (CDSCO):** CDSCO's Schedule Y: This document outlines the requirements for conducting clinical trials and the quality control of pharmaceutical products in India. It includes guidelines for analytical method validation and verification.

***

CHAPTER 3

Design of Experiments (DoE)

3.1 Introduction

Following the Quality by Design (QbD) concept, quality should be integrated into the product or method during pharmaceutical or analytical development. Typically, numerous input factors have the potential to impact the quality of both the product and the method. In recent times, Design of Experiments (DoE) has gained widespread usage in comprehending the multifaceted interactions of these input factors on the output responses of pharmaceutical products and analytical methods.

Traditionally, the development and optimization of pharmaceutical products and analytical methods have been carried out by analysing one factor at a time (OFAT approach). In the One-Factor-at-a-Time (OFAT) approach, a single factor is altered within a suitable range (or levels) while the remaining factors are held constant. However, this approach not only requires a substantial number of experiments but also fails to account for potential interactions between the factors, potentially undermining the effectiveness of development and optimization efforts. To address these shortcomings, DoE can yield superior outcomes with a reduced number of experiments.

It is a set of statistical tools which include screening and optimization designs. DoE constitutes a fundamental element of both pharmaceutical and analytical Quality by Design (QbD) frameworks. It furnishes both theoretical and practical guidance for implementing DoE within the context of pharmaceutical and/or analytical Quality by Design. When conducting optimization, multiple methods can be employed to establish a mathematical relationship or model.

The choice of DoE tool should be guided by factors such as the quantity of input variables, understanding of controlled parameters, and the scientific correlation between variables and outcomes. A solid grasp of statistics is pivotal for interpreting variable interactions and contributions (Xn) to responses (Yn), facilitating the identification of optimal variable levels.

The work of Sir Ronald Aylmer Fisher in the 1920s gave rise to statistical experimental design as well as the fundamental principles of DOE. Fisher, a statistician, laid the groundwork for contemporary statistical research. With the work of Box and Wilson, who applied the concept to industrial experiments and created the response surface methodology (RSM), the second phase of statistical experimental design got underway in 1951. RSM is used to determine the relationships between different process parameters and one or more responses. Despite being very contentious, Dr. Genichi Taguchi's work in the 1980s had a considerable influence on popularising statistical experimental design and highlighting its significance in terms of quality improvement.

3.2 DoE Vital Principles

DoE is defined as "a Multidimensional combination and interaction of input variables that have been demonstrated to assure the quality". It enables an analyst to systematically alter parameters in accordance with a predetermined design to get the optimum results.

DoE is a methodical and structured approach that establishes connections between input factors (x_i, independent variables) influencing one or more output responses (y_i, dependent variables) by constructing mathematical models ($y = f(x_i)$). Within the DoE framework, controlled input factors are methodically altered to assess their impact on output responses. This process facilitates the identification of crucial input factors, the determination of factors leading to optimized output responses, and the comprehension of interactions among input factors. Experimental data often involve inherent variability or noise, which can substantially impact results. Therefore, analyzing the data using suitable statistical techniques is advisable.

There are three vital principles of statistical methods in experimental design, which include,

Replication	It involves conducting the experiment multiple times to achieve a more accurate result (sample mean value) and to assess the experimental error (sample standard deviation).
Randomization	It pertains to the arbitrary sequence in which the experiment runs are carried out. This ensures that the conditions in one run do not rely on or predict the conditions in preceding or succeeding runs.
Blocking	It aims at isolating a known systematic bias effect and preventing it from obscuring the main effects. This is achieved by arranging the experiments in groups that are like one another. In this way, the sources of variability are reduced, and the precision is improved.

contd…

Advantages of DoE

- Significantly more data can be gathered using fewer resources (experiments, time, materials, etc.).
- The assessments of the impact of individual factors (variables) on the response are more accurate.
- It offers a methodical approach to assess interactions between process factors.
- It yields experimental insights across a broader region of the factor space.

3.3 DoE Basic Terminology

Before beginning the discussion on the applications of statistical tools in the optimization of analytical methods, it is pertinent to introduce and define some key terms.

Key terms of DoE

Experimental domain	It is the experimental field that must be investigated. It is defined by the minimum and maximum limits of the experimental variables studied.
Experimental runs or trials	Experiments conducted according to the selected experimental design under defined conditions, i.e., combinations of factors at varied levels for each of the CAAs to be measured.
Levels of a variable	These are distinct values of a variable at which experiments need to be conducted. For instance, in optimizing a spectrophotometric method, the pH variable can be examined at five levels: 4, 5, 6, 7, and 8.
Input factors or independent variables	They are experimental variables that can be changed independently of each other. Typical independent variables comprise the wavelength, scan speed (UV spectrophotometry), buffer pH, column temperature, flow rate, etc (HPLC).
Output factors or dependent variables	These are the observed outcomes obtained from experiments. Common responses include analytical signals (such as absorbance, net emission intensity, and electrical signal), analyte recovery, chromatographic peak resolution, residual carbon percentage, final acidity, and more.
Residual	It is the disparity between calculated and experimental results for a specific set of conditions. An effective mathematical model aligned with experimental data should yield minimal residual values.
Optimization	Implementation of systematic approaches to achieving"the best" combination of method characteristics under a given set of conditions.

3.4 DoE Basic Techniques

Several DOE techniques are available to the experimental designer. However, there is no best choice in the optimization of method conditions. Choosing the appropriate DOE technique depends on the nature of the problem at hand and the experimentation's objectives. It necessitates taking into account multiple factors, including clearly defined goals, the quantity of input factors and interactions under investigation, and the statistical soundness and efficiency of each design option. Fig. 3.1. depicts the Classification & Graphical representation of various experimental designs. In order to provide a better understanding of DoE application, it is necessary to know more about various experimental designs, which may be divided into two types: screening designs and optimization designs.

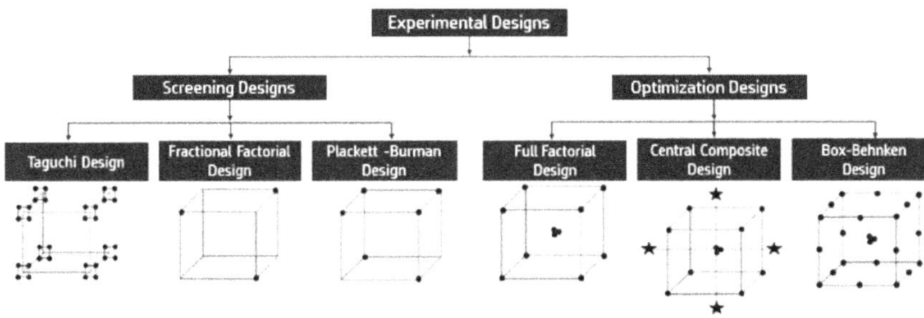

Fig. 3.1. Classification & Graphical depiction of Experimental Designs

3.5 Screening Designs

They are often used in the first step of DoE to select the most important input factors and reject the insignificant ones. Screening designs are efficient tools for identifying significant main effects of factors. The term "screening" signifies an experimental plan aimed at uncovering a handful of influential factors from a pool of many potential ones. Low-resolution designs (III or IV), such as fractional factorial design (FrFD), Plackett-Burman design, and Taguchi design, are mainly employed for screening purposes. These designs involve a limited number of experimental runs, allowing for efficient use of time and resources. Detailed explanations of each of the aforementioned screening designs are provided below.

They facilitate the exploration of numerous input factors with a reduced number of experiments. Nevertheless, they do come with certain limitations that need to be considered to ensure a comprehensive understanding of the effects of input factors on output responses. A Comparative summary of screening designs is depicted in Table 3.1.

Taguchi design

Genichi Taguchi, a Japanese engineer, created the Taguchi design for examining numerous variables with different factor levels based on the orthogonal array (OA), which offers a collection of trials that are properly balanced (minimum) and serve as objective functions for optimisation. This design proposed three steps (concept design, parameter design and tolerance design) to achieve a rugged optimization design. Without the need for any centre point runs, it starts with a minimum of three factors and generates four experimental runs at two levels. This approach makes use of mixed-level, two-, and three-level FrFDs.

To illustrate, consider a process involving 8 variables, each with 3 possible states. Testing all variables using conventional methods would require 6561 (3^8) experiments. However, by leveraging Taguchi's orthogonal arrays, only 18 experiments are needed, which is less than 3% of the initial experiment count. This approach enables the identification of critical parameters that significantly impact performance characteristics. Consequently, further experimentation can be focused on these influential parameters, while those with minimal impact can be disregarded.

Advantages:

- Allows the analysis of many different parameters without a prohibitively high amount of experimentation.
- It emphasizes a mean performance characteristic value close to the target value rather than a value within certain specification limits.
- It offers a straightforward and uncomplicated application to various engineering scenarios, rendering it a potent and user-friendly tool.
- It serves as a rapid means to narrow down the scope of research endeavours or detect issues within a manufacturing process using existing data.

Disadvantages:

- Results obtained are only relative and do not exactly indicate which parameter has the highest effect on the performance characteristic value.
- since orthogonal arrays do not test all variable combinations, this method should not be used with all relationships between all variables needed.

Fractionate factorial design (FrFD)

It falls under the category of factorial designs and is commonly employed for factor screening. FrFDs are denoted as X^{k-p}, where X represents the number of levels per factor investigated, k signifies the count of factors under examination, and p indicates the fraction of the full factorial design used. In formal terms, p indicates the number of generators or assignments confounding effects or interactions that cannot be independently estimated.For instance, a 2^{5-2} design constitutes a quarter of a two-level, five-factor factorial design, requiring only 8 runs instead of the complete 32 runs. FFDs are particularly suitable when the number of factors in an experiment range between 3 and 7. These designs typically utilize two factor levels for screening purposes. The designation +1 indicates a high level, while -1 signifies a low level. Additionally, a three-level factor with an intermediate coded value of 0 can also be incorporated for augmentation when the screening designs require it.

Advantages

- Most frequently utilised for screening purpose, as it allows for the evaluation of a large number of input factors with a minimal number of tests.

Disadvantages

- More attention should be paid to the estimation of main effects and interaction effects, because some of them are aliased (or confounded).

Plackett-Burman designs

In 1946, this design was developed by two statisticians R.L. Plackett and J.P. Burman that gives information on the single factor and not on the interactions. They are a specialized form of two-level fractionate factorial designs, specifically of resolution III. They enable the exploration of up to N-1 input factors using N experiments, where N must be a multiple of 4.

Starting with a minimum of 11 factors, Plackett-Burman designs generate 12 experimental runs without necessitating any center point runs. These designs are also available for 20-run, 24-run, and 28-run configurations, as well as higher numbers. With a 20-run design, it's feasible to screen up to 19 factors, up to 23 factors in a 24-run design, and up to 27 factors in a 28-run design. It is also called "saturated design" because the number of experiments is equal to the number of parameters in the first-order RSM model, and the degree of freedom of such a design is equal to zero.

Advantages

- It is most popular because it is both economical and efficient.

Disadvantages

- It does not consider any two-factor interaction effect i. e. itš not possible to evaluate the effects of the interaction terms.

Table: 3.1. Comparative summary of screening designs.

S. No	Design	Level	No. of Experiments	Factors	Orthogonality	Rotatability
1.	Taguchi design	N	2^N	N	Yes	No
2.	FrFD	2	2^{k-p} Res	K>4	Yes	Yes
3.	PBD	2	N	<N-1	Yes	Yes

Model building for screening

The general approach to the statistical analysis of screening design for every response being analysed includes

- estimating factor effects and examining their signs and magnitudes,
- building an initial model for the response
- performing statistical tests,
- refining the model removing any non-significant variable from the initial model, and
- analysing residuals in order to check model adequacy and assumptions.

The effect of each factor on each response is estimated as the difference between the average response of the experiments with positive signs and the average response of the experiments with Negative signs. An alternative to determine the factor effect is estimating the coefficients of the model.

3.6 Optimization Designs

Optimization stands as a subsequent step in experimental design, wherein optimal conditions for conducting an experiment are established. Factors deemed significant through screening designs undergo further optimization using these specific designs. Commonly referred to as response surface designs, they play a crucial role in optimizing factors identified through risk assessment and/or screening studies. These designs necessitate sufficient experimental runs to ascertain both main and interaction effects of the factors. Response surface designs can be categorized into symmetrical and asymmetrical designs.

Symmetrical designs, which cover the experimental domain around the center point to estimate experimental errors, encompass variations like full factorial design, central composite design (CCD), Box-Behnken design (BBD), and Doehlert design. On the other hand, asymmetrical designs, like D-optimal design, adopt an asymmetrical shape when investigating an uneven experimental domain. Table. 3.3. describes the 3-factor comparison between

FFD, CCD and BBD with three levels designated as '+', '–', '0' and the star point 'α' in CCD. Where α' represents factors at different levels.

A significant drawback of screening designs is their constraint to modeling only 1st order (linear) response surfaces due to the two-level setup for each input factor. In contrast, optimization designs incorporate 3 to 5 levels for each input factor, enabling the modeling of 2nd order (quadratic) response surfaces. However, due to the increased number of experiments required, they are usually used to study a reduced number of input factors. A comparative summary of optimization designs is depicted in Table 3.2.

Full Factorial Designs (FFDs)

In comparison to experiments that focus on a single factor or parameter, factorial experiments provide numerous benefits. Notably, they permit the assessment of a factor's effects across various levels of other factors. This results in conclusions that remain applicable across a spectrum of experimental conditions. Moreover, factorial experiments expedite the identification of optimal conditions more efficiently than One-Factor-at-a-Time (OFAT) experiments.

Two-level full factorial design

This design holds the distinction of being both an effective screening and optimization tool, enabling the estimation of main effects and interactions of input factors on output responses. The requisite number of experiments for a two-level full factorial design can be computed as 2^k, where k denotes the count of input factors under investigation. Below, matrices for two-level full factorial designs encompassing 2, 3, and 4 input factors are displayed.

Three-level full factorial design

These designs are commonly employed when studying two or three input factors, primarily due to the escalated number of experiments they necessitate. The required number of experiments can be computed as 3^k, where k represents the count of input factors under scrutiny. As an instance, a three-level full factorial design examining three input factors mandates $3^3 = 27$ experiments. A three-dimensional spatial illustration of a factorial design is depicted in Figure 3.1.

Advantages

allow additional factors to be studied without additional cost.

Disadvantages

They rely on the large number of experiments required, when compared to FrFD and PBD.

Central composite designs (CCD)

Developed by Box and Wilson in 1951, this design combines a two-level factorial design with a star design and center points (G. Box & Wilson, 1951). The experimental number of CCD is as per 2^k+2k+C where C is the replicate number of centre points and k is the factor number. They are among the most extensively employed optimization designs. They utilize 5 levels for each input factor, requiring a smaller number of experiments. CCD employs a second-order (quadratic) model for the response variable without employing a complete three-level factorial experiment. A three-dimensional spatial depiction of CCD for three input factors is presented in Figure 3.1. This design encompasses factorial design points, axial points, and the center point. The CCD matrix is additionally provided in Table 3.2, encompassing factorial design points (experiments 1-8), axial points (experiments 9-14), and the central point (experiments 15-20, including 6 replicas).

Advantages

- Its major advantage over factorial design is, it provides similar results with a short number of experiments.
- It can be employed when factorial designs detect the presence of curvature in the data.

Disadvantages

- Depending upon the Design, the squared terms in the model will not be orthogonal to each other.
- Inability to estimate individual interaction terms, i.e., linear by quadratic or quadratic by quadratic.

Box-Behnken design (BBD)

Developed by Box and Behnken in 1960 (G. E. Box & Behnken, 1960), this design involves three levels and is suitable for problems featuring three or more factors. This design necessitates $2k (k-1) + C$, here k is factor numbers and C is the central point number. In this design, the treatment combinations are at the midpoints of the edges of the process space and at the centre. These designs are rotatable (or near rotatable) and require three levels of each factor.

It is a special type of three-level FrFD, which allows modeling 1st and 2nd order response surfaces. It is possible to see all points used in BBD. The simplest model which can be adjusted is based on a linear function.

Advantages

- more cost-effective than 3-level FFD, particularly for large number of input factors.

Disadvantages

- limited capability for orthogonal blocking compared with the CCD.

Table: 3.2. Comparative summary of Optimisation designs.

S. No	Design	Level	No. of Experiments	Factors	Orthogonality	Rotatability
1.	3- level FFD	3	3^k	$2<K<3$	Yes	No
2.	CCD	5	$2^k + 2k + C$	$2K<5$	Yes/No	Yes/No
3.	BBD	2	$2k\,(k-1) + C$	$3<K<3$	Yes	Yes

Table: 3.3. Design matrix of 3-level FFD, CCD, and BBD for input factors (X_1, X_2, and X_3).

Runs	3-level FFD (3^3)			CCD			BBD		
	X_1	X_2	X_3	X_1	X_2	X_3	X_1	X_2	X_3
1	-	-	-	+	+	+	-	-	0
2	-	-	0	+	+	-	+	-	0
3	-	-	+	+	-	-	-	+	0
4	-	0	-	-	-	+	+	+	0
5	-	0	0	-	+	+	-	0	-
6	-	0	+	-	+	-	+	0	-
7	-	+	-	+	-	+	-	0	+
8	-	+	0	-	-	-	+	0	+
9	-	+	+	0	0	0	0	-	-
10	0	-	-	0	0	0	0	+	-
11	0	-	0	0	0	0	0	-	+
12	0	-	+	0	0	0	0	+	+
13	0	0	-	0	0	0	0	0	0
14	0	0	0	0	0	0	0	0	0
15	0	0	+	$-\alpha$	0	0	0	0	0
16	0	+	-	$+\alpha$	0	0	0	0	0
17	0	+	0	0	$-\alpha$	0	0	0	0
18	0	+	+	0	$+\alpha$	0			
19	+	-	-	0	0	$-\alpha$			
20	+	-	0	0	0	$+\alpha$			
21	+	-	+						
22	+	0	-						
23	+	0	0						
24	+	0	+						
25	+	+	-						
26	+	+	0						
27	+	+	+						

3.7 Other Optimization Designs

Doehlert Design

It is a practical and economical alternative in relation to other second-order experimental matrices and was developed by Doehlert, It characterizes a circular domain for two variables, a spherical domain for three variables, and a hyper-spherical domain for more than three variables, emphasizing the uniform distribution of studied variables within the experimental domain. While its matrices lack rotatability like previous designs, it offers several benefits. These include demanding fewer experimental points for implementation, along with displaying high efficiency compared to CCD and BBD.

Other characteristics:

- Requires an experiment count defined by $N = k^2 + k + cp$, where k signifies the factor count and (cp) denotes the replicate count of the central point.
- Investigates each variable at distinct levels, a vital feature when certain variables are constrained due to factors like cost or instrumental limitations, or when examining variables at varied levels is intriguing.
- Ensures uniform intervals between its levels.
- Facilitates the relocation of the experimental matrix to different regions through the use of adjacent points from previous setups.

Mixture design

In mixture experiments, the independent factors represent proportions of various components within a blend. Conversely, the requirement that these proportions must sum up to 100% adds complexity to both the design and analysis of such experiments.

Mixture experiments come in various types, including simplex-lattice designs, simplex-centroid designs, and optimal designs. Optimal designs are particularly prevalent for factor optimization. Within the realm of optimal designs, different types exist such as D-optimal, I-optimal, and A-optimal. These designs employ three levels for each chosen factor and are widely employed for factor optimization investigations. Among these, the D-optimal design has garnered significant attention over time.

D-optimal design

This design proves valuable when dealing with a substantial number of chosen experiments. It ensures a reduced experiment count while maintaining the precision equivalent to a full design. The design matrix furnishes significance, lack of fit, coefficient information, and P-values, contributing to a comprehensive comprehension of the results.

Traditional experimental designs (FFD, FrFD, CCD, BBD) are appropriate for calibrating linear models in experimental settings where factors are relatively unconstrained in the region of interest. In some cases, however, models are necessarily nonlinear. In other cases, certain treatments (combinations of factor levels) may be expensive or infeasible to measure. D-optimal designs are model-specific designs that address the limitations of traditional designs.

3.8 Software Employed in Experimental Design

Experimental design software listed in Table 3.4. plays a crucial role in planning, executing, and analyzing experiments efficiently and effectively. These software packages provide a range of features and capabilities for experimental design and analysis, catering to different user preferences and needs. The choice of software often depends on factors such as the specific needs of the study, complexity of the experiment, available resources, and the level of statistical expertise of the user.

Key features of the software used in experimental design

Design Capabilities	provides a range of design options to suit different experimental scenarios. This includes factorial designs, response surface designs, mixture designs, and more. The software enables users to select the appropriate design based on the specific objectives of their experiment.
Statistical Analysis	One of the primary functions is to perform statistical analysis on the data generated from the experiment. The software includes a suite of statistical tools and techniques to analyze factors, interactions, and response variables. It enables users to determine the significance of effects, optimize conditions, and generate predictive models.
Visualization	It offers graphical visualization capabilities to help users understand and interpret the experimental results. Graphical displays, such as scatter plots, contour plots, and surface plots, aid in visualizing the relationships between factors and responses. Visualization tools assist in identifying patterns, trends, and optimal regions within the design space.
Customization and Flexibility	Many software packages provide flexibility and customization options. Users can tailor the designs to their specific needs, add constraints, and modify the experimental setup accordingly. This enables researchers to adapt the software to various experimental scenarios and accommodate complex experimental requirements.

contd…

User-Friendly Interface	They offer user-friendly interfaces with drag-and-drop functionality, intuitive menus, and interactive features. This makes it easier for researchers and practitioners, even those without extensive statistical training, to use the software effectively. A user-friendly interface facilitates seamless experiment design, execution, and analysis.
Integration with Other Tools	It often integrates with other statistical and data analysis tools, allowing users to import and export data from various sources. This integration enables seamless workflows and enhances data management capabilities. Users can leverage the software's analytical power in conjunction with other data analysis tools to gain deeper insights and improve decision-making.
Documentation and Reporting	They usually provide options for generating comprehensive reports and documentation of the experimental design and results. This documentation aids in reproducibility, regulatory compliance, and sharing results with stakeholders. It allows researchers to communicate their findings effectively and present clear evidence of the experimental design and its outcomes.

It is important to select experimental design software based on the specific requirements of the experiment, the complexity of the design, the level of statistical expertise available, and the software's compatibility with other data analysis tools used in the organization.

Table: 3.4. Commonly employed software packages in experimental design.

S. No	Software	Company and web link
Software specialized in experimental design		
1.	Design-Expert	Stat-Ease Inc., www.statease.com/dx11.html
2.	Fusion Pro	S-Matrix Corporation, www.smatrix.com/fusion_pro.html
3.	Modde	Umetrics, https://umetrics.com/product/modde-pro
4.	Unscrambler	Camo AS, www.camo.com/p2_tuf.htm
5.	DOE++	Reliasoft Corporation, https://www.reliasoft.com
6.	DOE	wisdom Launsby Consulting, www.launsby.com/BookIM.html
7.	DOEpack	Productivity-Quality Systems, Inc., pqsystems.com
Statistical software with experimental design compatibility		
8.	SPSS	IBM, www.ibm.com
9.	JMP	SAS Institute Inc., sas.com/en_us/home.html
10.	Minitab	Minitab Inc., www.minitab.com/
11.	STATISTICA	StatSoft, www.statsoft.com/
12.	Matlab	The Mathworks Inc., www.mathworks.com/
13.	Origin	Microcal Software, www.originlab.com
14.	Statgraphics	Startpoint Technologies, www.statgraphics.com/

3.9 Selection of DOE Tools

Throughout the optimization process, various approaches can be employed to establish a mathematical relationship (model). The selection of a Design of Experiments (DoE) tool hinges on factors like the number of input variables, knowledge of controlled parameters, and the scientific link between results and variables (if applicable). Statistical acumen plays a pivotal role in comprehending interactions and variable contributions (Xn) in method responses (Yn), guiding the selection of variables at optimal levels. For instance, when measuring the effects of all input variables and their interactions, a factorial design can be utilized, followed by optimization with Response Surface Methodology (RSM). The Taguchi method offers a lower number of experimental runs compared to factorial designs (e.g., 50%, 25%, etc.), albeit with confounded interactions that require resolution. In cases involving a substantial number of input variables without interaction effects, Plackett-Burman Design (PBD) can be a suitable choice. A typical selection of DoE techniques is shown in Table 3.5.

Table: 3.5. Selection of DOE tools in analytical quality by design.

Design	Considerations
Factorial Design	These designs allow us to assess the main effects of individual variables as well as potential interactions between them. They are suitable to understand the main effects and interactions of a moderate number of variables.
Fractional Factorial Designs	These are useful when the number of variables is large, and evaluating all possible combinations becomes impractical. These designs allow us to evaluate a fraction of the total combinations, while still providing information about the main effects and some interaction effects. Fractional factorial designs are often used for screening experiments to identify the most influential factors.
Response Surface Methodology (RSM)	RSM is used to model and optimize complex relationships between variables and responses. It involves conducting multiple experiments at different levels of the variables and fitting a response surface model to predict the optimal combination of variables for achieving desired responses. RSM is suitable in case of a smaller number of variables and to optimize the response of the analytical method.
Central Composite Designs (CCD)	CCD is an extension of the factorial design that includes additional runs at the center point and axial points to allow for the estimation of curvature in the response surface. CCD is commonly used when non-linear relationships between variables and responses are expected.

contd...

Plackett-Burman Designs (PBD)	These are economical screening designs that allow for the identification of main effects of variables when the number of factors is large. These designs require fewer runs compared to factorial or fractional factorial designs but do not provide information about interaction effects.
Taguchi Designs	These, specifically the orthogonal arrays, are useful when you want to optimize a process or method under conditions of noise or variability. Taguchi methods focus on robustness and aim to minimize the effects of noise factors on the response.

When selecting DOE tools for AQbD based on the number of variables:

- Few variables (up to a moderate number): Consider using Factorial Designs to evaluate the main effects and interactions between variables.
- Large number of variables: Fractional Factorial Designs are useful for screening experiments, allowing you to evaluate a fraction of the total combinations.

When considering the usage in AQbD:

- Optimizing complex relationships: Response Surface Methodology (RSM) helps model and optimize the relationship between variables and responses.
- Non-linear relationships: Central Composite Designs (CCD) account for curvature in the response surface.
- Screening experiments: Plackett-Burman Designs are cost-effective and identify main effects of variables.
- Robustness against noise: Taguchi Designs, particularly orthogonal arrays, focus on minimizing the effects of noise factors on the response.

3.10 Basic Approach to a Design of Experiments

Design of Experiments (DoE) is a systematic and efficient approach for planning and conducting experiments to gather data and draw valid conclusions. The following are the basic steps involved in designing an experiment using the DoE approach:

1. Define the problem(s)
2. Determine objective(s)
3. Brainstorm
4. Design experiments
5. Conduct experiments and collect data
6. Analyze data
7. Interpret results
8. Verify predicted results

These steps provide a systematic approach to designing and conducting experiments, analyzing data, and drawing conclusions to address the defined problem(s) and achieve the desired objectives.

Step 1: Define the problem(s)

In the context of DoE, the first step is to clearly define the problem(s) or objective(s) which is to be addressed through the experiment. This step is crucial as it sets the foundation for the entire DoE process. Defining the problem involves understanding the specific issue or area that needs improvement, optimization, or investigation. It requires a clear understanding of the aim to be achieved or learnt from the experiment. By defining the problem(s), one can establish a clear focus and purpose for conducting the DoE.

In the example of the drug assay, the problem could be related to the accuracy and precision of the assay method. Perhaps there is a concern about inconsistent or inaccurate results, or there may be a need to streamline and optimize the assay process. By defining the problem, the scope of the experiment can be narrowed down and a specific target for improvement can be provided.

To define the problem(s) effectively, the following steps can be considered:

Identify the specific area of concern

↓

Gather relevant information

↓

Engage with stakeholders

↓

Formulate clear objectives

By effectively defining the problem(s), one can establish a solid foundation for the subsequent steps in the DoE process. This step ensures that the experiment is focused, relevant, and aligned with the goals of the organization or project. It helps to identify the key factors and variables that need to be investigated, laying the groundwork for the subsequent steps of the DoE, such as identifying factors, designing experiments, and analyzing data.

Step 2: Determine objective(s)

After defining the problem(s) in Step 1, the next step in conducting a DoE is to determine the objective(s) of the experiment. This step involves identifying the specific goals or outcomes one wants to achieve through the DoE process. Determining the objective(s) helps to provide clarity and focus to the experiment, guiding the selection of factors, design of experiments, and analysis of data. It allows the analyst to align the experiment with the desired outcomes and ensure that the results obtained are meaningful and relevant.

To determine the objective(s) effectively, the following can be considered:

Reflect on the defined problem(s)

↓

Identify measurable goals

↓

Prioritize objectives

↓

Consider constraints and trade-offs

By determining the objective(s) of the DoE, one can set a clear direction for the experiment and enable the subsequent steps to be conducted with purpose. The objectives serve as benchmarks for evaluating the success of the experiment and guide decision-making throughout the DoE process.

For example, in the drug assay context, the objective could be to determine the optimal combination of factors (such as pH, temperature, and reaction time) that maximize the accuracy and precision of the assay. Additionally, the objective could involve streamlining the assay process to reduce time and resources required. These objectives help guide the selection of factors, design of experiments, and subsequent analysis to achieve the desired outcomes. The determined objective(s) should be documented clearly, as they will shape the subsequent steps and serve as a reference point for the interpretation and evaluation of the experiment's results.

Step 3: Brainstorm

Once the problem(s) are defined and the objective(s) are determined in Steps 1 and 2 of the DoE process, the next step is to conduct a brainstorming session. Brainstorming involves generating a list of potential factors that may influence the response variable or outcome of interest.

Brainstorming is an important step as it allows one to tap into the collective knowledge and expertise of a group, fostering creativity and generating diverse ideas. It helps to identify relevant factors that should be considered in the experimental design and subsequent analysis.

One can conduct a productive brainstorming session by:

Assemble a diverse group
↓
Clearly communicate the problem and objective
↓
Encourage open discussion
↓
Generate a list of factors
↓
Stimulate creativity
↓
Encourage independent thinking
↓
Evaluate and refine the list

By conducting a thorough brainstorming session, one can gather a comprehensive list of factors that may influence the response variable or outcome of interest. This list forms the basis for the subsequent steps of the DoE process, such as designing the experiments and selecting the appropriate factors and their levels.

For example, in the drug assay context, factors identified during the brainstorming session could include pH, temperature, concentration of reagents, reaction time, sample preparation techniques, or even factors related to the equipment used for the assay. These factors will be further analyzed and selected in the subsequent steps to determine their effects on the assay performance. All the factors generated during the brainstorming session should be documented, as they will influence the experimental design and subsequent analysis.

Step 4: Design experiments

After conducting the brainstorming session and identifying the potential factors that may influence the outcome of interest, the next step in the DoE process is to design the experiments. This step involves selecting an appropriate experimental design and determining the number of experimental runs needed.

Designing the experiments is crucial as it allows one to systematically explore the effects of the identified factors and their interactions on the response variable. A well-designed experiment ensures efficient data collection and facilitates accurate analysis of the results.

One can design the experiments effectively by:

Select an appropriate experimental design

↓

Determine the number of experimental runs

↓

Define the factor levels

↓

Randomize the experimental runs

↓

Consider blocking or stratification

↓

Plan for control or baseline runs

↓

Document the experimental design

By designing the experiments effectively, one can ensure a structured and systematic approach to gathering data and investigating the effects of the factors on the response variable. The design allows us to efficiently explore the factor space and obtain meaningful results.

In the drug assay example, the experimental design could involve selecting factor levels for pH, temperature, and reaction time, based on the identified factors. For instance, a full factorial design may be chosen, where each factor is tested at multiple levels. The number of experimental runs would depend on the design and could range from a few runs to a larger number, depending on the available resources and objectives. The chosen design should be carefully considered and tailored to the specific problem and objectives of DoE.

Step 5: Conduct experiments and collect data

After designing the experiments in Step 4 of the DoE process, the next step is to actually conduct the experiments and collect the relevant data. This step involves implementing the planned experimental conditions, following the design parameters, and recording the observations or measurements of the response variable.

One can effectively conduct the experiments and collect the data by:

Prepare the experimental setup

↓

Implement the factor settings

↓

Conduct the experimental runs

↓

Collect data on the response variable

↓

Document experimental details

↓

Quality control and validation

↓

Adhere to safety protocols

By conducting the experiments carefully and collecting the data systematically, one can ensure the reliability and quality of the data. This data serves as the foundation for subsequent analysis and interpretation in the DoE process.

In the drug assay example, the analyst would implement the designed experimental conditions, such as applying the predetermined pH, temperature, and reaction time to each assay run. The established assay protocol should be followed, the drug concentrations or related parameters should be carefully measured, and the data for each experimental run should be recorded. Accuracy, consistency, and attention should be maintained to detail during the data collection process. Accurate and reliable data is essential for obtaining meaningful insights and drawing valid conclusions from the subsequent data analysis steps.

Step 6: Analyze data

After conducting the experiments and collecting the data in Step 5 of the Design of Experiments (DoE) process, the next step is to analyze the data. Data analysis involves applying appropriate statistical techniques to examine the relationships between the factors and the response variable, determine the significance of these relationships, and draw meaningful conclusions from the results.

One can effectively analyze the data by:

Organize and prepare the data

↓

Perform exploratory data analysis

↓

Apply statistical techniques

↓

Assess main effects and interactions

↓

Interpret the results

↓

Draw conclusions & make recommendations

↓

Document and report the findings

By conducting a thorough and systematic data analysis, one can extract meaningful insights from the collected data, understand the relationships between factors and the response variable, and draw valid conclusions. The data analysis step is crucial for identifying the key factors influencing the outcome and guiding decision-making for process improvement or optimization.

In the drug assay example, analyst would analyze the collected data to determine the effects of factors such as pH, temperature, and reaction time on the drug concentration. Analyst would use statistical techniques like ANOVA or regression analysis to assess the significance of these effects and understand their magnitude. This analysis helps identify the factors that significantly impact the assay performance and guide recommendations for optimizing the assay conditions.

The data analysis process and findings should be documented thoroughly. Clear documentation ensures transparency, reproducibility, and enables others to understand and validate the analysis performed.

Step 7: Interpret results

After analyzing the data in Step 6 of the DoE process, the next step is to interpret the results derived from the data analysis. Interpretation involves understanding the implications of the findings and drawing meaningful conclusions about the effects of factors on the response variable.

One can effectively interpret the results by:

Examine significant factors

↓

Consider effect sizes

↓

Assess interactions

↓

Understand the direction of effects

↓

Consider limitations and assumptions

↓

Relate findings to the objective(s)

↓

Communicate implications & recommendations

By effectively interpreting the results, one can gain a deeper understanding of the relationships between factors and the response variable. This understanding informs decision-making and allows for informed actions to be taken to optimize processes, improve outcomes, or address the defined problem(s).

In the drug assay example, analyst would interpret the results of the data analysis, considering factors such as pH, temperature, and reaction time, and their effects on the drug concentration.

Analyst would determine the significance and magnitude of these effects and identify any interactions. Based on the interpretation, analyst would conclude which factors have a substantial impact on the assay performance and provide recommendations for optimizing the assay conditions.

The interpretation process and findings should be documented thoroughly. Clear documentation ensures transparency, allows for replication of the interpretation, and supports the validation of the conclusions drawn.

Step 8: Verify predicted results

After interpreting the results in Step 7 of the DoE process, the next step is to verify the predicted results. This step involves testing the validity of the statistical model developed during the data analysis by comparing the predicted results with the actual experimental outcomes.

One can effectively verify the predicted results by:

Utilize the statistical model

↓

Determine the predicted factor settings

↓

Conduct additional experiments

↓

Compare predicted and actual results

↓

Evaluate the accuracy of predictions

↓

Validate the statistical model

↓

Iterate and refine if necessary

↓

Finalize the statistical model

By verifying the predicted results, one can assess the accuracy and reliability of the statistical model developed during the data analysis phase. This verification step helps ensure that the model can effectively predict outcomes for untested factor combinations and can guide decision-making and optimization efforts.

In the drug assay example, analyst would use the statistical model derived from the data analysis to predict the drug concentrations for untested factor combinations. Then, analyst would conduct additional experiments using these predicted factor settings and compare the actual drug concentrations with the predicted values. If the predicted and actual results are in good agreement, it confirms the validity of the model for predicting drug concentrations under different assay conditions. The verification process and outcomes should be documented thoroughly.

***

CHAPTER 4

Implementation of QbD in Analytical Procedure Development

4.1 Introduction

QbD is the heart of modern pharmaceutical and analytical method development. The implementation of QbD provides a cost-efficient approach to delivering high-quality medicines to patients. QbD gained importance in the pharmaceutical industry and is supported by several regulatory authorities like ICH, FDA, EU and accepts new drug applications (NDA) with an AQbD-based approach. There is an increasing demand to analyse samples with a wide range of polarities in a variety of applications, including environmental analysis, biomarker discovery and proteomics.

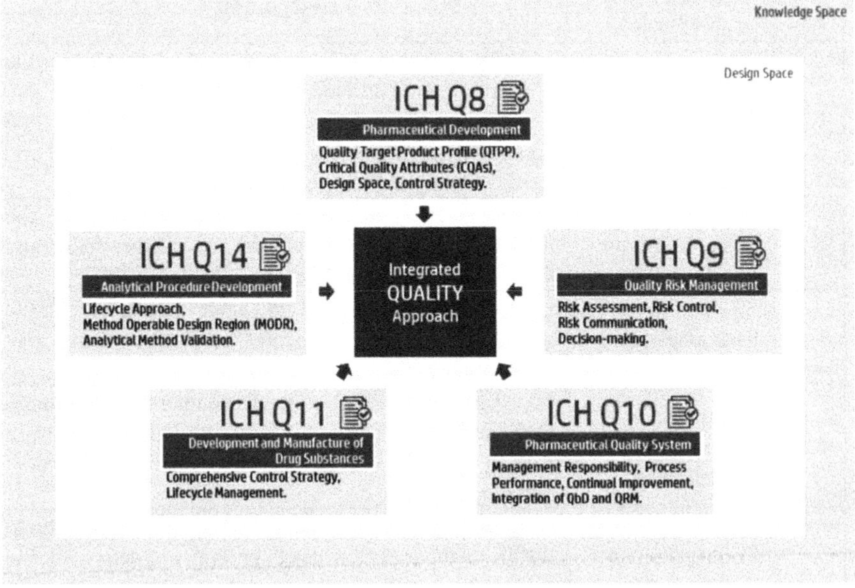

Fig. 4.1. Integrated application of ICH Q8, Q9, Q10, Q11, and Q14 guidelines.

The stagewise implementation AQbD paradigm in pharmaceutical quality system is presented in Table 4.1. The ICH published a series of quality guidelines such as Q8 (Pharmaceutical Development), Q9 (Quality Risk Management), Q10 (Pharmaceutical Quality System), Q11 (Development and manufacture of drug substances), Q14 (Analytical procedure development) for implementation of systematic quality by design principles. Among these guidelines, Q8 particularly describes the principles of quality by design (QbD), where DoE is considered as a pivotal element for optimizing the product and process performance. Fig. 4.1. illustrates the integrated quality approach revolving around the ICH Q8–Q14 guidelines.

The adoption of AQbD starts by defining the target measurement, encompassing the Analytical Target Profile (ATP) and Critical Analytical Attributes (CAA) of the product. This is followed by selecting an appropriate analytical technique, conducting risk assessments for variables, implementing method development via Design of Experiments (DoE), and validating the model and control strategy. In the final phase, AQbD addresses life cycle management, encompassing control strategy and ongoing improvement efforts.

Table 4.1 Stagewise Implementation of QbD in analytical Procedure development.

S. No.	Implementation stagewise	Description
1.	Target measurement	Identifying what to measure and determining the appropriate time and location for measurement. Defining the Analytical Target Profile (ATP) and creating measurement requirements based on ATP and Critical Analytical Attributes (CAA).
2.	Select technique	Selecting the suitable analytical technique for the intended measurement as outlined in the ATP, and specifying method performance characteristics.
3.	Risk assessment	Evaluating risks related to input variables, sample variation, and environmental conditions using risk assessment tools.
4.	Method development and validation	Investigating potential multivariate interactions through DoE and establishing the Method Operable Design Region (MODR) to comprehend method robustness and ruggedness.
5.	Control strategy	Outlining the control space and system suitability to fulfill method performance criteria aligned with the ATP.
6.	Continual improvement	Continuously monitoring method performance in compliance with ATP criteria, enabling analysts to

contd...

		proactively identify and address any out-of-trend method performance. Updating methods and analytical technology as needed.

4.2 Steps involved in AQbD Lifecycle

AQbD facilitates the establishment of a robust design space where all procedure performance objectives are achieved. The application of Quality by Design (QbD) principles for method development based on risk is detailed in the ICH Q14 guidelines. AQbD not only aids in developing dependable methods but also ensures method performance. This approach enhances data quality, strengthens interactions with regulatory authorities, elevates the efficacy of method validation and transfer, and reduces queries during regulatory submissions.

The AQbD life cycle commences with constructing the knowledge space for analytical method development and concludes with its ongoing monitoring. The sequence of steps within AQbD is illustrated in Fig. 4.2.

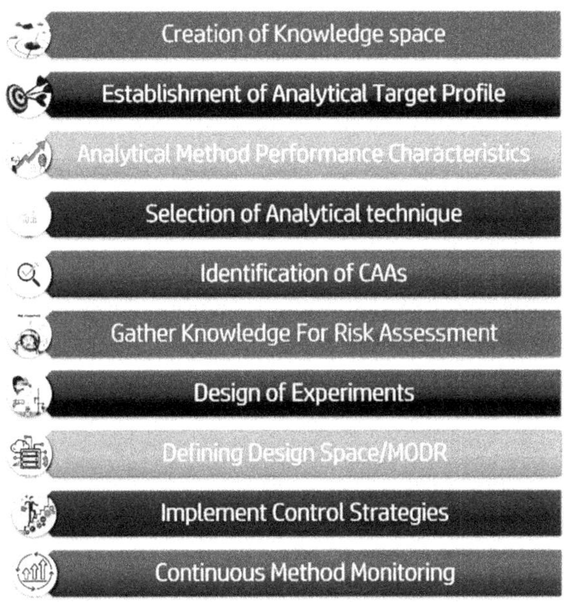

Fig. 4.2. AQbD elements.

4.3 Creation of Knowledge Space

The establishment of a knowledge space is a fundamental cornerstone for embedding quality within a procedure. The triad comprising knowledge space, design space, and control space constitutes the method's comprehension. The knowledge space encompasses insights into procedure development. If Critical Analytical Attributes (CAAs) lie beyond the design space but within the knowledge space, they often fail to meet acceptance criteria. Selecting an appropriate analytical technique and target elements hinges on familiarity with the substances' physicochemical properties, chemical structure, existing analytical methods, and toxicological considerations. This foreknowledge expedites the risk assessment phase in Quality Risk Management (QRM). Additionally, it aids in conducting risk assessments and identifying Critical Method Parameters (CMPs) that can impact analytical procedure development through tools like Ishikawa diagrams and process maps, which may be available for common analytical techniques.

4.4 Establishment of Analytical Target Profile (ATP)

A subsequent phase in the AQbD implementation involves ATP. It serves as a gauge of method effectiveness. PhRMA and EFPIA have defined ATP as a statement guiding method selection, design, and development activities. Put simply, ATP outlines what needs to be measured (e.g., active pharmaceutical ingredient), the context of measurement (e.g., pharmaceutical dosage form), and the purpose and timing of measurement (e.g., during stability studies). To ensure result quality, the ATP definition should incorporate a desired level of confidence.

An alternate approach for ATP definition is the Total Analytical Error (TAE) method. TAE encapsulates the comprehensive error stemming from both imprecision and inaccuracy. In procedure development, the specification limit may serve as the target. ATP entails distinct criteria for accuracy and precision, per ICH Q14, as it encompasses both systematic procedure error and random measurement error. Various statistical measures, like comparing TAE (combined accuracy and precision) to the specification limit, can evaluate method capability.

Traditionally, procedure development focuses on achieving accuracy, precision, Limit of Detection (LOD), Limit of Quantitation (LOQ), and robustness targets. Further exploration of these performance characteristics underscores that bias and accuracy are the primary aspects of measurement under consideration. Recognizing the interplay between these performance characteristics and overall bias and precision during procedure development enhances the understanding of factors influencing bias and accuracy, along with a more effective risk assessment and management strategy.

ATP should establish appropriate limits for bias and precision. Subsequently, the distribution of the reportable value should fall within this combined range. This approach combines bias and accuracy to yield a range of potential measurement results. Table 4.2 in the document lists ATPs, chosen techniques, and DoEs employed in some reported methods.

Table 4.2. ATP, Selected techniques for the ATP requirement & DoEs used in Analytical Procedure Development.

Drug	ATP			Selected technique	DoE
	Formulation	Accuracy	Precision		
Paliperidone HCl	Tablets	100%±3%	NMT 2%	UV	CCD
Trospium Chloride	Capsules	100%±2%	NMT 2%	UV	PCA
Raloxifene HCl	Tablets	100%±2%	NMT 2%	HPLC	CCD
Valsartan	Rat plasma	100%±3%	NMT 2%	HPLC	BBD
Aliskerin	Tablets	100%±2%	NMT 2%	UPLC	BBD
Telaprevir	Tablets	100%±2%	NMT 2%	UFLC	BBD
Mangiferin	Human plasma	100%±2%	NMT 2%	HPTLC	CCD
Fluoxetine	Human plasma	100%±2%	NMT 2%	LC-MS	BBD

Based on the information provided, the application of AQbD to UV-visible spectrophotometry and HPLC methods can be illustrated as follows:

For UV-visible spectrophotometry:

The ATP can be defined to accurately quantify Trospium chloride in its capsule dosage form within a range of 20-100 μg/ml in the drug substance. The accuracy target is set at 100% ± 2%, and the precision requirement is an RSD (Relative Standard Deviation) of no more than 2% for the reportable value.

For HPLC:

The ATP for HPLC could entail the accurate and precise quantification of Raloxifene HCl drug substance in tablets across a range of 0.5-100 μg/ml. The accuracy and precision criteria mandate that reported measurements must fall within ± 2% of the true value with at least a 95% probability.

Both these scenarios highlight the concept of ATP and its critical role in specifying the desired measurement outcomes for analytical methods. Additionally, the Total Analytical Error (TAE) approach is mentioned, which combines accuracy and precision. In this approach, the procedure should be capable of quantifying Trospium chloride in the capsule dosage form within a range of 20 to 100 μg/ml, even in the presence of degradation products. The distribution of TAE for the reportable value must align with the total allowable analytical error range of ± 2%. This approach ensures that the method's results remain within acceptable limits, accounting for both bias and precision considerations.

4.5 Analytical Method Performance Characteristics (AMPCs)

AMPCs are essential parameters evaluated during analytical method validation. These parameters, including accuracy, precision, specificity, linearity, range, detection limit, and quantitation limit, are defined to meet the requirements of the Analytical Target Profile (ATP). Various AMPCs are outlined by organizations such as USP and ICH, as presented in Table 4.3. These characteristics are categorized into systematic and random sources of error. Systematic characteristics include accuracy, specificity, and linearity, which evaluate the method's bias, selectivity, and proportionality, respectively. On the other hand, precision, LOD, and LOQ are categorized as random characteristics, assessing the method's repeatability and sensitivity.

Accuracy and precision are fundamental for quantifying pharmaceuticals, while specificity and linearity are necessary attributes for accuracy and precision to be meaningful. However, specificity and linearity don't inherently imply method robustness. Characteristics like range and robustness fall outside the systematic and random categories.

For inclusion in the ATP, it's advisable to consider composite conditions involving multiple procedure performance variables. This approach ensures a comprehensive evaluation of method performance aligned with the defined requirements.

Table 4.3. Type of Procedure performance characteristics as per USP & ICH Q2 (R1).

S. No.	Procedure Performance Characteristics	Type of variability
1.	Accuracy, specificity, and linearity	Systematic variability
2.	Precision, detection limit, and quantification limit	Inherent random variability
3.	Range and robustness	Not applicable

4.6 Selection of Analytical Techniques

While there is some overlap in the application of analytical techniques, each technique comes with its own advantages and limitations. Analytical procedures are utilized for various purposes such as identification, purity assessment, assay determination, bio-performance evaluation, and more. Table 4.4. provides a breakdown of the applicability of different analytical methods. When selecting an analytical technique, it's important to align with the specified requirements of the Analytical Target Profile (ATP). The technique chosen should fulfill the characteristics outlined in the ATP. Furthermore, even characteristics not explicitly included in the ATP should be met by the selected technique. For instance, while ATP might not explicitly mention specificity, the analytical procedure should still ensure specificity.

In some cases, an analytical technique may fulfill the ATP requirements but fall short of meeting the validation criteria specified by ICH Q2. For example, a chromatographic method can satisfy the required performance characteristics in the ATP as well as ICH validation requirements. On the other hand, a UV spectrophotometric approach might meet ATP needs but not fully meet ICH Q2 requirements. In essence, the choice of analytical technique should be driven by a careful consideration of both ATP requirements and broader validation criteria to ensure accurate and reliable results for the intended purpose.

Table 4.4. Applicability of analytical methods.

Analytical methods	Applicability
Identity	Raw material, excipients, drug substance, dosage form
Purity	Process related, stability related, heavy metals, solvent, water
Assay	API assay, dosage form potency/ content uniformity, blend composition, dissolution
Bio-performance	Dissolution, disintegration, hardness, particle size

4.7 Identification of CAAs and CMPs

According to ICH Q8, Critical Analytical Attributes (CAAs) are defined as "physical, chemical, biological, or microbiological property or characteristic that must be within an appropriate limit, range, or distribution to have the required product quality." CAAs encompass a range of factors including identification, assay, content uniformity, product deterioration, residual solvents, dissolution, moisture content, microbial limits, and physical properties like color, shape, and size.

Once the most suitable analytical technique has been selected, the focus shifts to evaluating the risks associated with various method parameters. This evaluation includes factors related to the instrument configuration, sample characteristics, sample preparation, and environmental conditions. A method parameter is deemed critical when its variability has a direct impact on a CAA, and thus it should be monitored or controlled to ensure the method consistently produces the desired results. In this phase, analysts must identify Critical Method Parameters (CMPs) that directly influence method performance. This requires a deep understanding of the method, which can be obtained through literature research or retrospective data analysis of the analyte. CMPs are grouped into three categories: those relating to the analyte, those relating to the instrument, and those relating to operational conditions. Examples of typical CMPs for chromatographic experiments include aspects like sampling, sample preparation, standards, reagents, column chemistry, mobile phase composition, pH and flow of the mobile phase, column temperature, and detector selection.

The responses (CAAs) associated with these parameters would include metrics such as resolution, retention time, tailing factor, detection limit, and robustness. Through a risk management process, both Critical Analytical Attributes and Critical Method Parameters are identified to manage the variability of materials and methods. These CAAs and CMPs are unique to each analytical method. For instance, the success of a UV-visible spectrophotometric method can hinge on factors like solvent selection, wavelength of analysis, slit width, scan speed, sampling interval, and the type and concentration of chromogenic reagents. Similarly, for an HPLC method, CMPs might include aspects like column dimensions, stationary phase, mobile phase composition, flow rate, run time, pH of buffer, and the organic modifier in the mobile phase.

Table 4.5 illustrates typical CMPs and CAAs for various analytical techniques. The identification of potential CAAs derived from the ATP plays a crucial role in guiding the development of new analytical procedures.

Table 4.5. Analytical techniques with their CMPs and CAAs.

Analytical Technique	CMPs	CAAs
UV	Solvent, Wavelength, slit width, Scan speed, sampling interval	λ_{max}, Absorbance, Spectral Shape & sharpness

contd...

Analytical Technique	CMPs	CAAs
Colorimetry (Visible)	Solvent, Wavelength, slit width, Scan speed, sampling interval, Type & concentration and volume of chromogenic reagent	λ_{max}, Absorbance, Spectral shape & sharpness
FT-IR	Wavenumber, moisture levels	% Transmittance, peak shape
HPLC	Column (dimensions, SP, make, ageing), MP composition, Flow rate, run time, pH of the buffer, organic modifier in MP	t_R, N, Rs, PA, As
GC	Column (dimensions, SP, make, ageing), Type of carrier gas, Flow rate, oven temperature program, split flow, run time, injector and detector temperature	t_R, N, Rs, PA, As
GC	Column (dimensions, SP, make, ageing), Type of carrier gas, Flow rate, oven temperature program, split flow, run time, injector and detector temperature	t_R, N, Rs, PA, As
HPTLC	Plate dimensions, SP and coating thickness, MP composition, saturation time, development time & distance, sample volume (spot), drying time, visualization technique, band length	Rf, t_R, N, Rs, PA, H, k
LC-MS	MP composition, Flow rate, run time, pH of buffer, type of column, heat block temperature	t_R, N, Rs, PA, As
GC-MS	Type of carrier gas, Flow rate, oven temperature (initial & final), inj. vol., type of column	t_R, N, Rs, PA, As

SP: stationary phase; MP: mobile phase; λmax: absorption maxima; Rf: Retardation factor; t_R: retention time; N: theoretical plates; Rs: resolution; PA: peak area; As: asymmetric factor; H: Peak Height; K: Capacity factor.

4.8 Risk Assessment

Critical Method Parameters (CMPs), which are the attributes or variables that have an impact on the ATP, are identified through a process of risk assessment. One commonly used tool for this purpose is the Ishikawa diagram, also known as the fishbone diagram. The Ishikawa diagram helps in identifying and classifying the primary sources of method-related risks. It consists of a main arrow representing the intended outcome, and the crossing arrows represent various strategies and causes to be considered when designing a method. This diagram facilitates the collection of multiple variables for a single level by reviewing all the aspects that may have been overlooked in previous processes. It offers a comprehensive way to gather a wide range of potential factors at one level. The Ishikawa diagram assists in identifying and analyzing risks through cause and effect (C & E) analysis. In the context of different analytical methods like UV-spectrophotometry, HPLC, and HPTLC, Ishikawa fishbone diagrams are used for risk assessment. These diagrams help visualize the potential causes and effects of various risks in each method.

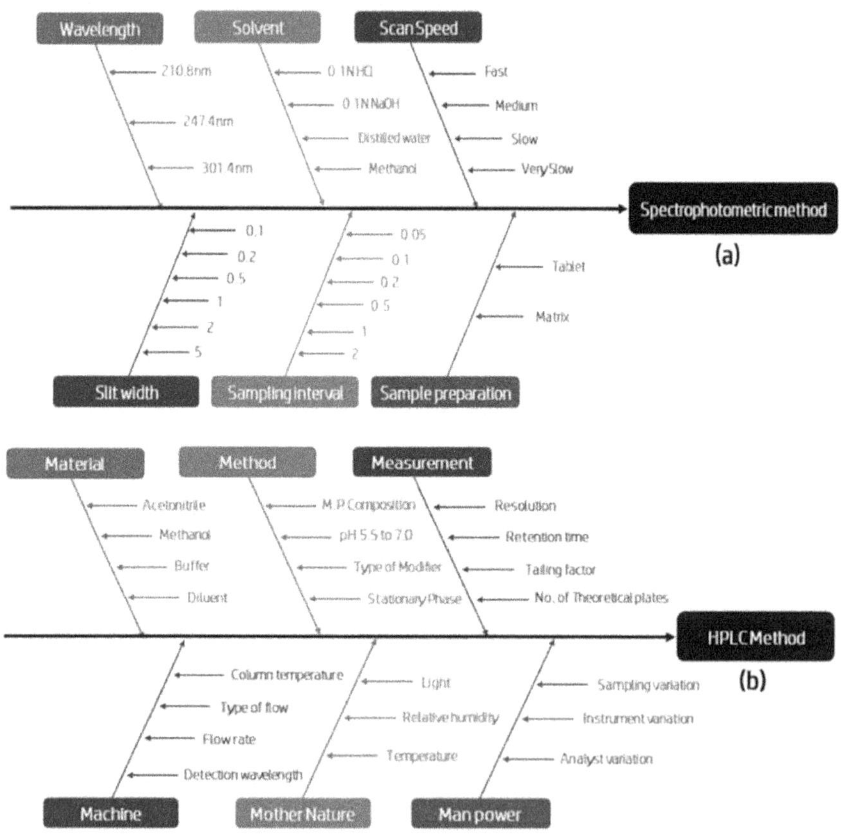

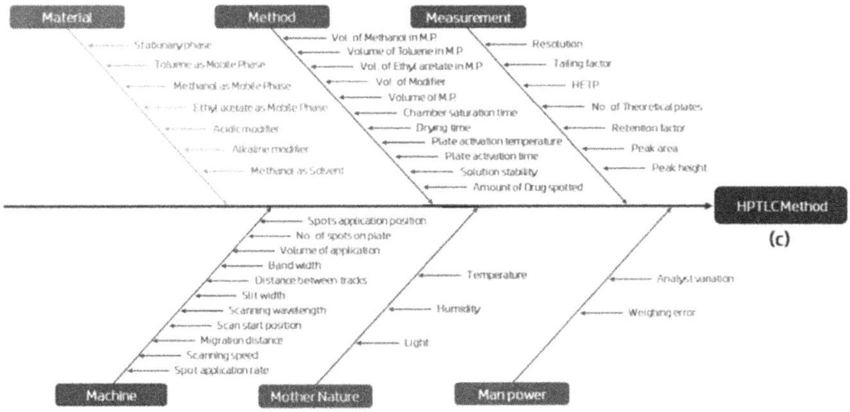

Fig. 4.3. Ishikawa fishbone diagram for the risk assessment in (a) UV-spectrophotometry method (b) HPLC method (c) HPTLC method.

The Risk Priority Number (RPN) is often used as a threshold score for an attribute. If the RPN exceeds this threshold, it indicates that further investigation is required for that risk factor. Researchers have reported using fishbone diagrams for risk assessment of CMPs in different analytical techniques. DoE is often conducted to establish the cause-and-effect relationship between procedure performance and method parameters. This helps in determining the robustness of a method. Some researchers have utilized Failure Mode Effect Analysis (FMEA) for identifying CMPs. FMEA assigns a Risk Priority Number (RPN) to combinations of occurrence of failure mode (O), severity of failure (S), and detectability (D). RPN can help prioritize high-risk failure modes for further investigation or risk control strategies.

After conducting FMEA, strategies can be developed to mitigate high-risk failure modes by adopting risk control measures. Alternatively, FMEA outcomes can be used to identify the design space. Table 8 provides an illustration of the risk assessment of HPLC method parameters and their impact, categorized as severe, intermediate, and weak.

Risk assessment is an essential phase of the risk management process (Fig. 4.4.). This phase improves the quality of the process. It can be defined as a single or combined view of the occurrence of any impairment or the degree of impairment to the process. Risk assessment plays a crucial role in enhancing the quality of the development process, especially in the context of analytical method development. It involves evaluating the potential impact of initial variables on the entire analytical development process. The main objective of risk assessment is to identify attributes or factors that could potentially jeopardize the quality of the final product.

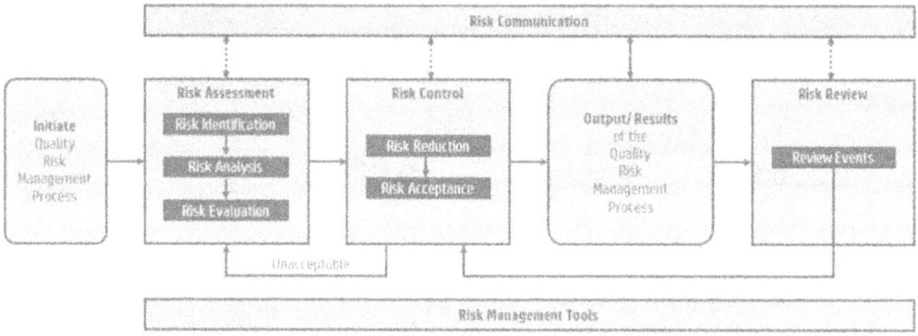

Fig. 4.4. Overview of Quality Risk Management process.

The process of risk assessment involves three essential elements:

a) **Risk Identification:** This step involves systematically gathering and analyzing information to identify potential sources of hazards. This information can be derived from historical data, theoretical analysis, and concerns raised by stakeholders. By identifying these hazards, it becomes possible to understand the potential risks associated with them.

b) **Risk Analysis:** After identifying potential hazards, the next step is to estimate the level of risk associated with each hazard. This involves analyzing the probability and consequences of each hazard occurring. Through risk analysis, it becomes possible to quantify the potential impact of these hazards on the overall process.

c) **Risk Evaluation:** Once the risks associated with identified hazards are estimated, the next step is to evaluate these risks. This involves comparing the estimated risks using either a quantitative or qualitative scale. The purpose of risk evaluation is to determine the significance of each risk in relation to the entire process.

By following these steps, it becomes possible to systematically identify potential risks and their impacts on the quality of the process or product. This process allows for informed decision-making, prioritization of risks, and the implementation of appropriate risk management strategies to mitigate or eliminate identified hazards.

Methods of Risk Assessment:

Quality risk management supports a scientific and practical approach to decision-making. It provides documented, transparent and reproducible methods to accomplish steps of the quality risk management process based on current knowledge about assessing the probability, severity and sometimes detectability of the risk. Traditionally, risks to quality have been assessed and managed in a variety of informal ways (empirical and/ or internal procedures) based on, for example, compilation of observations, trends and other information. Such approaches continue to provide useful information that might support topics such as handling of complaints, quality defects, deviations and allocation of resources. Additionally, the pharmaceutical industry and regulators can assess and manage risk using recognized risk management tools and/ or internal procedures (e.g., standard operating procedures). As per ICH Q9, risk assessment tools are as follows:

- Basic risk management facilitation methods (flowcharts, check sheets etc.),
- Cause and effect analysis (C & E),
- Failure Mode Effects Analysis (FMEA)
- Failure Mode, Effects and Criticality Analysis (FMECA)
- Fault Tree Analysis (FTA)
- Hazard Analysis and Critical Control Points (HACCP)
- Hazard Operability Analysis (HAZOP)
- Preliminary Hazard Analysis (PHA)
- Risk ranking and filtering
- Supporting statistical tools.

Both the Ishikawa (fishbone) diagram and Failure Mode and Effects Analysis (FMEA) are widely used tools for conducting risk assessments in various fields, including analytical method development. They serve different purposes and offer distinct approaches to identifying and managing risks:

Ishikawa (Fishbone) Diagram:

It is also known as the fishbone diagram or cause-and-effect diagram, is a visual tool used for qualitative risk assessment. It helps to systematically identify and categorize potential sources of hazards or problems. It allows you to analyze the relationships between various factors that might contribute to a specific issue.

The diagram is structured around a central "spine" that represents the problem or effect. Branches extending from the spine represent different categories of potential causes, such as people, processes, equipment, materials, environment, and management. This tool is particularly useful for brainstorming and identifying a wide range of possible hazards or factors that could impact a process or outcome.

Failure Mode and Effects Analysis (FMEA):

FMEA is a structured approach to quantitative risk assessment that focuses on identifying potential failure modes, their causes, and their effects on a process or system. It assigns numerical values to three factors: Occurrence (likelihood of failure), Severity (consequences of failure), and Detection (likelihood of detecting the failure before it reaches the customer). By multiplying these three factors (RPN = P x S x D), a risk priority number (RPN) is calculated for each potential failure mode. Higher RPN values indicate higher levels of risk.

FMEA is a systematic way to prioritize risks by considering both the probability of failure and the potential impact of that failure. This tool is valuable for quantifying risks and prioritizing actions to address high-risk areas within a process or system.

In FMEA the variables are ranked on the basis of the likelihood failure will occur (probability), affect on the analytical results (severity), and difficulty of detection (detectability), resulting in a risk priority number (RPN). Factors with an RPN above a cut-off level can then be evaluated by subsequent studies whereas factors with a lower RPN can be eliminated from further study.

Therefore, Ishikawa diagram is a qualitative tool that helps identify and categorize potential sources of hazards, while FMEA is a quantitative tool that assigns numerical values to factors affecting risk and calculates a risk priority number.

Both tools provide valuable insights for risk assessment and can be used in combination to comprehensively address potential hazards and their consequences.

4.9 Design of Experiments (DoE)

It is a, "Multidimensional combination and interaction of input variables that have been demonstrated to assure the quality". It allows an analyst to systematically adjust parameters according to a predetermined design to achieve optimal outcomes. The choice of the appropriate DoE technique depends on the specific problem under investigation and the experimentation goals. Several factors need consideration, including defined objectives, the number of input factors, anticipated interactions, and the statistical validity and efficacy of each design.

The DoE method serves two distinct purposes: screening parameters used in a method and optimizing parameters already established for a method. Screening designs aim to pinpoint critical factors from a vast array of possibilities based on statistical findings obtained from DoE software. On the other hand, optimization designs strive to determine the ideal experimental conditions by predicting response values for all permutations of critical factors. Within the AQbD methodology, DoE encompasses tool selection, screening, and optimization. Detailed descriptions of different types of screening and optimization designs and their selection can be found in chapter 3.

It's crucial to evaluate product robustness throughout the product lifecycle. This aspect is pivotal when selecting the most suitable plan for authorization. It is a credible approach that bridges the gap between raw materials and the final products of a process. Typically employed in the QbD process, DoE defines measurement and attribute limits during the development phase. Experts can employ DoE to determine the operational ranges of the process, which is essential for minimizing the number of experiments and avoiding wastage of time and resources in development. When correctly applied, DoE can significantly enhance precision and robustness, leading to reduced errors during the development process.

DoE finds its utility in three primary applications:

- Enhancing processes, whether they are novel procedures or existing ones in need of improvement.
- Verifying analytical processes for their reliability and accuracy.
- Assessing the influence of analytical methods on the products they are applied to.

Numerous analytical studies have utilized experimental design methodologies such as factorial or fractional factorial designs and response surface methodologies. However, these studies often focused on constructing mathematical models to establish relationships between input variables (Xn) and output responses (Yn). The successful integration of DoE in the method development phase necessitates a comprehensive understanding of the proper selection of input variables and output responses.

4.10 Defining Design Space/MODR and Surface Plots

It is defined as "the set of method parameters over which robustness and ruggedness experimentation has demonstrated the method's capability to meet the requirements of the AT)." This concept allows for flexibility in adjusting various input procedure parameters to achieve the desired procedure performance criterion and its corresponding response. It employs a risk-based, multivariate approach to evaluate the impact of numerous factors on procedure performance. The design space, essentially synonymous with the control space, defines the typical operating ranges within which critical quality attributes can be reliably ensured. By navigating within the MODR, the risks associated with critical procedure parameters are mitigated, leading to alignment with the ATP. For example, in the context of an HPLC method, conducting a thorough analysis of all input parameters and their interactions through DoE can lead to the creation of a design that encompasses a range of combinations involving mobile phase composition, buffer strength, pH, column specifications, flow rate, column temperature, and more. These combinations collectively contribute to achieving results that closely align with the predefined goals. Any HPLC method operating within the parameter values defined by the MODR boundaries can consistently yield quality results. This approach enables the effective management of all potential sources of variability through an appropriate control strategy. The MODRs for various methods are visually presented in Figure 4.5.

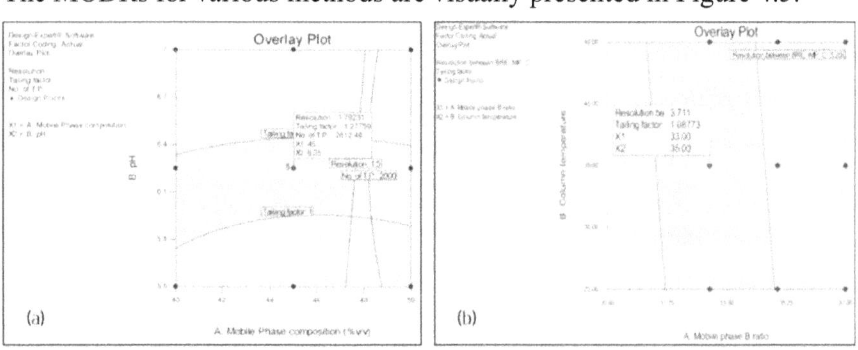

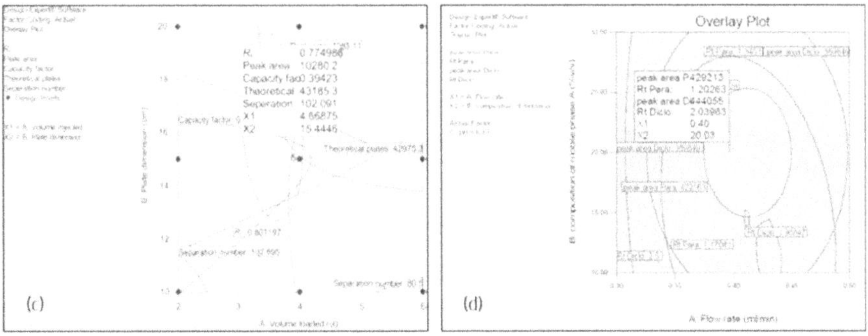

Fig. 4.5. Design Space Plot for (a) Telmisartan by HPLC (b) Brexpiprazole by UPLC (c) Mangiferin by HPTLC (d) Paracetamol and Diclofenac by LC-MS.

In alignment with the ICH Q8 guidelines concerning "design space" in the realm of product development, the concept of MODR can also be applied during the method development phase. This strategic implementation of MODR holds the potential to yield robust and cost-effective analytical methods. Similar to the Critical Quality Attributes (CQAs) in product development, MODR defines the operational range for critical method input variables that consistently yield results in line with the objectives outlined in the ATP.

This concept introduces a degree of flexibility into the manipulation of various input method parameters, ensuring that the anticipated method performance criteria and corresponding responses are achieved without necessitating resubmission to regulatory authorities like the FDA. This approach is rooted in a scientific foundation, employing a risk-based and multivariate methodology to comprehensively evaluate the impact of diverse factors on method performance.

In this context, the FDA has recommended that the establishment of the MODR should ideally coincide with the method validation process. By defining the MODR, appropriate controls can be established for the method, and subsequently, the method validation can be conducted. This integrated approach aids in the development of analytical methods that are not only robust but also compliant with regulatory standards.

The illustration of the MODR concept is visually represented in Figure 4.5 through a model contour plot, a two-dimensional graphical representation. This contour plot showcases the interplay between two factors: pH (on the x-axis) and the percentage of the aqueous phase (on the y-axis), concerning their impact on the retention time of the analyte. Notably, factors like flow rate and other instrument configurations are held constant. The numerical values of -1, -2, +1, and +2 along both axes denote the coded levels of variables employed in the DOE plan.

The contour plot's effectiveness is particularly notable when the relationship between the input variable and the method response exhibits nonlinearity and a pronounced curvature effect. The MODR can be deduced from these contours utilizing mathematical models. It's essential to validate the predicted method response by conducting actual experimental runs as part of the model validation process.

Alternatively, a surface model can also be generated through simulation. This surface model offers insights into how the method response changes concerning the variables, making it more suitable for scenarios where a linear relationship between the variables and the response exists. This approach enhances the understanding of the intricate dynamics between input variables and method responses, aiding in the selection of optimal operational ranges and the establishment of a robust analytical method.

Mathematical Modeling in Experimental Design

After gathering responses through experiments conducted under varying conditions, the multivariate data is fitted into linear or quadratic models based on the predefined objectives. Mathematical models, as previously mentioned, are developed to elucidate the relationship between experimental factors and observed responses. These models are typically characterized by their polynomial order, which can be either a first-order model (linear model) or a second-order model (quadratic model). For three factors (x_1, x_2, x_3), linear and quadratic models can be expressed using equations 1 and 2, respectively:

$$y = b_0 + b_1x_1 + b_2x_2 + b_3x_3 + b_{12}x_1x_2 + b_{23}x_2x_3 + b_{13}x_1x_3 + b_{123}x_1x_2x_3 + \varepsilon$$

$$y = b_0 + b_1x_1 + b_2x_2 + b_3x_3 + b_{11}x_{12} + b_{22}x_{22} + b_{33}x_{32} + b_{12}x_1x_2 + b_{23}x_2x_3 + b_{13}x_1x_3 + b_{123}x_1x_2x_3 + \varepsilon$$

In these equations, y represents a measured response, b0 denotes the intercept, b1, b2, and b3 are linear terms (first-order parameters), b12, b23, and b13 indicate interaction parameters, and b11, b22, and b33 denote quadratic terms (second-order parameters). The residual term ε accounts for the differences between observed and predicted response values. The coefficients in the model are computed from the model matrix, as explained in references. The magnitude of a coefficient provides insight into the impact of a factor, where a positive or negative coefficient signifies whether the response increases or decreases with an increase in the factor's value. Residuals represent the discrepancies between the observed and predicted response values. Ideally, all residuals would be 0, indicating a perfect fit within the investigated experimental range. For designs involving factors examined at two levels (screening designs), only a linear model can be applied, resulting in a lack of curvature. Consequently, neither response minimums nor maximums can be identified in three-dimensional graphs. Although the linear model isn't suitable for selecting optimal experimental conditions, it is valuable for determining the significance of factor effects When factors are studied at three levels, a quadratic relationship can be established, incorporating significant curvature. This curvature, stemming from quadratic terms, enables analysts to grasp the system's behavior and pinpoint optimal experimental conditions by identifying response minima or maxima. In scenarios where multiple responses of interest exist, multi-criteria decision-making techniques should be employed to identify optimal conditions. It's important to note that one model should be dedicated to a single response, ensuring effective decision-making and optimization.

Model Validation

Before making a decision based on contour plots or graphs, it's crucial to validate the predicted values for the desired method response through actual experimental runs. This validation process ensures that the model's predictions align with real-world outcomes. Subsequently, a regression analysis should be conducted to statistically validate the model's accuracy. A representative graph illustrating this process is depicted in Figure 4.6.

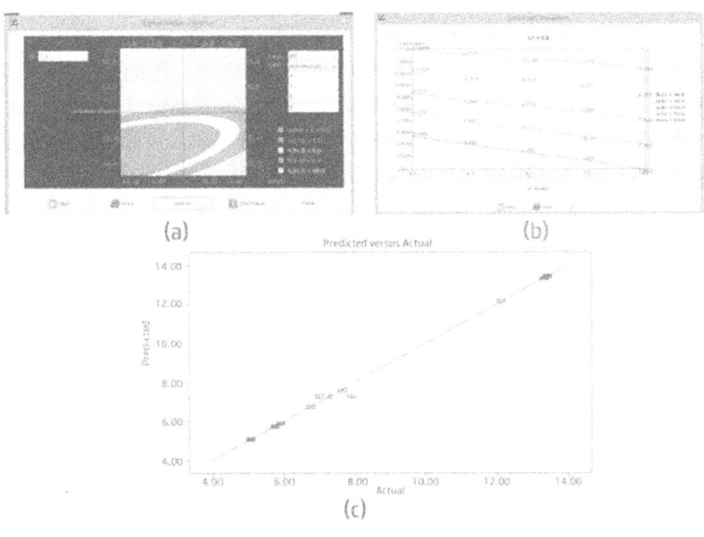

Fig. 4.6. Contour plot for MODR (retention time as method response).

4.11 Control Strategy

It is a "pre-determined set of controls based on the type of analyte and MODR knowledge" is established. This set of controls can be formulated using the statistical information collected throughout the stages of DoE and MODR. The knowledge gained about the developed method serves as the foundation for the procedure's control strategy. Notably, the procedure control strategy demonstrates minimal variations between the AQbD methodology and the traditional approach. Constructing analytical procedure controls is grounded in experimental data derived from "CAA," "DoE," and "MODR," ensuring a closer alignment between the procedure's objectives and its actual performance.

The method control strategy is defined in cases where risks are low and manageable. However, when risks are high and difficult to manage, a more appropriate method should be employed. For instance, in the context of HPLC, the control strategy revolves around managing input factors to meet system suitability requirements and any other performance-related criteria, if applicable. The assessment of system suitability testing in HPLC instrumentation serves as a fundamental control element for the method's overall performance.

In a study involving the QbD approach for the quantification of ceftriaxone using an HPLC method, the analytical control strategy was developed to encompass various aspects such as sample preparation, measurement, and the control of replicates.

It is a pre-determined set of controls based on type of analyte and MODR knowledge. The whole statistical data obtained during the DoE and MODR stages can be used to develop a method control plan. Correlations between technique and analyte properties for the capacity to meet ATP criteria can be drawn using this statistical experimental data.

The inconsistency in method parameters will be resolved by using a control technique (e.g., reagent grade, instrument brand or type, and column type). When comparing the AQbD methodology to the traditional approach, the method control strategy does not appear to be significantly different.

To ensure a tighter link between the method purpose and performance, method controls are constructed based on CQA, DoE, and MODR experimental data. The role of analytical method in control strategy is critical, and it begins from raw material testing (before manufacturing) to stability testing's (after marketing), as shown in Table 4.6.

Table 4.6. Role of analytical method in pharmaceutical testing and control strategy.

Pharmaceutical testing	Control strategy
Testing of raw material	Specification is derived from the Product QTPP and CQA to ensure the desired product quality. The impact of variability, encompassing factors like supplier variations, on both process and method development is comprehensively grasped.
In-process testing	Real-time measurements, conducted at-, on-, or in-line, provide valuable insights into the ongoing process. The process is actively controlled to minimize variations in the final product. The establishment of criteria based on a thorough understanding of multivariate processes ensures quality control.
Release testing	Quality attributes are reliably predicted from inputs within the process's design space. Specifications, while crucial, form just one facet of the comprehensive quality control strategy. Moreover, these specifications align with patient requirements, encompassing aspects of quality, safety, efficacy, and performance.
Stability testing	Predictive models employed during release aid in minimizing stability-related issues. Specifications are set to reflect the desired product performance over time, ensuring long-term consistency and reliability.

Continuous Method Monitoring / Lifecycle Management

It marks the final stage of the AQbD life cycle. During this phase, the process of sharing information and insights gathered throughout the development and testing stages remains ongoing. This continuous exchange of information ensures that any irregular or unexpected performance of the analytical approach can be detected and addressed promptly. Continuous improvement is a key focus of the CMM phase. This involves vigilantly monitoring the consistency of product quality, conducting regular maintenance on HPLC equipment, computers, software, and other laboratory apparatus. By implementing these practices, the laboratory can uphold the reliability and efficiency of its analytical processes.

The CMM phase serves as the culmination of the AQbD process, bringing together critical components such as CQA, ATP, the MODR, and risk assessments from preceding phases. This integrated approach ensures a comprehensive control strategy that extends into the commercial stage.

Life cycle management, which is integral to this phase, entails the ongoing sharing of knowledge gained during both the development and implementation of the design space. This encompasses the outcomes of risk assessments, assumptions based on prior knowledge, statistical design considerations, and the linkages between design space, MODR, control strategy, CQA, and ATP.

Once method validation is successfully completed, the method becomes ready for routine use. Continuous monitoring of method performance is carried out to ensure its sustained reliability. This monitoring involves the use of control charts, tracking system suitability data, conducting method-related investigations, and more. By continuously monitoring method performance, analysts can promptly identify and address any unusual or concerning trends in the analytical results.

***

CHAPTER 5

AQbD for UV-Visible Spectrophotometric Method Development

5.1 Introduction

Light consists of electric & magnetic components which intersect each other at a right angle as they move through a vacuum. The distance between successive crests/ toughs of either the electric field or the magnetic field is the wavelength. Radiation is released as photons, which are bundles of light energy that travel at the speed of light as quantized harmonic waves.

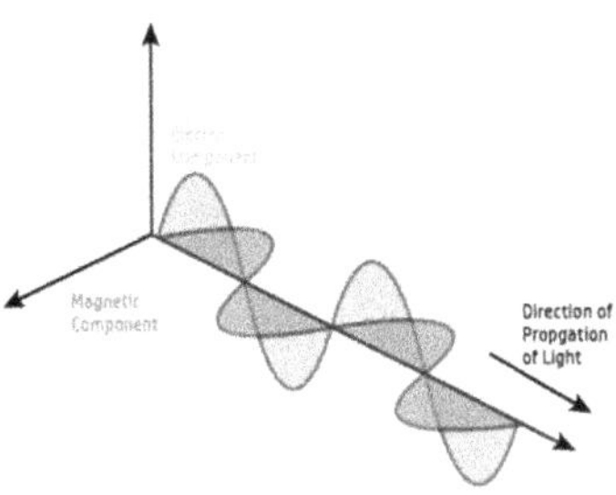

Fig. 5.1. Electric & Magnetic components of Light.

This energy is then grouped into categories based on its wavelength into the electromagnetic spectrum. The different types of electromagnetic radiation consist of radio waves, microwaves, infrared waves, visible light, ultraviolet radiation, X-rays, and gamma rays. A wide variety of information about a substance can be obtained by irradiating it with light. With a UV-VIS spectrophotometer, irradiating a substance with ultraviolet and visible light (200nm – 80nm) makes it possible to obtain information about the electrons in that substance, and it is even possible to measure its quantity.

Up on absorption of light an energy results in switching of an electron from ground state (E_0) to excited states (E_1). Electrons have particular energy levels, and rays of ultraviolet and visible light have the energy to change the energy states of the electrons. Because the higher energy state, E_1, is unstable, the electron soon returns to the ground state, E_0. The energy discharged when the electron returns from E_0 to E_1 (E_1 - E_0) is converted to heat. If, for some reason, it is not converted to heat, the energy is discharged as light. The phenomenon of light emission is well known as fluorescence or phosphorescence.

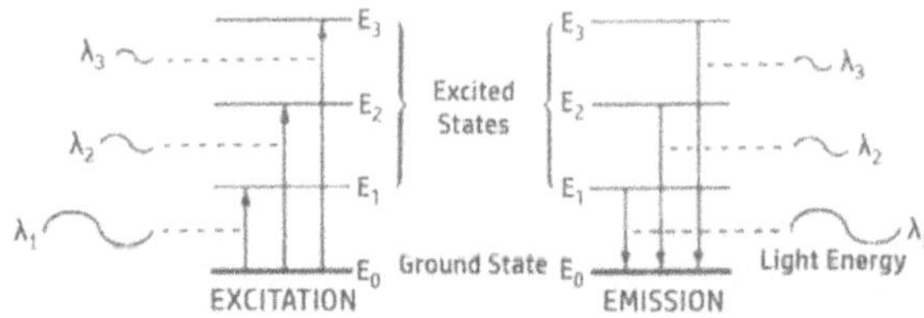

Fig. 5.2. Excitation and Emission phenomena.

UV-Visible spectrophotometers use a light source to illuminate a sample with light across the UV to the visible wavelength range (typically 190 to 900 nm). The instruments then measure the light absorbed, transmitted, or reflected by the sample at each wavelength. The design of the UV-Vis spectrophotometer includes both the parts of the spectrometer and photometer. The spectrometer part contains a light source, sample cell, monochromator, and slits. The microcontroller controls grating in the monochromator, whereas the photometer part consists of a photodiode, preamplifier, and data acquisition system.

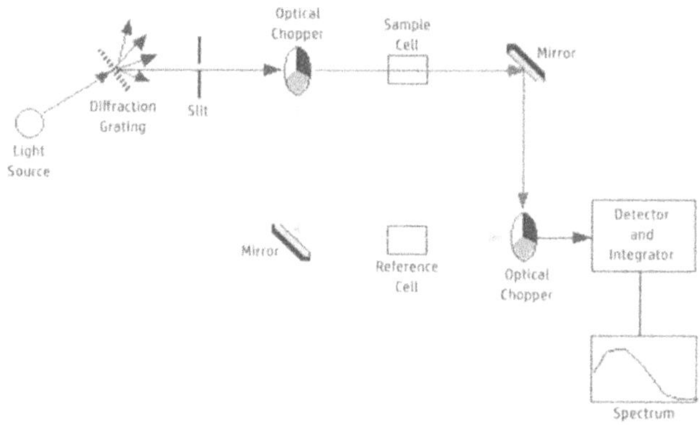

Fig. 5.3. Double beam UV- Visible spectrophotometer.

UV absorption spectrophotometry is a commonly employed technique for quantifying molecules that contain chromophore groups. These chromophore groups are specific parts of the molecule characterized by unsaturation and covalent bonding, leading to distinctive absorption patterns in the ultraviolet (UV) or visible spectrum. This method is known for its reliability, rapidity, and user-friendly nature, making it a preferred choice for various analytical applications. It is based on the fundamental law of absorption i.e the Beer-Lambert's law which establishes a direct relation between the absorbance and concentration at a given wavelength of maximum absorption.

$$A = \varepsilon b c$$

where, A = Absorbance; Ɛ = molar absorptivity, $mol^{-1}.lit.cm^{-1}$; b = pathlength, cm; c = concentration, $mol.lit^{-1}$

Colorimetry, also known as visible spectrophotometry, is a technique employed to quantify the concentration of colored compounds within a solution. This method relies on the Beer-Lambert's law, which establishes a direct relationship between absorbance and concentration at a specific wavelength of maximum absorption. A colorimeter or visible spectrophotometer is a device used to assess solution concentration by measuring the absorbance of light at a particular wavelength.

The selection of a reagent for colorimetric analysis hinges on factors like specificity and sensitivity. In spectrophotometric methods, the selectivity is influenced by various factors such as the reagent's nature, oxidation state of the metal ion, pH of the medium, temperature, order of reagent mixing, reagent aging, and careful evaluation of chromophore properties and stability.

Colorimetry finds diverse applications, including the study of complex molar compositions, determination of indicator pKa values, analysis of inorganic complexes, and quantitative analysis. Another significant application of visible spectrophotometry is determining the formula and stability constants of metal complexes. Methods commonly used for optimizing colorimetric procedures and determining the formula of metal complexes include Job's method of continuous variation and mole ratio method. Colorimetric or spectroscopic procedures are typically adopted for the following reasons:

- The use of visible spectrophotometric methods instead of UV procedures can be driven by cost considerations.
- Indirect spectroscopic techniques enhance the selectivity of UV-absorbing substance assays in samples containing other UV-absorbing components.
- When the analyte weakly absorbs in the UV region, higher sensitivity can be achieved by converting the substance to a derivative with a more strongly absorbing chromophore.
- Conversion of the analyte to a derivative can help eliminate interference from irrelevant absorption.

5.2 Selecting Optimum Parameters for UV-Vis Measurements

Selection of suitable sample holder, solvent and instrument parameters is critical for the success of measurement.

- Optical cell selection
- Thermostatting the samples

- Selection of solvent (Solvent transparency)
- Optimum spectral band width
- The linear range of a UV-Vis instrument.

Optical cell selection

The choice of optical cell depends on factors such as sample volume, sample type (liquid or solid), and the path length required for the analysis. Quartz cuvettes are commonly used for UV-Vis measurements due to their high transparency in the UV range. Plastic or glass cuvettes may be suitable for visible range measurements but can have limited UV transparency. Specialized cells, such as flow cells or solid-state holders, are available for specific applications.

Thermostatting the samples

Temperature control is important if measurements are temperature-sensitive or if we want to investigate the effects of temperature on the sample. Some UV-Vis spectrophotometers offer temperature control options, allowing to maintain a constant temperature during measurements. This is particularly important for kinetic or time-dependent studies.

Selection of solvent (Solvent transparency)

The choice of solvent is crucial as it should be transparent in the wavelength range of interest and not contribute significant absorption. For UV measurements, solvents such as water, ethanol, methanol, or acetonitrile are commonly used. However, it's important to consider the solvent's compatibility with the sample and its potential interactions.

Careful consideration is necessary when choosing solvents and substrates for UV-Visible experiments. When dealing with liquid samples, it's important that they can readily dissolve in the chosen solvent while aiding in the preservation of sample stability. Ideally, the selected solvent or substrate should possess transparency within the wavelength range in which the sample's chromophore absorbs.

This approach helps minimize the possibility of any extra absorbance that might approach the boundaries of the instrument's photometric range.

Optimum spectral bandwidth

The spectral bandwidth determines the range of wavelengths detected simultaneously by the spectrophotometer. A narrow bandwidth provides better spectral resolution, allowing to resolve closely spaced absorption peaks.

However, a wider bandwidth increases sensitivity. The choice of bandwidth depends on the spectral features we want to study and the trade-off between resolution and sensitivity.

The linear range of a UV-Vis instrument

The linear range refers to the concentration range where the instrument's detector response is directly proportional to the analyte concentration. It's important to determine the linear range of your UV-Vis instrument for accurate quantitative analysis. If the concentration exceeds the linear range, sample dilution or adjustments to the instrument's settings may be necessary to obtain reliable measurements.

Response and Scanning Speed

The response corresponds to the duration during which data is integrated or the time span for which the detector accumulates photons before transmitting the signal to the A/D converter for processing. The square root of the response maintains proportionality to the signal-to-noise ratio (S/N), thereby indicating that extended response times yield improved S/N ratios. This effect is more pronounced when the sample's signal is minimal, due to reduced light throughput. The pace of scanning determines how swiftly the monochromator moves across the designated wavelength range to gather data points according to the specified data pitch. In continuous scan mode, it's crucial to select an appropriate scanning speed that aligns with the chosen response to prevent distortion in the measured spectrum. A helpful guideline in choosing the response and scanning speed is as follows:

$$\text{Response} \times \text{Scanning speed} < \text{FWHM}/10$$

Here, FWHM stands for the full width at half the peak height of the target peak.

5.3 Classical Approach for UV-Visible Spectrophotometric Method Development

As most of the UV-visible applications are single-component quantitative analyses, in this chapter we focus on the optimization of such methods. Method development involves selecting the wavelength or wavelengths that yield the best results for a particular analysis on a particular instrument. Here, best is defined by parameters such as accuracy, precision, sensitivity, linearity, range, selectivity, and ruggedness. Because all of these parameters cannot be optimized at the same time, the parameter or parameters for optimization must be determined and the requirements defined prior to analysis. The scheme for UV-Visible spectrophotometric method development is depicted in the following Table No. 5.1.

Table 5.1. Scheme for UV-Visible spectrophotometric method development.

UV Spectroscopic method development	Visible Spectroscopic method development
Collection and identification of drug(s) ↓ Literature ↓ Define a goal ↓ Experimental work ↓ Analytical method development ↓ Solubility studies ↓ Selection of Solvent ↓ Selection of wave length/s for best linearity/ accuracy/ selectivity/ sensitivity. ↓ Optimization of Concentration ↓ Check for problems and requirements for special procedures ↓ Optimizations of conditions ↓ Method development report ↓ Validation report ↓ Use of developed method for regular analysis	Collection and identification of drug(s) ↓ Literature ↓ Define a goal ↓ Experimental work ↓ Analytical method development ↓ Solubility studies ↓ Selection of Solvent ↓ Selection of Chromogenic Reagent ↓ Formation of Colored product ↓ Selection of wave length/s for best linearity/ accuracy/ selectivity/ sensitivity. ↓ Optimization of Reaction Conditions ↓ Optimization of concentration ↓ Check for problems and requirements for special procedures ↓ Optimizations of conditions ↓ Method development report ↓ Validation report ↓ Use of developed method for regular analysis

5.4 AQbD Elements for UV-Visible Spectrophotometric Method Development

Creation of Knowledge Space

ICH guideline provides three aspects to build a method understanding which are knowledge space, design space, and control space. The knowledge space is the widest region in which knowledge and understanding of procedure or method development exist. Critical Quality Attributes will often fail to fulfil acceptance requirements if they are located outside of the design space but within the knowledge space.

The selection of a suitable analytical technique and the target elements for the quantitation of drug substances in their dosage forms is based on having prior knowledge about their physico-chemical properties, chemical structure, existing analytical methods, toxicological aspects etc.

Analytical Target Profile

The first step in the implementation of AQbD is ATP. It defines the goal of the spectroscopic method development process, and is the indicator of method performance. It involves the determination of amount of drug in API or in formulation accurately and precisely by employing a simple, sensitive and economical analytical method.

Analytical Method Performance Characteristics

AMPCs are the validation parameters/ characteristics that are normally evaluated during spectrophotometric method validation. The characteristics such as accuracy, precision, specificity, linearity, range, detection limit, quantitation limit.

Selection of Analytical Techniques

With reference to ATP defined in the step 2, UV-Visible spectrophotometric technique is selected to meet the goals as it is simple and economical.

Identification of Critical Analytical Attributes (CAAs)

After the selection of spectrophotometric technique, detailed assessment of the risks associated with method parameters, viz., Solvent, Wavelength, instrument configuration, viz., slit width, Scan speed, sample characteristics, sampling interval, sample preparation are focussed. To control the "Variability" of materials and method, Critical Analytical Attributes (CAA) and Critical method parameters (CMP) are identified through Risk Management process. For spectrophotometric technique, typical CAAs are Spectral shape, sharpness, and absorbance intensity, absorption maximum. It helps to have better understanding of method & its performance thus helping Life Cycle Management of the method (LCM).

Risk Assessment

It plays a crucial role in identifying the critical variables within a method, as well as the parameters that exert an influence on the ATP. An extensively used tool for risk assessment in spectrophotometric techniques is the Ishikawa (fishbone) diagram. This diagram effectively aids in the identification and classification of primary risk sources linked to the method. In the Ishikawa diagram, the main arrow symbolizes the intended final outcome, while the intersecting arrows represent various levels, strategies, and causes to be taken into account during method development. Employing this approach involves revisiting overlooked factors from previous stages, thereby offering ample opportunities to identify numerous factors at a single level.

The Ishikawa diagram serves as a method to ascertain risk through cause and effect (C and E) analysis. In this process, risk factors are assigned a risk priority number (RPN), which signifies their criticality. Factors or attributes exceeding a certain RPN score warrant further investigation. Accuracy and precision are commonly considered as method parameters to enhance the method's robustness and ruggedness. To evaluate the robustness of a method, DoE is conducted, revealing the cause and effect relationship between method performance and its parameters.

Design of Experiments (DoE)

It is defined as, "Multidimensional combination and interaction of input variables that have been demonstrated to assure the quality". it allows the analyst to modify parameters in a systematic manner according to a pre-determined design to obtain best suited results. Various DoE tools used in spectrophotometric method development are Principal component analysis, two level and three level factorial designs, central composite design etc

MODR

MODR is defined as the set of method parameters over which the robustness and ruggedness experimentation has shown the method can meet the requirements of the ATP. It allows for the adaptation of different input method parameters to achieve the desired method performance criteria and response without necessitating resubmission to the FDA. This approach is rooted in a scientific, risk-based, and multivariate methodology that assesses the impact of various factors on method performance. The design space represents the normal operating ranges whereby critical quality attributes can be assured - which essentially is control space.

Control strategy

Control strategy is a pre-determined set of controls based on analyte type and MODR knowledge. The whole statistical data obtained during the DoE and MODR stages can be used to develop a method control plan. Method Control Strategy is based on the knowledge gained about the developed method. When comparing the AQbD methodology to the traditional approach, the method control strategy does not appear to be significantly different. To ensure a tighter link between the method purpose and performance, method controls are constructed based on CQA, DoE, and MODR experimental data.

Continuous Method Monitoring

CMM is the last step in the AQbD life cycle; it is a never-ending process of sharing information obtained throughout development and testing. The continuous monitoring allows an analyst to detect, identify & address any abnormal or out of trend performance of analytical method.

***

Practical Examples of AQbD applied to UV - Visible Spectrophotometric method development

Estimation of Trospium chloride in capsule dosage form

Drug Profile

Trospium Chloride, an antispasmodic, antimuscarinic agent used in the treatment of overactive bladder with urge incontinence, official in B.P. 2012. It is chemically [(1R,5S)-spiro [8-azoniabicyclo [3.2.1] octane-8,1'-azolidin-1-ium]-3-yl] 2-hydroxy - 2,2-diphenylacetate, soluble in organic solvents such as ethanol and DMSO, which should be purged with an inert gas.

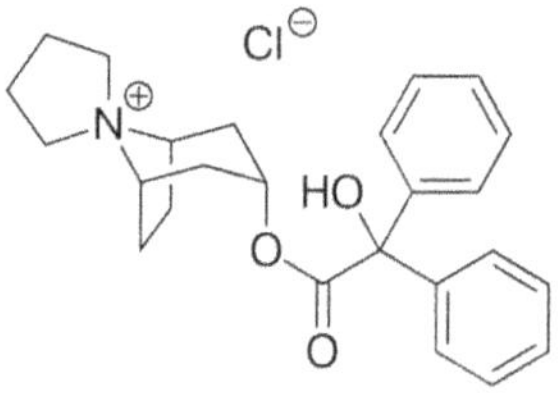

Fig. 5.4. Trospium chloride structure.

The solubility of drug in these solvents is approximately 0.2 and 0.16 mg/ml, respectively.

Literature

The chosen drug was quantified employing advanced techniques such as LC-MS/MS, RP-HPLC, fluorimetry, and a Stability Indicating RP-UFLC method. These methods involve complex and highly advanced techniques, resulting in increased costs and time consumption. Hence, a decision was made to develop a straightforward spectrophotometric method (Method-I) and a first derivative spectrophotometric method (Method-II) using the QbD approach outlined in the ICH Q8 (R2) guidelines.

ATP

Two robust spectrophotometric methods (Simple & First derivative) must be able to accurately quantify Trospium chloride in its capsule dosage form in a range from 20-100 mcg/ml in the drug substance with an accuracy 100%±2% and a precision of RSD NMT 2% for the reportable value.

CAAs

The Ishikawa diagram incorporated various factors including sample preparation method, choice of solvent, wavelength selection, and instrumental parameters such as slit width, scan speed, and sampling interval.

These parameters were identified through observation and Principal Component Analysis (PCA) to assess their impact on spectral characteristics such as shape, sharpness, and absorbance intensity. Extracted CAAs are enlisted in Table 5.2.

Table 5.2. Extracted critical parameters.

Method-I: Simple spectrophotometric method			
By observation (By comparing the spectral shape, sharpness and absorbances of linearity, the critical parameters were selected in case of sample preparation, solvent and wavelength.)			
Parameter	**Trials**	**Extracted CAA**	**Reason**
Solvent	0.1 N NaOH, 0.1N HCl, Distilled water	0.1 N NaOH	The spectrum was sharp in 0.1 N NaOH.
Wavelength	231.0 nm and 258.0 nm	258 nm	The absorbances at 231.0 nm were not reproducible, while the absorbances at 258.0 nm were reproducible
Sample preparation	Matrix (lactose monohydrate, microcrystalline cellulose and starch), tablet, Capsule	Capsule (Rospium XR)	The precise results were obtained in the capsule preparation
By PCA			
Parameter	**Trials**	**Extracted CAA**	**Reason**
Scan speed	fast, medium, slow, very slow	Medium	Critical Parameters were extracted using SPSS software
Slit width	0.1, 0.2, 0.5, 1.0, 2.0, 5.0 nm	1.0	
Sampling interval	0.05, 0.1, 0.2, 0.5, 1.0, 2.0 nm	0.2	

Contd...

Method-II: First derivative spectrophotometric method			
By observation			
Parameter	**Trials**	**Extracted CAA**	**Reason**
Solvent	0.1 N NaOH, 0.1N HCl, Distilled water	0.1 N NaOH	The spectrum was sharp in 0.1 N NaOH.
Wavelength	210.6 nm and 226.6 nm	226.6 nm	The absorbances at 226.6 nm were reproducible
Sample preparation	Matrix (lactose monohydrate, microcrystalline cellulose and starch), tablet, Capsule	Capsule (Rospium XR)	The precise results were obtained in the capsule preparation
By PCA			
Parameter	**Trials**	**Extracted CAA**	**Reason**
Scan speed	fast, medium, slow, very slow	Medium	Critical Parameters were extracted using SPSS software
Slit width	0.1, 0.2, 0.5, 1.0, 2.0, 5.0 nm	1.0	
Sampling interval	0.05, 0.1, 0.2, 0.5, 1.0, 2.0 nm	0.2	
Delta lambda	2, 4, 6, 8	2	
Scaling factor	1, 2, 3, 4, 5	5	

RA tool

Structured methodologies for risk assessment, such as Fishbone diagram was implemented to identify the potential risk of the method due to a small change in method parameters or under a variety of conditions such as different analysts, instruments, reagents, days, etc. In this stage of QbD approach, critical parameters that affect the overall quality of method were identified such as slit width, scan speed and sampling interval and were fitted into Ishikawa fishbone diagram to determine their interaction effects.

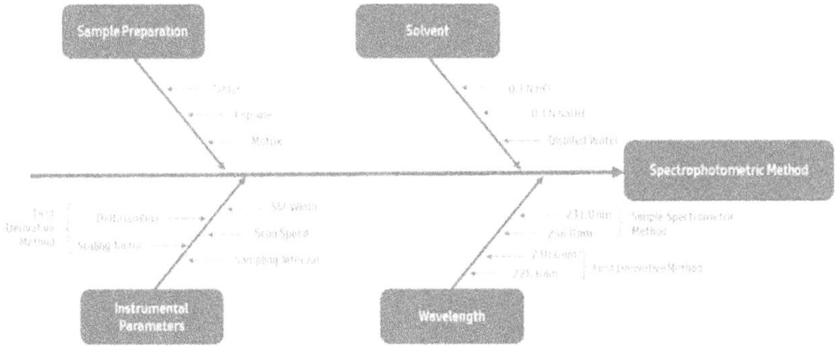

Fig. 5.5. Ishikawa (fishbone) diagram.

DoE

In this method, statistical tool known as principal component analysis was utilized for extraction of critical parameters using SPSS software.

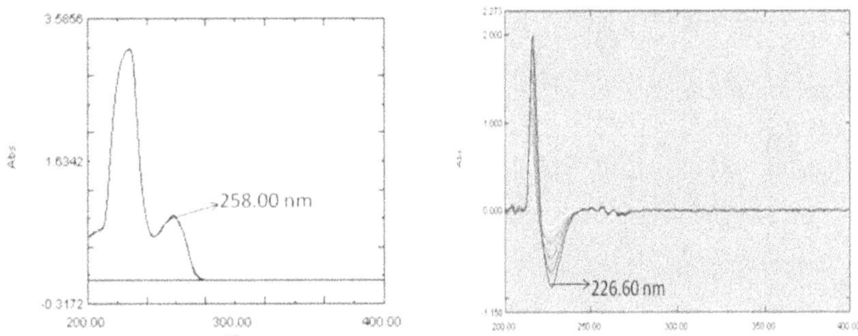

Fig. 5.6. UV Spectrum (Normal) & First Derivative Spectrum in 0.1 N NaOH.

Based on the extracted parameters, a solvent of 0.1 N NaOH solution and Rospium XR capsules as the dosage form were utilized for both Method-I and Method-II. The chosen wavelengths were 258.0 nm for Method-I and 226.6 nm for Method-II. In Method-I, the instrumental parameters consisted of a slit width of 1.0, medium scan speed, and a sampling interval of 0.2. For Method-II, a delta lambda of 2 and a scaling factor of 5 were employed.

The developed methods underwent validation in accordance with the guidelines provided by ICH Q2 (R1) for analytical method validation. The validation process confirmed their accuracy, precision, and cost-effectiveness. These methods are suitable for routine quality control analysis of trospium chloride in pharmaceutical dosage forms. The application of the QbD approach led to the creation of robust methods capable of producing consistent, reliable, and high-quality data throughout the analytical process, while also saving both time and resources.

Table 5.3. Statistical data of Validation parameters.

Parameter	Method - I	Method - II
Wavelength (nm)	258	226.6
Linearity Range (µg/ml)	200-1000	20-100
Regression equation	Y = 0.00094 X + 0.019	Y = 0.0084 X + 0.030
Correlation coefficient (r^2)	0.9999	0.9999
Accuracy (% recovery)	98.8	99.2
Repeatability, (%RSD)	0.26	0.38
Intermediate precision, (%RSD)	1.63	1.58
Absorptivity (lit $mole^{-1}$ cm^{-1})	41682.60	37278.80
Sandells Sensitivity ($\mu g/cm^2/0.001$)	0.0102	0.0154
LOD (µg/ml)	0.71	2.57
LOQ (µg/ml)	2.17	7.81
Specificity (% RSD)	0.73	0.58
Robustness (% RSD)	0.34	0.21

***

Practical Examples of AQbD applied to UV - Visible Spectrophotometric method development

Determination of Chlorpheniramine maleate in bulk & tablet dosage form

Drug Profile

Chlorpheniramine Maleate, chemically 1-(N, N-Dimethyl amino)-3-(p-chlorophenyl)-3-(alpha-pyridyl) propane maleate. It is a halogenated amine used as antihistamine, to treat common cold, conjunctivitis and acute allergic symptoms like rhinitis and urticaria, sneezing etc. it is Freely soluble in water, soluble in alcohol and in chloroform, slightly soluble in ether and in benzene.

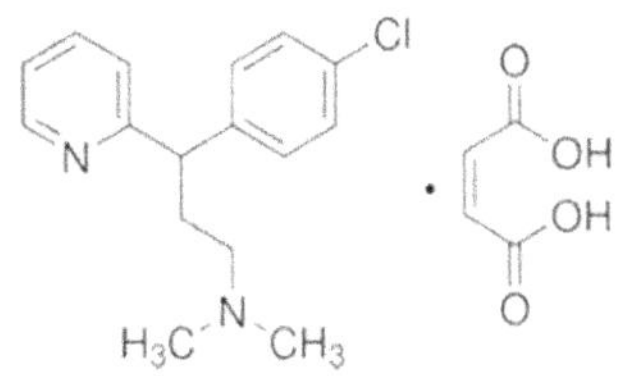

Fig. 5.7. Chlorpheniramine maleate structure.

ATP

Novel, alternative and simplified UV-Spectrophotometric method must be able to accurately quantify Chlorpheniramine maleate in its bulk and tablet dosage form with the following targets.

Table. 5.4. Defining ATP to Chlorpheniramine maleate in bulk and tablet dosage form.

ATP element	Target	Justification
Accuracy	The experimental results should be close to the true value.	It should be 100 ± 2%
Linearity	The method should have the ability to elicit test results that are directly proportional to the concentration of the analyte in the samples within a given range.	It should be in a range from 10-50 mcg/ml
Repeatability (Intra-day precision)	The method's test results should exhibit strong consistency when utilizing identical operating conditions within a specified brief timeframe, typically lasting for 1 day.	It should be established with %RSD NMT 2

Contd...

Intermediate Precision (Inter-day precision)	Similarly, the method's test results should demonstrate substantial consistency when using the same operating conditions, usually within the same laboratory, over an extended period, often exceeding 1 day.	It should be established with %RSD NMT 2
LOD	The lowest possible concentration of an analyte in the sample that can be detected with accuracy and precision.	It should be established with S: N ratio 3:1
LOQ	The lowest possible concentration of an analyte in the sample that can be determined with accuracy and precision.	It should be established with S: N ratio 10:1

CAAs

CCD was performed based on 27 randomized experimental runs on UV spectrophotometer to observe the effect of CMPs such as solvent, scan speed and sample interval on CAA viz., Absorbance.

RA tool

In this method, Ishikawa fishbone diagram was employed to determine the effects of CMPs on CAAs.

DoE

It involves the use of Central Composite Design (CCD) for the simultaneous evaluation of three critical method variables viz., solvent, scanning speed and sampling interval at three levels (33) using Design-Expert Software.

The drug exhibited solubility in water, 0.1N HCl, and 0.1N NaOH. The absorption maximum of its standard solution was observed at 261 nm in water and 245 nm in both 0.1N HCl and 0.1N NaOH, which were selected as the detection wavelengths. The experimental investigation utilized a CCD model, and the resulting data were analyzed using ANOVA. Notably, for the critical analytical attribute (CAA), minimal interaction was observed between the critical method variables (CMVs), as indicated by non-intersecting factor lines.

For interpretation and optimization purposes, both 3-D surface profiling and 2-D contour analysis were performed. The contours derived from the optimized conditions were then subjected to further investigation with the chosen values for the CMVs. An evident curvilinear increase in the response was noticed at low levels of scanning speed, while the sampling interval did not exhibit a significant effect.

The experimental investigation employed a CCD model, and the resulting data were subjected to analysis using ANOVA (Analysis of Variance), parameter estimates, and prediction profiler. The analysis of the obtained outcomes indicated the suitability of a Quadratic model for both wavelengths, namely 261 nm and 245 nm.

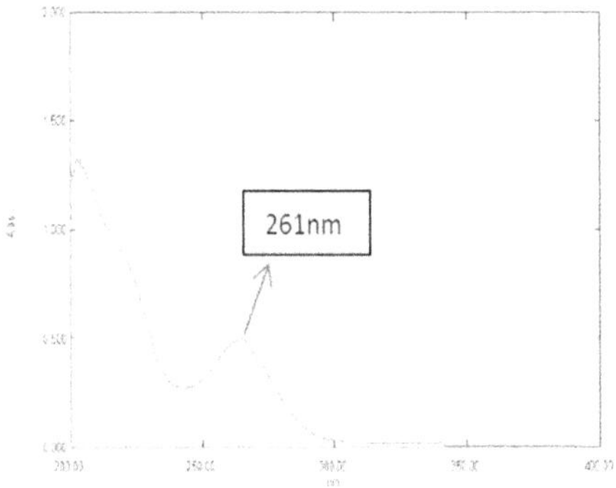

Fig. 5.8. Absorption spectrum in 0.1N HCl.

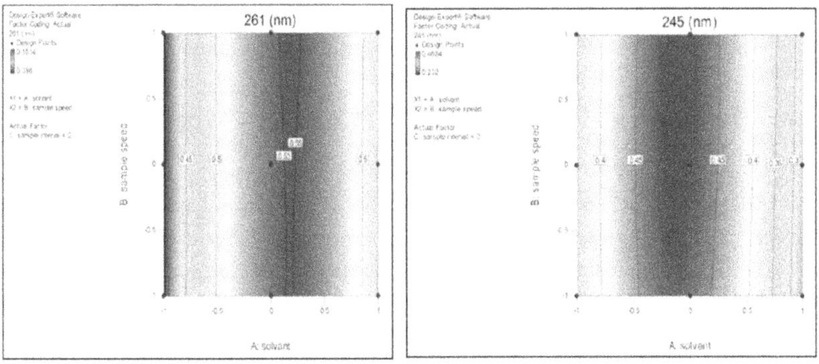

Fig. 5.9. 2-D contour plot at 261 nm and 245 nm.

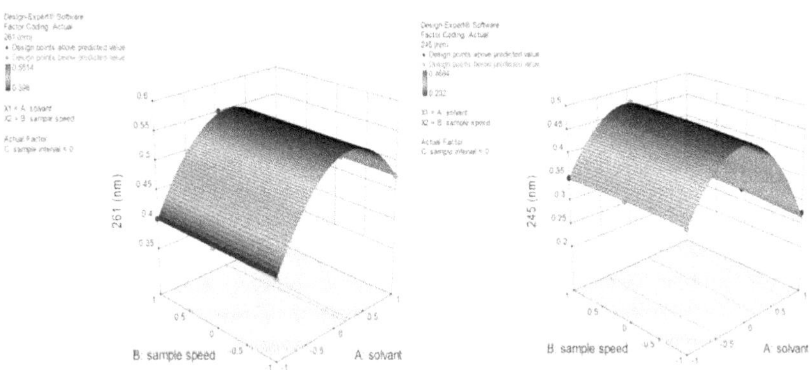

Fig. 5.10. 3D Contour plots showing the effect of solvent & scanning speed on wavelength (at 261 nm and 245 nm).

The ANOVA analysis, with a p-value of less than 0.05, along with a satisfactory R-squared value exceeding 0.9, suggests that the selected mathematical model is appropriate for deriving optimum values of CAAs.

Notably, there was minimal interaction observed among the critical method variables (CMVs) in relation to the critical attribute, as indicated by the non-intersecting factor lines. Furthermore, the ANOVA analysis showed satisfactory p-values, and the predicted residual sum of squares (PRESS) value indicated that the model was well-fitted and optimized. The prediction expressions for the adopted model are represented in the following quadratic polynomial equations for the wavelength of 261 nm and 246 nm.

$$y = 0.57 + 0.25\,A + 0.009\,B - 0.0073\,C + 0.013\,AB - 0.011\,AC + 0.012\,BC - 0.12\,A^2 - 0.010\,B^2 - 0.0048\,C^2$$

$$y = 0.26 + 0.11\,A + 0.002\,B - 0.0013\,C + 0.0026\,AB - 0.0022\,AC + 0.0025\,BC - 0.083\,A^2 - 0.0026\,B^2 - 0.0074\,C^2$$

A = Solvent B = Scanning speed C = Sampling interval

Table 5.5. Response 1- 261 nm : ANOVA for Response Surface Quadratic model.

Analysis of variance table [Partial sum of squares - Type III]					
Source	**Sum of squares**	**d.f.**	**Mean square**	**F - Value**	**P – value (Prob > F)**
Model	0.096000000	9	0.011000000	2173.97	< 0.0001 significant
A- Solvent	0.026000000	1	0.026000000	5236.66	< 0.0001
B- Sample speed	0.00000280	1	0.00000280	0.57	0.4606
C- Sample interval	0.00000123	1	0.00000123	0.25	0.6236
AB	0.00000645	1	0.00000645	1.31	0.2676
AC	0.00000102	1	0.00000102	0.21	0.6543
BC	0.00000005	1	0.00000005	0.011	0.9182
A^2	0.07000000	1	0.07000000	14325.94	< 0.0001
B^2	0.00000093	1	0.00000093	0.19	0.6684
C^2	0.00000299	1	0.00000299	0.61	0.4463
Residual	0.00008352	17	0.00000491		
Cor Total	0.096000000	26			

Table 5.6. Response 1- 245 nm : ANOVA for Response Surface Quadratic model.

Analysis of variance table [Partial sum of squares - Type III]					
Source	**Sum of squares**	**d.f.**	**Mean square**	**F - Value**	**P – value (Prob > F)**
Model	0.17000000	9	0.01900000	408.94	< 0.0001 significant
A- Solvent	0.02700000	1	0.02700000	574.07	< 0.0001
B- Sample speed	0.00015780	1	0.00015780	3.38	0.0837
C- Sample interval	0.00010760	1	0.00010760	2.3	0.1477
AB	0.00025390	1	0.00025390	5.43	0.0324
AC	0.00016060	1	0.00016060	3.43	0.0813
BC	0.00011970	1	0.00011970	2.56	0.128
A^2	0.14000000	1	0.14000000	3086.64	< 0.0001
B^2	0.00003536	1	0.00003536	0.76	0.3966
C^2	0.00008868	1	0.00008868	1.9	0.1863
Residual	0.00079490	17	0.00004676		
Cor Total	0.17000000	26			

The developed method was validated as per ICH Q2 R1guidelines and their results were summarized below in Table 5.7.

Table 5.7. Summary of Method Validation Parameters.

Parameter	Water, 0.1N HCl	0.1N NaOH
Wavelength (nm)	261 nm	245nm
Linearity Range (µg/ml)	10-50	10-50
Regression equation	y = 0.0231x - 0.0129	y = 0.0142x + 0.0858
Correlation coefficient (R^2)	0.9995	0.9996
Precision (%RSD) - Repeatability	0.073765	0.069081
Intra-day precision	0.07715 ± 0.023145	0.081079 ± 0.061617
Intra-day precision	0.088454 ± 0.02568	0.093376 ± 0.080528
Accuracy at 80% level	95.36 ± 0.00030	96.54 ± 0.00043
Accuracy at 100% level	97.69 ± 0.00042	102.23 ± 0.00065
Accuracy at 120% level	101.34 ± 0.00032	103.48 ± 0.00046
LOD (µg/ml)	0.1527	0.1436
LOQ (µg/ml)	0.8235	0.7659

Practical Examples of AQbD applied to UV - Visible Spectrophotometric method development

Estimation of Ambrisentan in bulk and pharmaceutical dosage forms

Drug Profile

Ambrisentan, chemically (2S)-2-(4,6-dimethyl pyrimidin-2-yloxy) -3-methoxy-3, 3-diphenyl propionic acid, is an endothelin receptor antagonist used in the therapy of pulmonary arterial hypertension (PAH).

It is practically insoluble in aqueous solutions at low pH. and soluble at higher pH.

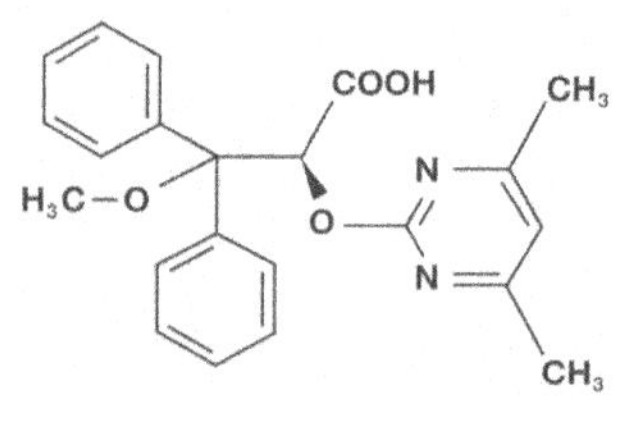

Fig. 5.11. Ambrisentan structure.

Literature

Literature survey showed LC–ESI–MS/MS, enantio-selective liquid chromatography, spectrophotometry and UV–HPLC methods for the estimation of ABN. But there is no method based on QbD for the estimation of selected drug with visible spectrophotometry.

ATP

Simple, accurate, precise, robust and stable DoE based visible spectroscopic method based on the principle of oxidation and coupling reaction of Ambrisentan in tablet dosage form with 3-methyl-2-benzothiazolinone hydrazone (MBTH reagent) in presence of $FeCl_3$ to form bluish-green chromogen (Fig. 5.12).

CAAs

The interaction effects of four distinct independent factors were examined: MBTH reagent concentration (X_1), volume of MBTH reagent (X_2), $FeCl_3$ concentration (X_3), and volume of $FeCl_3$ solution (X_4). These factors were carefully integrated into the Ishikawa fishbone diagram to assess their influence on the absorbance parameter, denoted as Y. The objective was to discern and evaluate the potential interaction effects among these variables and their impact on the absorbance outcome.

DoE

Two-level full factorial design was employed to evaluate the effect of CMPs on CAAs. Experimental design, data analysis and contour plots were developed using Minitab® 16.2.4 trial version (Minitab Inc). Upon analyzing the resulting design matrix, it was evident that the highest level of absorbance (Y) was achieved when the MBTH reagent concentration was 2%, and both the $FeCl_3$ concentration and the volume of $FeCl_3$ solution were set at 2 mL and 1.5–2 mL, respectively. The contour plots of absorbance vs. $FeCl_3$ and MBTH concentration and volume are presented in Fig. 5.13.

Table 5.8. 2- Level FFD with their Response Values.

Run	PT	Factors				Response
		X_1	X_2	X_3	X_4	Y
1	2	0	2	1	1	0.119
2	0	1	1	1	1	0.757
3	2	2	0	1	1	0.234
4	2	1	0	2	1	0.384
5	2	0	1	1	0	0.211
6	2	2	1	1	2	0.627
7	2	1	2	2	1	0.675
8	2	0	1	0	1	0.201
9	2	1	1	2	0	0.321
10	2	0	1	2	1	0.119
11	2	1	2	1	2	0.701
12	2	2	2	1	1	0.715
13	0	1	1	1	1	0.757
14	2	1	0	1	2	0.118
15	0	1	1	1	1	0.757
16	2	1	0	0	1	0.113
17	2	1	2	0	1	0.451
18	2	0	0	1	1	0.381
19	2	1	2	1	0	0.294
20	2	1	1	0	2	0.632
21	2	1	1	2	2	0.699

Contd...

22	2	1	1	0	0	0.471
23	2	2	1	1	0	0.511
24	2	2	1	2	1	0.712
25	2	1	0	1	0	0.11
26	2	2	1	0	1	0.213
27	2	0	1	1	2	0.114

PT = Pt type, B = blocks, X_1 *= MBTH reagent concentration,* X_2 *= MBTH reagent volume,* X_3 *= concentration of* $FeCl_3$*,* X_4 *=* $FeCl_3$ *volume, Y = Absorbance*

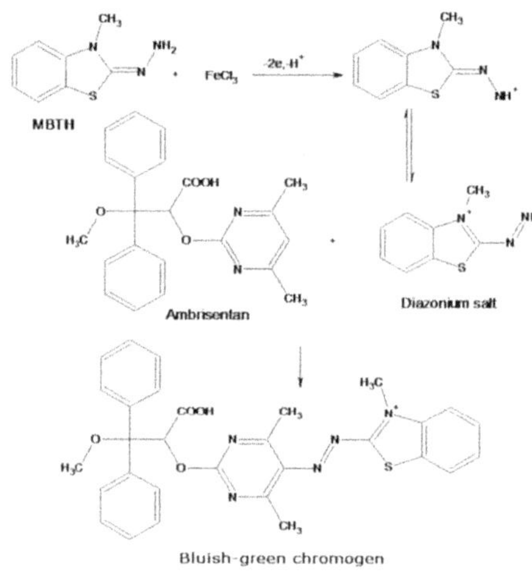

Fig. 5.12. Reaction scheme showing formation of bluish-green chromogen.

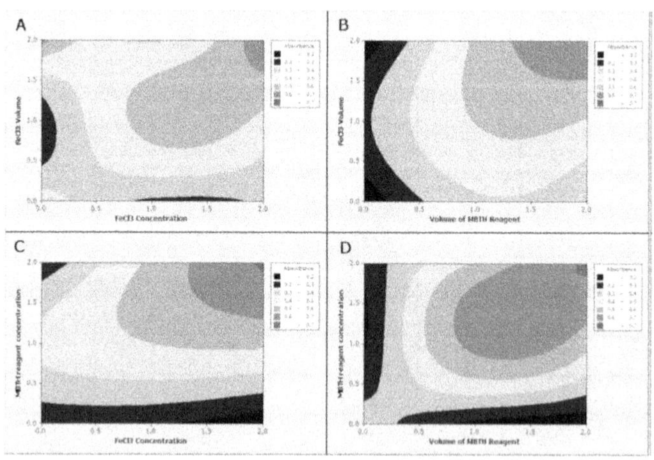

Fig. 5.13. Contour plots of (A) absorbance vs concentration and volume of FeC13, (B) absorbance vs. volume of FeC13 and MBTH, (C) absorbance vs. concentration of MBTH and FeC13, and (D) absorbance vs. concentration and volume of MBTH.

The method was validated as per ICH guidelines in terms of linearity, accuracy, precision, robustness, LOD and LOQ. The matrix of the two-level full factorial design and experimental runs for visible spectroscopy is provided in Table 5.9.

Table 5.9. Validation Summary of Ambrisentan by Visible Spectroscopy (n=6).

Parameter	Observed value
Specificity	Specific
Linearity, µg/mL	10–30
Accuracy (% recovery)	98.8–99.6
Precision (% RSD)	1.04
LOD (S: N Ratio), µg/mL	2.7 &
LOQ (S: N Ratio), µg/mL	8.3
Robustness at 623nm (% RSD)	1.02
Robustness at 627nm (% RSD)	1.74

***

Practical Examples of AQbD applied to

UV - Visible Spectrophotometric method development

Estimation of Cefixime Trihydrate using Ninhydrin Reagent

Drug Profile

Cefixime is obtained as a crystalline solid substance having solubility in organic solvents such as ethanol (5 mg/ml), DMSO and DMF (30 mg/ml) with poor solubility in water. It is a semi-synthetic broad-spectrum, third generation cephalosporin derived from the marine fungus Cephalosporium acremonium with antibacterial activity.

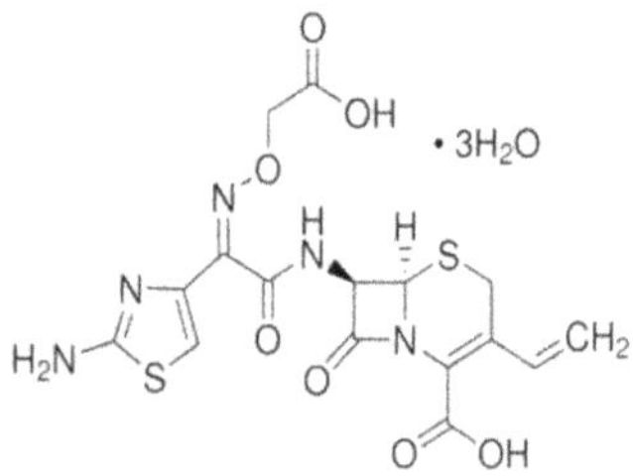

Fig. 5.14. Cefixime structure.

Its IUPAC name is (6R,7R)-7-{[2-(2-Amino-1,3-thiazol-4-yl)-2-(carboxymethoxyimino) acetyl] amino} - 3 - ethenyl - 8 - oxo - 5 - thia - 1- aza bicyclo[4.2.0]oct-2-ene-2-carboxylic acid with molecular weight of 507.5 g/mole.

Literature

Number of studies have been carried out on Cefixime like spectrophotometry, spectrofluorimetric, HPLC, HPTLC and voltammetry to estimate the content of CEF in single-component and multicomponent formulations. I.P., B.P., U.S.P. and E.P. described a liquid chromatographic method for estimating the CEF content in bulk form, oral suspension and tablet formulation. The visible spectrophotometric methods reported were based on the oxidative coupling reaction of CEF with 3-methyl-2-benzothiazolinon hydrazone hydrochloride in the presence of ferric chloride; the reaction of CEF with sodium nitrite in an acidic solution; the acidic oxidation of CEF with cerium at elevated heating temperature; Conversion of CEF into hydroxamic acid, which forms a coloured complex with iron (III); the derivatization of CEF with sodium 1,2-naphthoquinone-4-sulfonate; the reaction of CEF using ninhydrin reagent. The conventional experimental method was utilized to optimize the reaction variables in the above spectrophotometric methods. But, one variable at a time method was inefficient in giving accurate results. Therefore, a systematic and statistical way of optimizing the reaction variables in order to get significant and precise results was done by utilising the experimental methodology employed for the screening and optimization of experimental variables in the development of a spectrophotometric technique for quantifying the content of CEF in both bulk and pharmaceutical formulations, utilizing ninhydrin as a derivatizing reagent.

ATP

ATP of this method is development of a visible spectrophotometric technique based on the reaction of the amino group of cefixime with ninhydrin reagent in an alkaline medium to form a yellow-coloured derivative (Fig. 5.15).

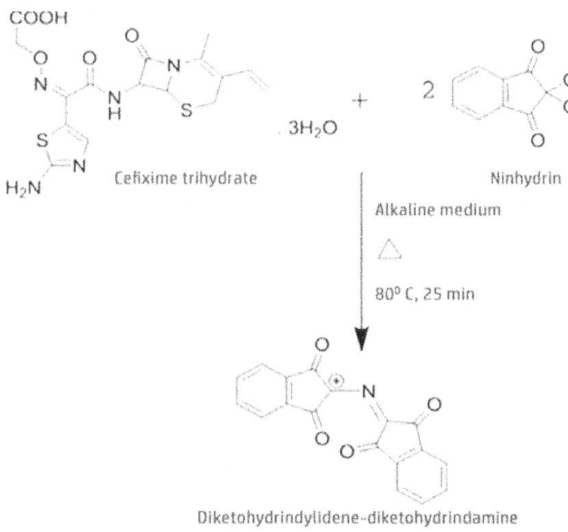

Fig. 5.15. Reaction of Cefixime with Ninhydrin reagent.

CAAs

Various experimental parameters, including the concentration of ninhydrin reagent, quantity of ninhydrin reagent, heating temperature, heating duration, and the choice of diluting solvent, were subjected to optimization using an experimental design methodology to achieve the highest absorption value in the resultant-colored reaction mixture.

When numerous factors could potentially impact a specific response, screening designs are commonly employed. In this context, a two-level full factorial design was employed to assess the main effects of four independent factors: ninhydrin reagent concentration (X_1), volume of ninhydrin reagent (X_2), heating temperature (X_3), and heating time (X_4) on the generation of the cefixime–ninhydrin complex (Y) absorbance.

The primary aim was to identify significant main effects with minimal runs. Various levels of the chosen factor are outlined in Table 5.10, and the design matrix for the two-level full factorial design can be found in Table 5.11. All experimental trials were executed in triplicate, and the outcomes are detailed in Table 5.11.

Table 5.10. Experimental factors and response variable for 2- level FFD.

Input factors	Code	Levels	
		Low	High
Ninhydrin reagent concentration (% W/V)	X_1	0.1	0.3
Volume of ninhydrin reagent (ml)	X_2	0.5	1.5
Heating temperature (°C)	X_3	70	90
Heating time (Min)	X_4	20	30
Absorbance *(Cefixime–ninhydrin complex)*	Y	Goal maximum	

Table 5.11. Experiment 2^4 and Response value.

Run	Factors				Response
	X_1	X_2	X_3	X_4	Y
1	0.3	0.5	90	30	0.181
2	0.3	1.5	90	20	0.194
3	0.3	1.5	70	30	0.179
4	0.1	0.5	90	20	0.178
5	0.1	0.5	90	30	0.178
6	0.1	1.5	70	20	0.177
7	0.3	1.5	90	30	0.195
8	0.3	0.5	90	20	0.194
9	0.1	0.5	70	20	0.163
10	0.3	0.5	70	30	0.176
11	0.3	0.5	70	20	0.167
12	0.1	1.5	70	30	0.176
13	0.1	1.5	90	20	0.191
14	0.1	1.5	90	30	0.191
15	0.3	1.5	70	20	0.180
16	0.1	0.5	70	30	0.163

On the basis of preliminary experiments, the ranges of values used in the design are the following:

Ninhydrin reagent concentration (X_1)	: 0.1–0.3% w/v
Volume of ninhydrin reagent (X_2)	: 0.5–1.5 mL
Heating temperature (X_3)	: 70–90 °C
Heating time (X_4)	: 20–30 min

Statistical analyses, including one-way ANOVA and Pareto ranking, revealed that the concentration of ninhydrin reagent (X_1), the volume of ninhydrin reagent (X_2), and the heating temperature (X_3) were statistically significant factors ($P < 0.05$) influencing the formation of the cefixime–ninhydrin complex Y (absorbance). Pareto charts (Fig. 5.16) were generated based on multivariate regression analyses, where the length of each bar in the Pareto chart represents the magnitude of the regression coefficient for that particular factor. The direction of the bar indicates whether the factor has a direct or inverse effect on the response. Specifically, the ninhydrin reagent concentration (X_1), volume of ninhydrin reagent (X_2), and heating temperature (X_3) directly affect the absorbance Y, and these effects are statistically significant ($P < 0.05$). On the other hand, the heating time (X_4) also has a direct effect on the response Y, but it is not statistically significant ($P > 0.05$).

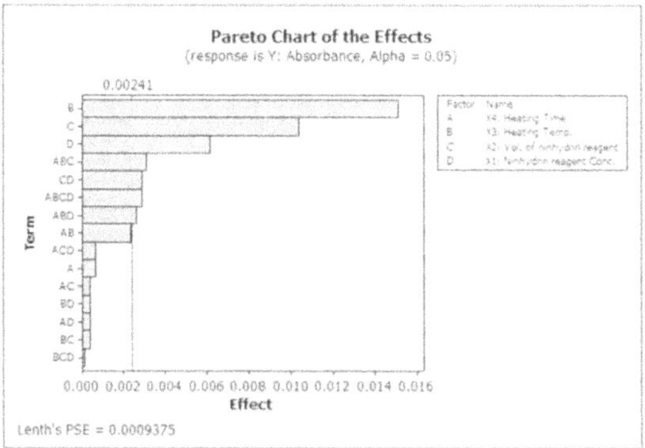

Fig.5.16. Pareto chart.

The main, interaction, and quadratic effects of these three factors on the selected response Y were assessed using a Box-Behnken experimental design in conjunction with response surface methodology. By employing response surface and contour plots, the optimal values for the chosen factors were determined. These values were fixed as

Ninhydrin reagent concentration (X_1) : 0.2% w/v

Volume of ninhydrin reagent (X_2) : 1 mL

Heating temperature (X_3) : 80 °C

Table 5.12. Optimization method parameters for BBD.

Run	Pattern (X_1, X_2, X_3)	X_1	X_2	X_3	Predicted response	Observed response Y
1	- - 0	0.1	0.5	80	0.209	0.219
2	- + 0	0.1	1.5	80	0.225	0.243
3	0 0 0	0.2	1.0	80	0.221	0.222
4	+ 0 +	0.3	1.0	90	0.234	0.223
5	0 - +	0.2	0.5	90	0.222	0.243
6	0 0 0	0.2	1.0	80	0.221	0.224
7	+ + 0	0.3	1.5	80	0.232	0.203
8	0 - -	0.2	0.5	70	0.203	0.198
9	- 0 -	0.1	1.0	70	0.207	0.215
10	+ - 0	0.3	0.5	80	0.216	0.203
11	+ 0 -	0.3	1.0	70	0.214	0.241
12	0 + +	0.2	1.5	90	0.238	0.221
13	0 + -	0.2	1.5	70	0.219	0.243
14	0 0 0	0.2	1.0	80	0.221	0.217
15	- 0 +	0.1	1.0	90	0.227	0.219

Using multivariate regression analysis, a fitted full quadratic model was obtained for the average response Y, given by the following equation:

$$\mathbf{Y = \beta_0 + \beta_1 X_1 + \beta_2 X_2 + \beta_3 X_3 + \beta_{11} X_1^2 + \beta_{22} X_2^2 + \beta_{33} X_3^2 + \beta_{12} X_1 x_2 + \beta_{13} X_1 X_3 + \beta_{23} X_2 x_3}$$

where, Y= selected response; β_0 = arithmetic mean response; andβ_1, β_2 and β_3 = regression coefficients of the factors X_1, X_2 and X_3, respectively.

Table 5.12 presented the regression coefficients along with their corresponding P-values. The results reveal that the ninhydrin reagent concentration (X_1), volume of ninhydrin reagent (X_2), and heating temperature (X_3) significantly influenced the absorbance (Y) of the CEF–

ninhydrin complex (P < 0.05). An interaction effect was noted between the ninhydrin reagent concentration (X_1) and the volume of ninhydrin reagent (X_2) (P = 0.078). Another interaction effect was observed between the volume of ninhydrin reagent (X_2) and the heating temperature (X_3) (P = 1.000), although this interaction was not statistically significant (P > 0.05). However, no significant interaction effect was observed between the ninhydrin reagent concentration (X_1) and heating temperature (X_3) (P = 1.000). To visualize the impact of the parameters on the selected response Y, response surface and contour plots were analyzed. Figure 5.17 illustrates the influence of the ninhydrin reagent concentration (X_1), volume of ninhydrin reagent (X_2), and heating temperature (X_3) on the chosen response Y. The contour plots depict nonlinear effects of these factors on the selected response Y. The surface diagram indicates that a ninhydrin reagent concentration (X_1) ranging from 0.2 to 0.25% w/v and a heating temperature (X_3) between 80 and 85 °C yield the maximum absorbance (Y) (Fig. 5.18a).

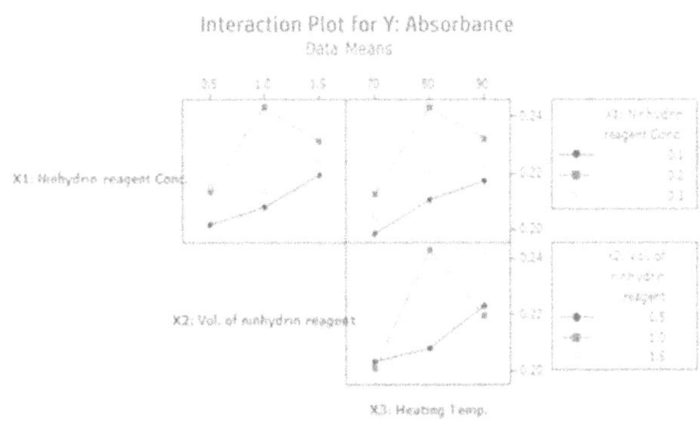

Fig. 5.17. Interaction plot of response Y.

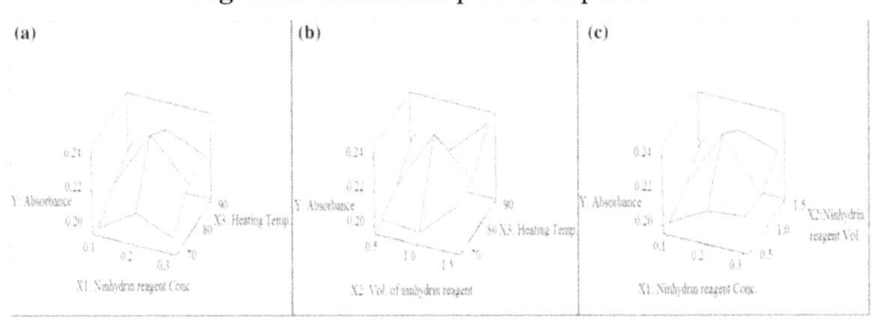

Fig. 5.18. Response surface plot of response Y.

(a) X_1: Ninhydrin reagent Conc. versus X_3: Heating Temp. (b) X_2: Vol. of Ninhydrin reagent versus X_3: Heating Temp. (c) X_1: Ninhydrin reagent Conc. versus X_2: Vol. of Ninhydrin reagent.

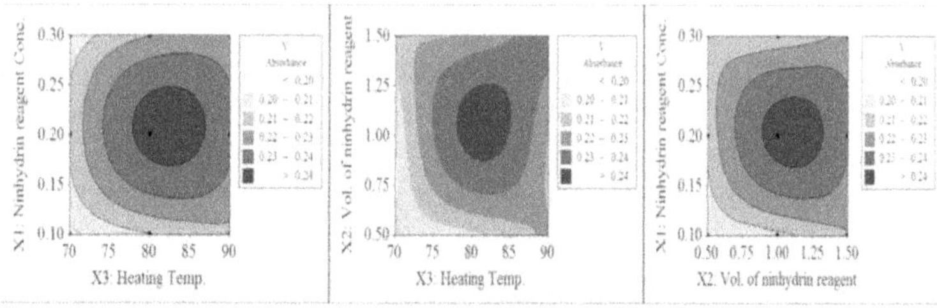

(a) (b) (c)

Fig. 5.19. Contour plots of response Y.
(a) X_3: Heating Temp. versus X_1: Ninhydrin reagent Conc. (b) X_3: Heating Temp. versus X_2: Vol. of Ninhydrin reagent (c) X_2: Vol. of Ninhydrin reagent versus X_1: Ninhydrin reagent Conc.

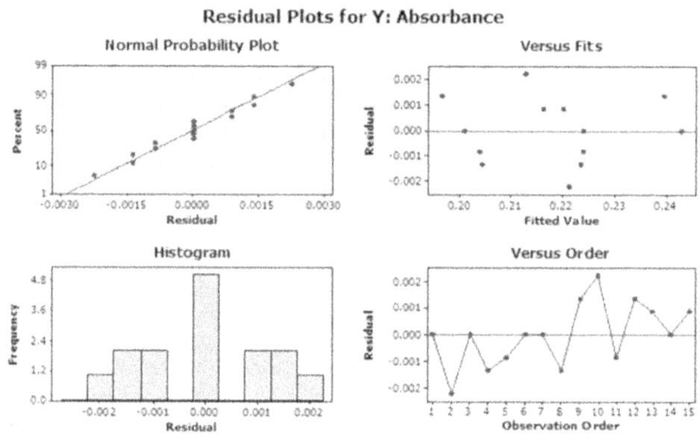

Fig. 5.20. Residual plots of response Y.

The predicted values of the response matched the experimental values reasonably well, with an R^2 of 99.41% and R^2 (adj) of 98.34% for the selected response Y. In order to gain a better understanding of the effects of the variables on the selected response Y, the predicted model was presented in the form of a response surface and contour plot design.

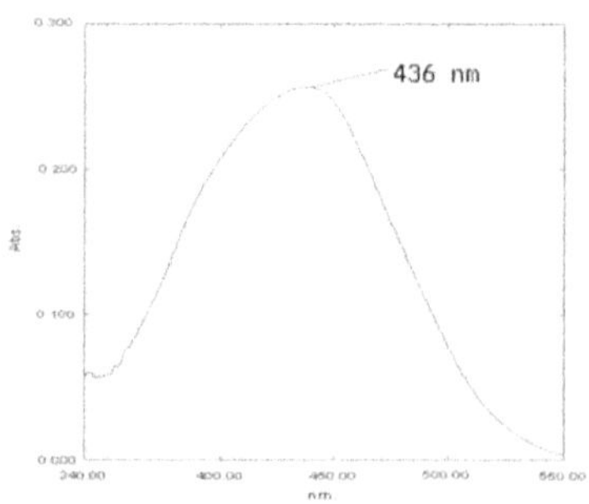

Fig. 5.21. UV–Visible spectrum of CEF-Ninhydrin complex.

Table 5.13. Optical characteristics and statistical data of the regression equations.

Parameter	CEF-Ninhydrin complex
pH	Alkaline borate buffer pH 10
Colour	Yellow
Stoichiometry of the Complex (ninhydrin to CEF molar ratio)	20:1
λmax (nm)	436
Beer–Lamberts law limit (μg/ml)	5–30
Molar absorptivity (L/mol cm)	2.13 X 10^4
Sandells sensitivity (μg/ml cm)	1.48
Slope	0.028
Intercept	0.001
Regression coefficient	0.9995

The proposed method was validated according to the ICH Q2 (R1) method validation guidelines.

Table 5.14. Validation Summary of developed method.

Parameter	Observed value
Specificity	Specific
Linearity (μg/mL)	5–30
Regression coefficient	0.9995
Accuracy (% recovery)	
80% Level	102.50
100% Level	102.48
120% Level	101.09
Intra-day Precision (% RSD)	1.12
Inter-day Precision (% RSD)	0.92
LOD (μg/mL)	1.4045
LOQ (μg/mL)	4.213

***

CHAPTER 6

AQbD for HPLC Method Development

6.1 Introduction

High Performance Liquid Chromatography is an analytical technique used to separate, identify or quantify each component in a mixture. The mixture is separated using the basic principle of column chromatography and then identified and quantified by spectroscopy. It is an incredibly useful analytical technique with a broad range of applications.

HPLC involves a column of adsorbent material (such as silica beads) through which a sample is passed under pressure. Each component of the sample mixture will interact differently with material in the column, and as such, have a different flow rate. As a result, the various components will leave the column at different times and can be collected separately.

Qualitative and quantitative analysis can determine the identity of each component and the composition of the sample. It is considered a crucial tool in a variety of pharmaceutical applications, including evaluating formulations, checking purity, and monitoring changes due to process adjustments or during scaleup.

6.2 Principle of HPLC

It is based on the distribution of the analyte (sample) between a mobile phase (eluent) and a stationary phase (packing material of the column). Depending on the chemical structure of the analyte, the molecules are retarded while passing the stationary phase. The specific intermolecular interactions between the molecules of a sample and the packing material define their time "on-column". Hence, different constituents of a sample are eluted at different times. Thereby, the separation of the sample ingredients is achieved. A detection unit (e.g., UV detector) recognizes the analytes after leaving the column. The signals are converted and recorded by a data management system (computer software) and then shown in a chromatogram. After passing the detector unit, the mobile phase can be subjected to additional detector units, a fraction collection unit or to the waste.

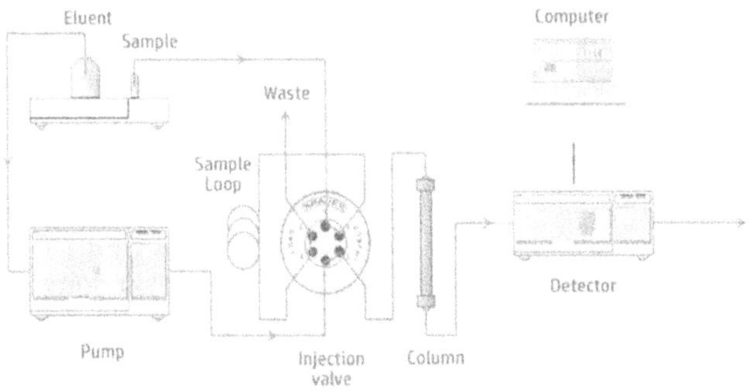

Fig. 6.1. Layout of a HPLC system.

In general, a HPLC system contains the following modules: a solvent reservoir, a pump, an injection valve, a column, a detector unit and a data processing unit (Fig. 6.1.). The solvent (eluent) is delivered by the pump at high pressure and constant speed through the system. To keep the drift and noise of the detector signal as low as possible, a constant and pulseless flow from the pump is crucial. The analyte (sample) is provided to the eluent by the injection valve.

The separated analytes which are transported by the mobile phase are recorded as signal peaks by the detector unit. The total amount of all peaks is called chromatogram. Each individual peak provides qualitative and quantitative information of the analyte. Qualitative information is given by the peak itself (e.g.: shape, intensity of the signal, time of appearance in the chromatogram). In addition, the area of a peak is proportional to the concentration of the substance. Hence, the chromatography data management software can calculate the concentration of the sample by integration. This provides quantitative information. Ideally the peaks are recorded as a Gaussian bell-shaped curve. A schematic example of chromatogram is illustrated in Fig. 6.2.

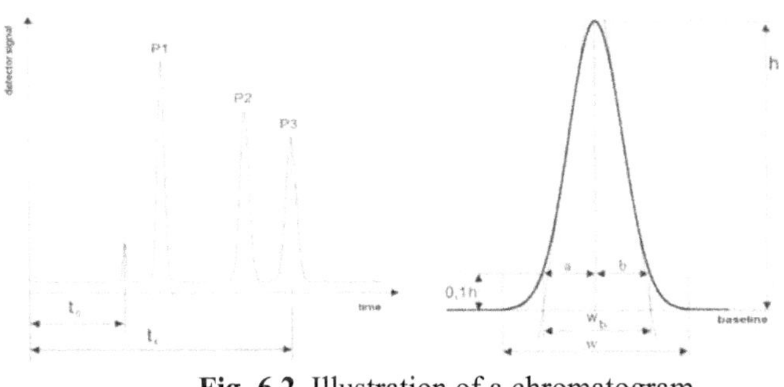

Fig. 6.2. Illustration of a chromatogram.

t_0: Delay time; t_R: Retention time; w: Peak width; P_1, P_2, P_3: Symmetric peaks; T: tailing factor = b/a; T = 1 represents a symmetrical peak. For T > 1 the peak profile is named tailing. For T < 1 the peak profile is named fronting.

6.3 Classical Approach for HPLC Method Development

The Classical approach for HPLC method development involves the scheme depicted in the Table. 6.1. The aim in HPLC method development is to optimize the resolution for the desired analyte(s) in the shortest possible time. Reversed-phase chromatography is the most common type of method used in HPLC - it probably accounts for 60% of all methods, and is used by nearly 95% of all chromatographers. In reversed-phase chromatography, we partition analytes between the polar mobile phase and the non-polar stationary phase – the opposite of normal phase chromatography. Typically, we get non-polar, non-specific interaction of analytes with hydrophobic stationary phase, meaning the sample partitions into the stationary phase. stationary phases like C18, C8, phenyl, or C3, which give polarity difference based on the aromatic structure of a molecule are used.

More polar analytes are less retained than non-polar analytes in reversed-phase chromatography. Retention is roughly proportional to the hydrophobicity of the analytes. The analytes which have large hydrophobic groups and with longer alkyl chains will be more retained than molecules that have polar groups (e.g., amine, hydroxyl) in their structure. If there are a series of fatty acids, such as C12, C14, C16 and C18, the C12 would be the least retained and the C18 would be the most retained. The mobile phase is comprised of two main parts, water with an optional buffer, or perhaps an acid or base to adjust pH and water-miscible organic solvent. Reversed-phase chromatography is quite versatile and it can be used to separate non-polar, polar, ionizable and ionic molecules, sometimes in the same chromatogram. Typically, with ionizable compounds, to improve retention and peak shape, it will be beneficial to add a modifier to the mobile phase to control pH and retention.

Table 6.1. Classical approach for HPLC Method Development.

Collection and identification of drug(s)
↓
Literature
↓
Define a Separation goal
↓
Experimental work
↓
Need for special HPLC procedure, Sample pre-treatment etc
↓
Selection of mode, Column and its packing dimensions, chemistry of stationary phase, mobile phase and its Ph, detector etc
↓

Contd...

Selection of LC method, Preliminary run, estimate best separation conditions

↓

Optimization of separation Conditions

↓

Check for problems or requirements for special procedures

↓

Recovery of purified material, qualitative and quantitative estimation

↓

Optimizations of results

↓

Method development report

↓

Validation of developed method

↓

Use of developed method for regular analysis

6.4 AQbD Elements for HPLC Method Development

The utilization of Design of Experiments (DoE) has become indispensable in contemporary drug analysis, particularly in High-Performance Liquid Chromatography (HPLC). DoE efficiently balances various chromatographic parameters to achieve optimal separation, making it an irreplaceable technique in modern pharmaceutical analysis. Despite its extensive application in pharmaceutical research, devising reliable HPLC methods remains a formidable challenge.

This challenge arises from the need to concurrently control numerous factors influencing analyte retention, which has traditionally been addressed through a time-consuming and resource-intensive trial-and-error approach. This conventional method also results in substantial reagent and toxic solvent consumption, with no guarantee of achieving the ideal working conditions. To streamline the process of HPLC condition optimization and explore the experimental space more systematically, chemometric approaches are increasingly being employed.

DoE, a multivariate statistical technique, plays a pivotal role in planning, executing, and analyzing data from experiments. In DoE studies, deliberate modifications are made to one or several input variables (factors) to understand their impact on the observed response or desired experimental outcome. In essence, applying DoE in HPLC analysis offers the advantage of obtaining objective and information-rich results with minimal experimental effort. It finds utility in chromatographic method development, optimization, and robustness testing.

While experienced analysts well-versed in the fundamentals of DoE can execute many DoE steps manually, the data analysis process is often simplified by employing specialized software or general statistical tools. Some popular software choices for interpreting chromatographic data include Design Expert (Stat-Ease Inc.), MINITAB (Minitab Inc.), MATLAB (The Mathworks Inc.), Statgraphics Centurion (Statpoint Technologies), and JMP (SAS Institute Inc.).

Creation of Knowledge Space

Prior knowledge plays an important role in identifying the appropriate analytical technique. Knowledge of best practices and current state-of-the-art technologies as well as current regulatory expectations contributes to the selection of the most suitable technology for a given purpose. Existing platform analytical procedures (e.g., estimation of drug substances in formulation by RP-HPLC) can be leveraged to evaluate the attributes of a specific method without conducting additional procedure development. As additional information is obtained, knowledge related to analytical procedures should be actively managed throughout the method lifecycle.

Analytical Target Profile

The first step in the implementation of AQbD is ATP. It defines the goal of the HPLC method development process, and is the indicator of method performance. It involves the determination of amount of drug in API or in formulation, accurately and precisely by employing a simple, sensitive and economical analytical method.it can also be used for determination drug in the presence of impurities (Stability Indicating Assay Method, SIAM), determination of amount of drug release in *in-vitro* dissolution studies.

Analytical Method Performance Characteristics

AMPCs are the validation parameters/ characteristics that are normally evaluated during HPLC method validation. The characteristics such as accuracy, precision, specificity, linearity, range, detection limit, quantitation limit, robustness, ruggedness can be determined as per ICH Q2 (R1) guidelines.

Selection of Analytical Techniques

with reference to ATP defined in the step 2, HPLC is selected to meet the goals, as it is a versatile technique and can be applied to a broad spectrum of compounds, including organic and inorganic substances, pharmaceuticals, biomolecules (e.g., proteins and nucleic acids), and more with suitable accuracy, precision and robustness.

Identification of Critical Analytical Attributes (CAAs)

After the selection of technique, detailed assessment of the risks associated with method parameters, viz., Mobile phase composition, pH, flowrate of mobile phase, run time, pH of buffer, type of column, column temperature, injection volume, type of detector etc. are focused. To control the "Variability" of materials and method, Critical Analytical Attributes (CAA) and Critical method parameters (CMP) are identified through Risk Management process.

For HPLC technique, typical CAAs are Retention time, NTP, Resolution, peak area, asymmetric factor. It helps to have better understanding of method & its performance thus helping Life Cycle Management of the method (LCM).

Risk Assessment

According to ICH Q9 Risk Assessment can be done in three steps- Risk identification, risk analysis and risk evaluation. Commonly used risk assessment tools for chromatographic technique are Ishikawa (fishbone) diagram and failure mode and effects analysis (FMEA) as they help to identify and classify main sources of hazards associated with the method.

Design of Experiments (DoE)

The DoE methodology evaluates how factors interact with each other, offering comprehensive insights, providing high-quality information across the entire experimental domain, and achieving the desired results with fewer experiments compared to classical approaches.

In HPLC method development, commonly employed screening designs include the 2-level full factorial design, fractional factorial design, Taguchi design, and occasionally the Plackett-Burman design. For optimization purposes, the preferred designs are the 3-level fractional factorial design, Box-Behnken design, and central composite design. In most research studies, the central composite design and D-optimal designs have been favored for optimizing HPLC systems when dealing with two critical method parameters (CMPs), while the Box-Behnken design is chosen when working with three or four CMPs.

MODR

MODR of any analytical method, also termed as Analytical Design Space (ADS), or Proven Acceptable Range (PAR), is the multidimensional combination and interaction of input variables that have been demonstrated to provide assurance of quality. Before validating a MODR, confirmatory validation runs should be performed to rectify the empirical model resulting from a DoE exercise.

It allows for adaptability in adjusting different input method parameters to achieve the desired method performance criteria and response, all without the need for resubmission to the FDA. It relies on a scientific, risk-based, and multivariate methodology to assess the impacts of various factors on method performance.

Control Strategy

A robust method control strategy is developed based on the extensive data gathered during the method development and verification phases. This data enables the establishment of connections between method attributes, such as resolution, and the ability to meet Acceptance and Tolerance Profile (ATP) criteria. The control strategy should encompass method parameters that influence variability and are set as constants (e.g., reagent grade, instrument brand or type, column type). It's worth noting that the method control strategy doesn't undergo significant changes when adopting the AQbD approach compared to the traditional approach. However, under the AQbD approach, method controls are established with a more comprehensive dataset, guided by ATP criteria, thus forging a stronger link between the method's purpose and its performance.

Continuous Method Monitoring

After implementing a method for routine use, continuous monitoring of method performance becomes essential to ensure ongoing compliance with ATP criteria. This can be achieved through tools like control charts or other mechanisms for tracking system suitability data, method-related investigations, and more. Periodic re-verification experiments aligned with the method's intended purpose may also be conducted as needed. Continuous monitoring empowers analysts to proactively detect and address any deviations from expected performance trends. Existing methods should undergo periodic re-evaluation to address any identified gaps or opportunities for improvement in the current methodology, potentially involving enhancements to the existing methodology or, as analytical technologies advance, the adoption of new technologies.

***

Practical Examples of AQbD applied to HPLC method development

Determination of Raloxifene HCl in Pure and Tablets

Drug Profile

Raloxifene (RLX) HCl, a 2nd generation selective oestrogen receptor modulator, used in the treatment of osteoporosis in postmenopausal women and breast cancer. Chemically, it is [6-hydroxy-2-(4-hydroxyphenyl)-1-benzothiophen- 3-yl]- [4-(2 piperidinyl ethoxy)-phenyl]-methanone.

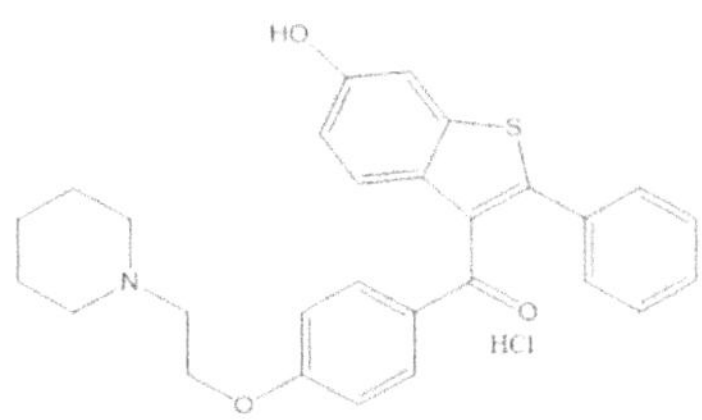

Fig. 6.3. Raloxifene HCl structure.

It is soluble in ethanol, DMSO, DMF and sparingly soluble in aqueous buffers.

Literature

Since RLX HCl became official in European pharmacopeia in 2007, various analytical methods like UV-Vis spectrophotometry, RP-HPLC, capillary electrophoresis, and Rayleigh scattering have been reported in the literature to detect, estimate and quantify it. However, invariably these documented techniques exhibit shortcomings such as extended retention times (RT), elevated operational expenses, as well as diminished sensitivity, accuracy, and precision. Consequently, there is a demand for the creation of a more sensitive, cost-effective, and reliable analytical method to assess the drug molecule.

ATP

An assay ATP should encompass a declaration regarding accuracy and precision, as demonstrated by the following example: The RP-HPLC method must demonstrate the capability to accurately and precisely measure the drug substance in tablets within the concentration range of 0.5-100 mcg/ml. This accuracy and precision should be such that the recorded measurements fall within ± 2% of the true value with a minimum confidence level of 95%. To meet the need of ATP, system suitability, linearity, LOQ, LOD, precision, accuracy, selectivity and robustness are selected as AMPCs. Through risk Management process, tailing factor (TF), % assay and theoretical plate count (TPC) are identified as CAAs and flow rate and mobile phase composition are identified as CMPs.

DoE

Screening design used was fractional factorial design (Fr FD) with eight runs to determine the influential factors for the systematic development. optimization studies were carried out by employing a second order central composite design (CCD).

Data optimization and model validation procedures were performed utilizing Design Expert® version 11 software (manufactured by Stat-Ease Inc., MN, USA). This involved fitting the experimental data into second-degree quadratic polynomial models to estimate the various response variables under investigation, in conjunction with the examined factors.

For the purpose of method optimization, a CCD was employed, followed by subsequent data analysis. The analysis involved the selection of second-order quadratic equations that encompassed both the primary and interaction effects for each of the studied CAAs. The coefficients of these various quadratic polynomial model terms, as well as the corresponding ANOVA parameters such as the model p-value and R2 value, are provided in Table 6.2.

$$Y = \beta_0 + \beta_1 X_1 + \beta_2 X_2 + \beta_3 X_1 X_2 + \beta_4 X_1 + \beta_5 X_2$$

where, β_0 represents the intercept, while β_1 and β_2 are the coefficients of factor X_1 and X_2, and β_3 represents the coefficient of an interaction term between factor X_1 and X_2 and β_4 and β_5 are the coefficients of the quadratic terms.

Among the numerous parameters considered, the model evaluation was centered on the correlation coefficient (R2) and the analysis of lack of fit. Coefficients with a significance level of $p < 0.001$ were then specifically taken into account for assessing the Analysis of Variance (ANOVA) model. Additionally, the exploration of the relationship between factors and responses was carried out through the utilization of 3-D response plots and 2-D contour plots.

Optimized conditions of the method are

Mobile phase : Methanol : Sodium acetate buffer (50:50 %v/v)

pH : 4

Flow rate : 1mL/min

Oven temperature : 40°C

Detection wavelength : 287 nm

The RP-HPLC method that was developed was employed to quantitatively determine RLX in a commercially available tablet formulation known as Ralista®.

This optimized method underwent validation to assess various parameters, including linearity, system suitability, limit of quantification (LOQ), limit of detection (LOD), precision, accuracy, selectivity, and robustness. This validation process was conducted following the guidelines outlined in ICH Q2 (R1) and Q14.

Table 6.2. 4-factor 8-run Fr FD for screening of method variables and process parameters.

Run	Flow rate	Injection volume	Mobile phase ratio	Temperature
1	-1	-1	+1	-1
2	-1	+1	+1	-1
3	+1	-1	+1	+1
4	+1	-1	-1	-1
5	-1	-1	-1	+1
6	+1	-1	-1	-1
7	-1	-1	-1	+1
8	+1	+1	+1	+1

Selected parameter	Levels of factors studied	
	Low	High
Flowrate (ml/min)	0.8	1.2
Injection volume (µl)	10	20
Mobile phase ratio (% v/v)	40: 60	60:40
Temperature (°C)	25	40

Table 6.3. Design matrix as per CCD for optimization of HPLC method.

Run	Coded factor Levels	
	Factor 1 (Mobile phase ratio)	**Factor 2 (Flowrate)**
1	+1	0
2	-1	-1
3	-1	+1
4	+1	-1
5	+1	+1
6	0	0
7	0	0
8	0	-1
9	0	0
10	0	+1
11	0	0
12	0	0
13	-1	0

Selected parameter	Decoded factor level		
	Low (-1)	**Intermediate (0)**	**High (+1)**
Flowrate (ml/min)	0.8	1.0	1.2
Mobile phase ratio (% V/V)	40: 60	50:50	60:40

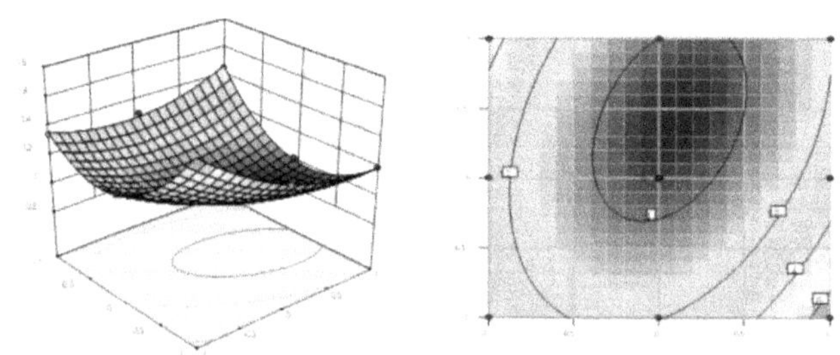

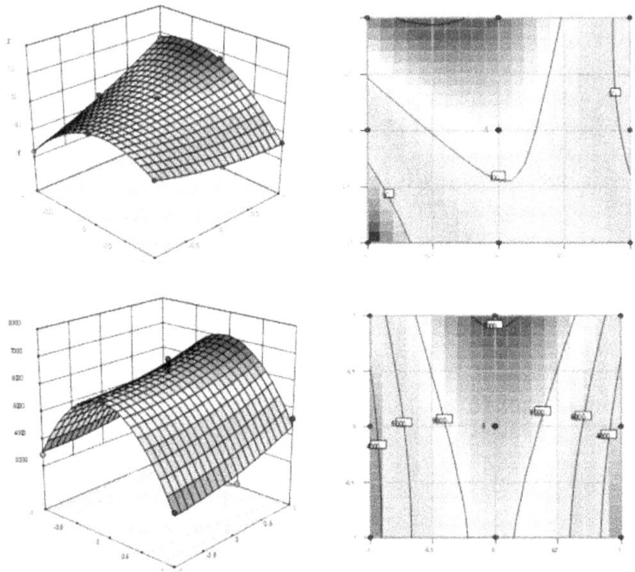

Fig. 6.4. 3D response surfaces and 2D contour plots for different CAAs, viz., tailing factor (a-b), % assay (c-d) and theoretical plate count (e-f).

Table 6.4. Coefficients of polynomial equation as per the second-order modified quadratic model for each CAA.

Coefficient code	Polynomial coefficients for critical analytical attributes		
	Tailing factor	**% Assay**	**Theoretical plate count**
β_0	0.95931	101.655	6386.52
β_1	0.0166667	-2.66667	-102
β_2	-0.0983333	4.5	506.333
β_3	-0.15	-8.5	110.5
β_4	0.332414	-10.7931	-2755.31
β_5	0.137414	1.7069	215.69
P-value	<0.0001	<0.0001	<0.0001
R^2	0.9824	0.9926	0.8497

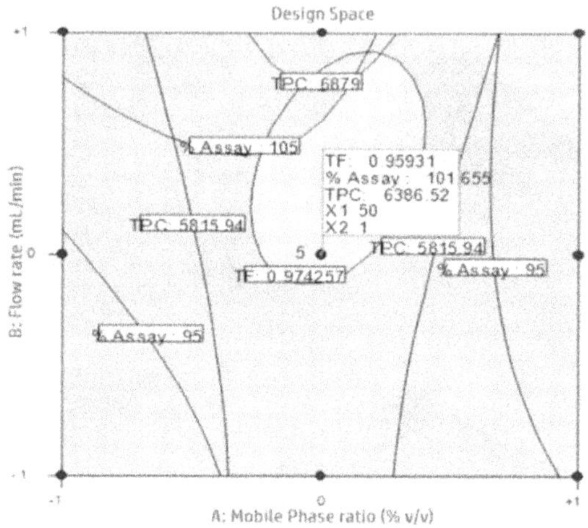

Fig. 6.5. Overlay plot showing the optimal analytical design space.

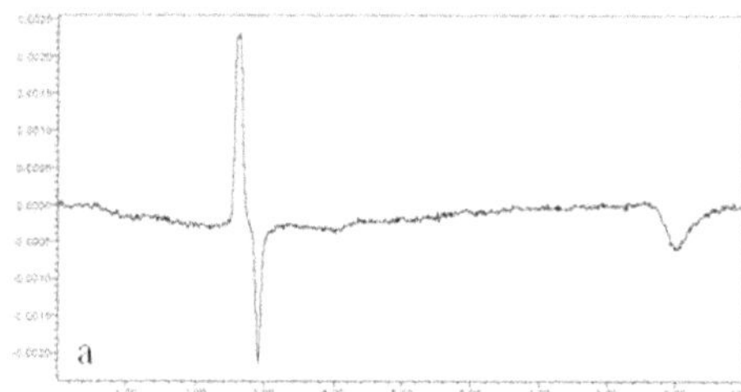

Fig. 6.6. (a) Chromatogram of blank.

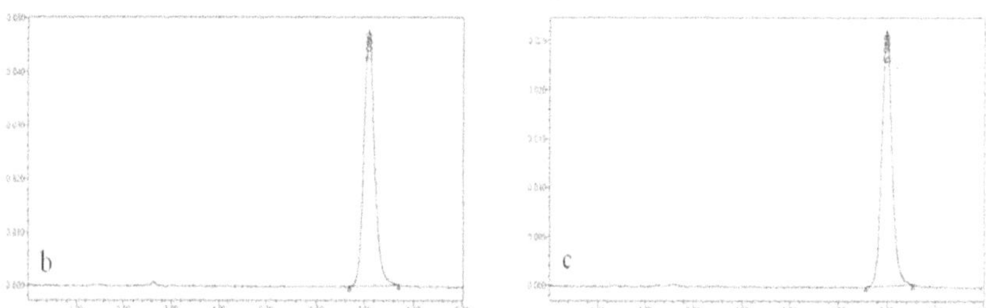

Fig 6.6. Chromatograms of (b) RLX standard and (c) Tablets.

Table 6.5. Summary of Validation parameters of RLX HCl.

Parameter	Observed value
Linearity (μg/ml)	0.5-100
Correlation coefficient (R^2)	0.999.

Contd...

Accuracy (% recovery)	98.24 – 102.80 %
Precision (% RSD)	< 2%
Robustness (% RSD)	< 2%
LOD (ng/mL)	0.5432
LOQ (ng/mL)	1.6461

***

Practical Examples of AQbD applied to HPLC Method Development

Estimation of Valsartan in Rat Plasma

Drug Profile

Valsartan, an Angiotensin - II receptor antagonist, is primarily used for the treatment of hypertension, congestive heart failure and other related cardiac disorders. Chemically, It is N-(1-oxopentyl)-N-[[2-(1H-tetrazol-5-yl) [1,1-biphenyl]-4-yl] methyl]-Lvaline with an empirical formula of $C_{24}H_{29}N_5O_3$ and molecular weight of 435.5. its pKa (acid) is 4.37.

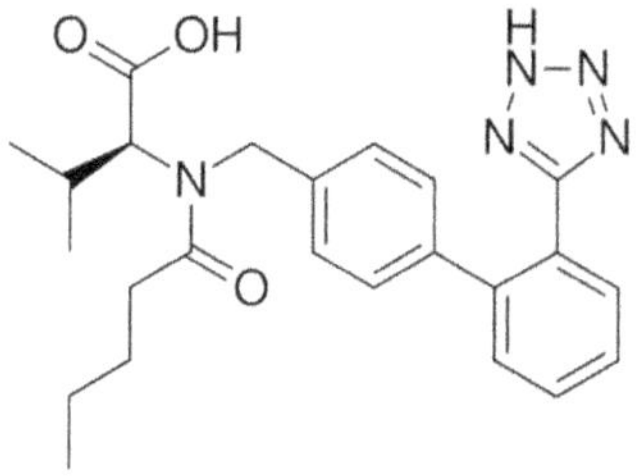

Fig. 6.7. Valsartan structure.

It occurs as white, crystalline powder and exhibits pH-dependent aqueous solubility (0.18 g/L in water) and is soluble in the neutral pH range.

Literature

Till date, several chromatographic methods have been developed for the separation and quantification of valsartan employing different instrumental techniques such as HPTLC, UV spectrophotometry, HPLC with fluorescence detector, HPLC with PDA detector, HPLC with UV detector, UPLC-ESI-MS-MS, LC-MS-MS, HPLC-MS (with time-off-flight), hydrophilic interaction liquid chromatography/electro spray ionization mass spectrometry, GC-MS, UPLC, stereo specific HPLC, and capillary electrophoresis. While these methods have proven to be effective in quantifying valsartan in biological samples, they still pose several challenges. These challenges include the extraction of the analyte from the biological matrix and its subsequent utilization in the developed method for pharmacokinetic and clinical studies.

ATP

QbD based simple, sensitive and cost-effective RP-HPLC analytical technique must be able to rapidly estimate valsartan drug substance in rat plasma with an accuracy of 100%±3% and precision of %RSD NMT 2 is the ATP of this method. To meet the need of ATP, system suitability, linearity, LOQ, LOD, precision, accuracy, selectivity and robustness are selected as AMPCs.

CAAs & CMPs

Through risk Management method i.e., Ishikawa fish bone diagram peak area, retention time, peak tailing and number of theoretical plates are identified as CAAs and mobile phase pH, flow rate and percentage of organic modifiers are identified as CMPs.

DoE

Quality risk management was utilized to identify the Critical Method Parameters (CMPs), followed by method optimization. The optimization involved a three-factor, three-level Box-Behnken Design (BBD) with mobile phase pH, flow rate, and the percentage of organic modifiers as the CMPs set at low (-1), intermediate (0), and high (+1) levels. Key Critical Analytical Attributes (CAAs) like peak area, retention time, peak tailing, and the number of theoretical plates were evaluated. A total of 15 experimental runs, including triplicate center points (0, 0, 0), were generated as per the selected BBD design.

Subsequently, the developed method was applied in bioanalysis, where a liquid-liquid extraction process was employed to separate the drug from rat plasma. The optimization of the extraction process was conducted using a Face-Centered Cubic Design (FCCD) with centrifugation speed and centrifugation time as the CMPs, aiming to maximize % recovery, signal-to-noise ratio, and the purity threshold of the drug peak post-extraction.

The optimum chromatographic solution was determined using mathematical and graphical search techniques, and a design space was delineated. This search for optimal chromatographic conditions was guided by a numerical desirability function that balanced the CAAs according to the desired target objectives. The optimal conditions identified included a mobile phase mixture comprising a 65:35 ratio of ACN and 0.01M Acetic acid at a pH of 3.2, a flow rate of 0.83 ml/min, and an organic modifier at the 64% level. These conditions yielded a peak area of 1,295, retention time of 6.76, peak tailing of 1.13, and theoretical plates of 11,616.

Other parameters, such as column oven temperature (30°C), sample volume (20 µl), and PDA detection (242 nm), remained constant throughout the study based on preliminary trial observations. The chosen conditions, as identified through numerical optimization, achieved a desirability value of 1, and the optimized conditions were depicted in the design space overlay plot (Fig. 6.13).

Using the optimized chromatographic conditions, the bioanalytical method development was carried out according to the suggested method parameters. A total of 13 experimental trials were conducted as per the selected FCCD design depicted in Table 6.6. The data obtained for the percentage recovery of the drug from the plasma were subjected to mathematical modeling using the quadratic model, which was found to be statistically valid based on high R2 values (0.934–0.999) and low values of PRESS and model parameters ($P < 0.05$). Optimization data analysis was performed through multiple linear regression analysis using Design Expert® 9.0.5.1 software (provided by Stat-Ease Inc., Minneapolis, USA), following a second-order quadratic polynomial model with interaction terms.

$$\mathbf{Y = \beta_0 + \beta_1X_1 + \beta_2X_2 + \beta_3X_1X_2 + + \beta_4X_{12} + \beta_5X_{22} + \beta_6X_{12}X_2 + \beta_7X_1X_{22} + \beta_8X_{12}X_{22}}$$

The influence of factors A (centrifugation speed) and B (centrifugation time) on both %recovery and the Signal-to-Noise (S/N) ratio displayed a similar trend, exhibiting linear increases as their values transitioned from low to high levels. In contrast, the impact of these factors on Peak Tailing (PT) was not as pronounced, with maximal PT occurring at intermediate levels for both factors. The presence of a pronounced curvature in the response surface, resembling a tomb shape, indicated a significant interaction effect between these factors on the studied response variable.

The quest for the optimal chromatographic conditions involved using a numerical desirability function, which balanced the Critical Analytical Attributes (CAAs). The optimal solution, identified as a combination of Centrifugation Speed at approximately 10,000 rpm and Centrifugation Time of 29 minutes, yielded a percentage recovery of 90.14%, an S/N ratio of 91.37, and a purity threshold of 2.0. The desirability function for this chosen condition closely approached a value of 1, and the optimal solution was illustrated in the design space overlay plot. A comparison between predicted and observed values of CAAs indicated minimal variation (%prediction error within ± 5%) in the results.

Following the optimization of conditions for both the HPLC and bioanalytical methods, validation was conducted according to the Q2 R1 guidelines of the ICH, covering various parameters such as linearity, accuracy, precision, Limit of Detection (LOD), and Limit of Quantification (LOQ). The results are presented below.

Table 6.6. Design Matrix for chromatographic method optimization as per the BBD.

Runs	CMPs			CAAs			
	Mobile phase pH	Flow rate (ml/min)	% Of Organic modifier	Peak area	Rt	PT	NTP
1	3	0.95	60	1310	6.72	1.15	12,610
2	3.5	1.2	65	1,257	7.24	1.19	11,587
3	4	0.95	60	1,158	7.98	1.28	10,475
4	3	0.95	65	1,425	5.98	1.01	11,234
5	3.5	1.2	60	1,314	7.05	1.07	12,987
6	4	0.7	62.5	1,208	7.58	1.21	11,035
7	4	0.95	65	1,144	7.88	1.09	10,457
8	3.5	0.95	62.5	1,258	7.29	1.18	11,587
9	3.5	0.95	62.5	1,229	7.31	1.17	11,410
10	3.5	0.7	65	1,169	7.64	1.11	12,001
11	4	1.2	62.5	1,158	7.97	1.02	10,658
12	3.5	0.7	60	1,084	7.47	1.15	11,235
13	3	0.7	62.5	1,258	6.29	1.25	11,458
14	3	1.2	62.5	1,389	6.99	1.04	10,478
15	3.5	0.95	62.5	1,298	7.27	1.15	11,385

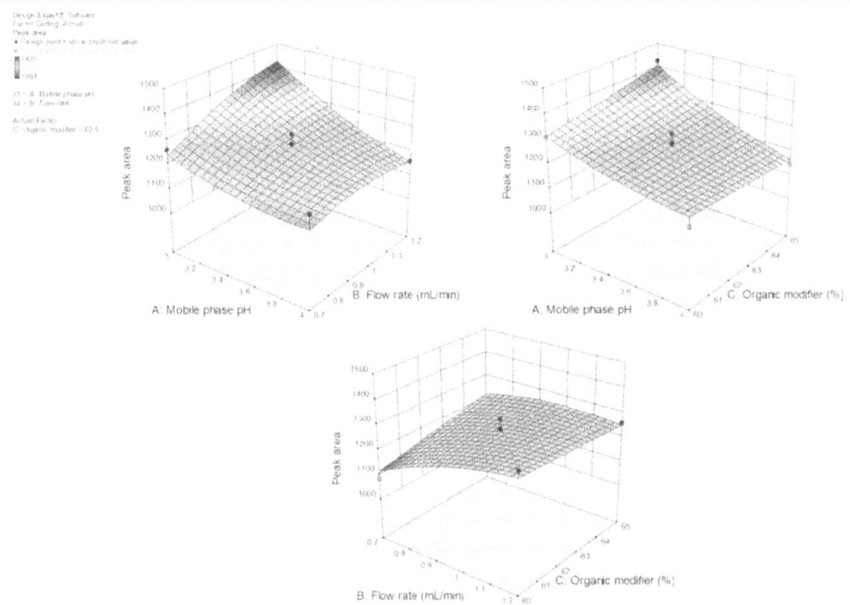

Fig. 6.8. 3D response surface plots depicting the influence of factors A and B, factors A and C, and factors B and C on peak area.

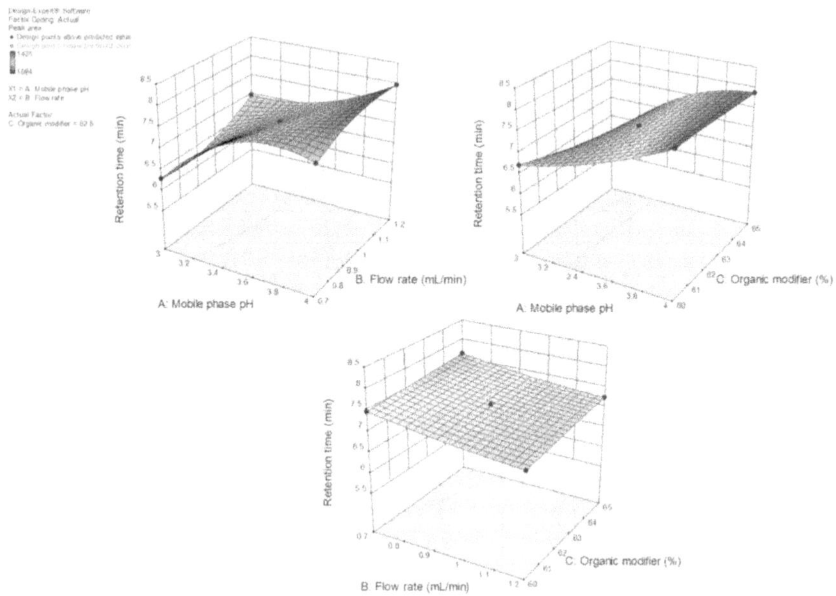

Fig. 6.9. 3D response surface plots depicting the influence of factors A and B, factors A and C, and factors B and C on retention time.

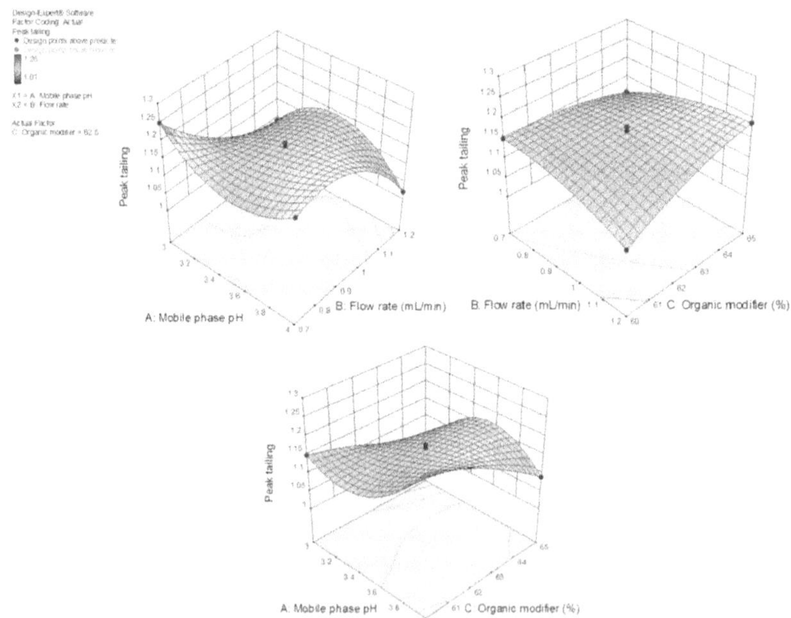

Fig. 6.10. 3D response surface plots depicting the influence of factors A and B, factors A and C, and factors B and C on peak tailing.

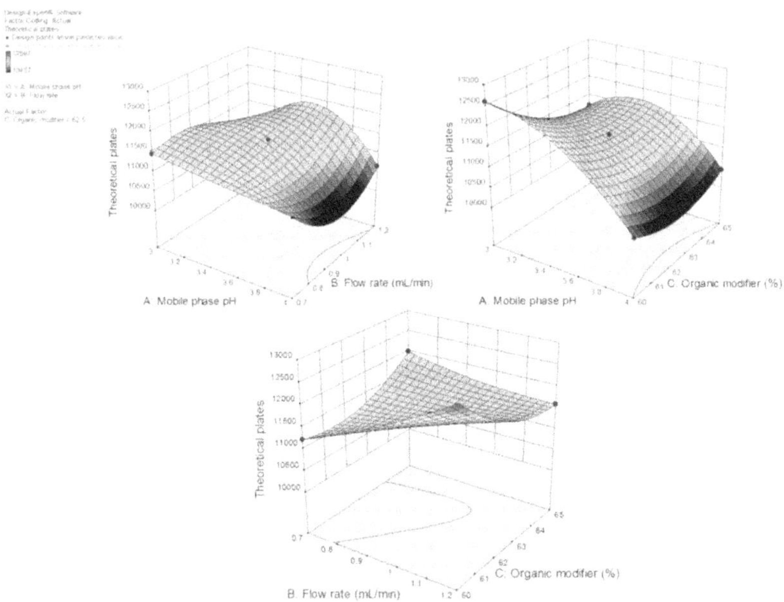

Fig. 6.11. 3D plots showing the influence of factors A and B, factors A and C, and factors B and C on No. of theoretical plates.

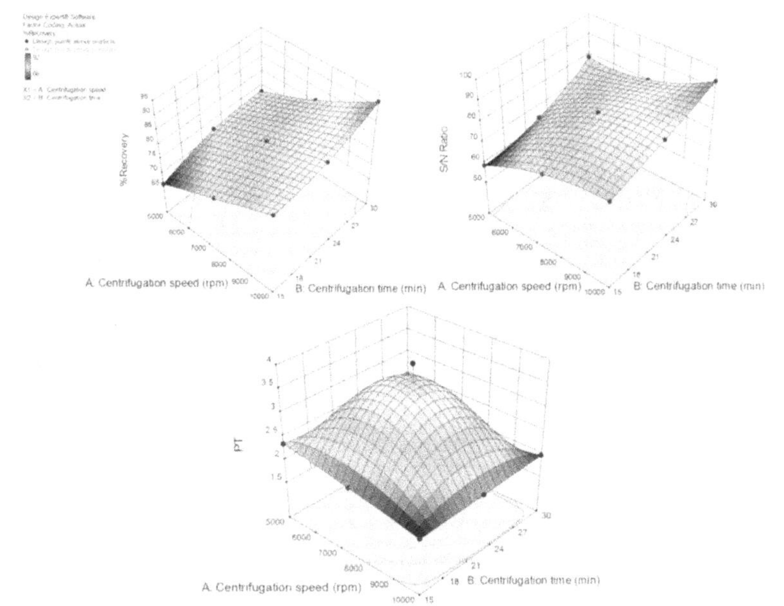

Fig. 6.12 3D response surface plots depicting the influence of factors A and B on %recovery, S/N ratio and PT.

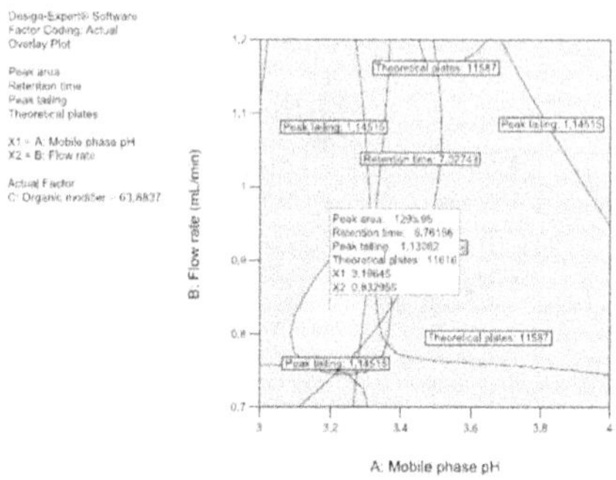

Fig. 6.13. Overlay plot showing design space & the flagged point.

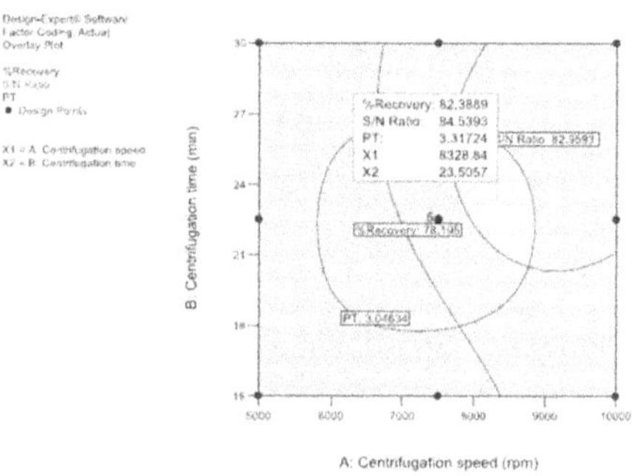

Fig. 6.14. Overlay plot showing design space for the bioanalytical extraction .parameters

Table 6.7. Design Matrix for Bioanalytical Method Extraction as Per the FCCD.

Trials	CMPs		CAAs		
	Centrifugation speed (rpm)	Centrifugation time (min)	% Recovery	S/N ratio	Purity threshold
1	5,000	22.5	72.0	64.29	2.33
2	5,000	15.0	66.0	58.68	2.35
3	10,000	15.0	84.0	76.35	1.89
4	7,500	22.5	79.0	81.25	3.24
5	7,500	15.0	75.0	71.51	2.15
6	7,500	22.5	80.0	81.57	3.39
7	5,000	30.0	73.0	78.68	2.45
8	7,500	22.5	79.5	81.87	3.97
9	10,000	30.0	92.0	93.67	1.97
10	7,500	22.5	80.2	80.58	3.36
11	10,000	22.5	86.0	84.57	1.93
12	7,500	30.0	81.0	80.6	1.91
13	7,500	22.5	80.0	81.65	3.95

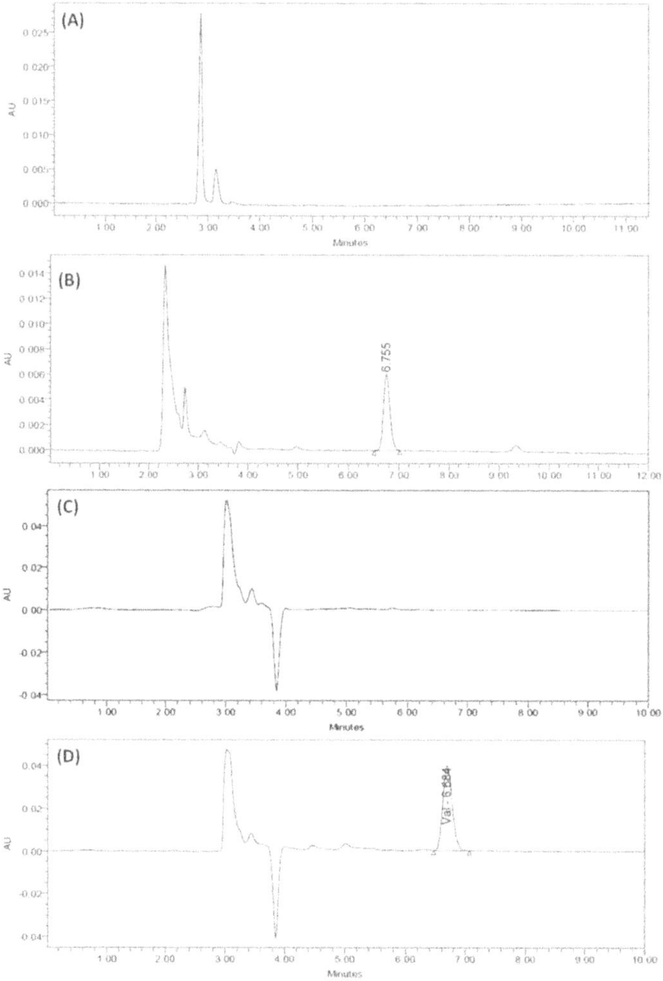

Fig. 6.15. Chromatograms of (A) blank, (B) valsartan at concentration (100 ng/ml) (C) blank plasma (D) valsartan in plasma (100 ng/ml).

Table 6.8. Summary of Validation parameters of Valsartan.

Parameter	HPLC method	Bio-analytical method
Linearity (ng/ml)	10 - 400	5 - 100
Correlation coefficient (R^2)	0.9999	0.9998
Accuracy (% recovery)	97 -100.8%,	99.7 -100.9%
Intra-day Precision (% RSD)	0.034 - 0.719	0.068 - 0.943
Inter-day Precision (% RSD)	0.028 – 0.857	0.042 - 0.613
LOD (ng/ml)	2.23	0.76
LOQ (ng/ml)	6.76	2.29

Practical Examples of AQbD applied to HPLC Method Development

Estimation of Gliclazide and its Impurity (Gliclazide Impurity A)

Drug Profile

Gliclazide, belongs to the sulfonylurea class, chemically 1-[(4-methylbenzene) sulfonyl]- 3 - {octa hydrocyclopenta[c]pyrrol-2-yl} urea is an oral hypoglycaemic compound used in the treatment of type-II diabetes mellitus.

Gliclazide Impurity A, (4-Methyl benzene sulphonamide) (GI- A) is a common process-related impurity that occurs during the synthesis of gliclazide.

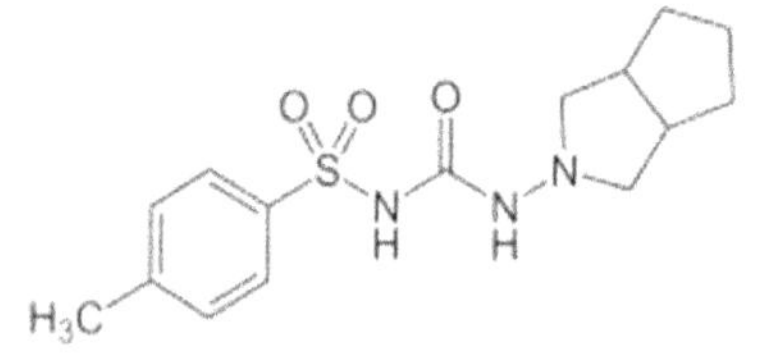

Fig. 6.16. Structure of Gliclazide.

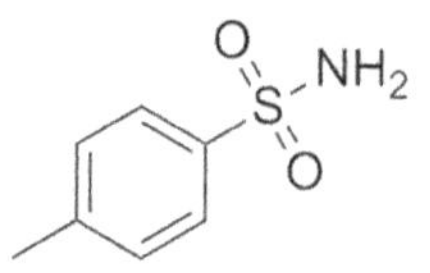

Fig. 6.17. Gliclazide Impurity A Structure.

Literature

Literature survey reveals the chromatographic procedures like TLC, Micellar electrokinetic chromatography, capillary zone electrophoresis, GC–FID and electroanalytical techniques like coulometry and voltammetry have been developed for the estimation of gliclazide in pharmaceuticals, LC method is a recommended method for the assessment of gliclazide purity as per pharmacopeia.

ATP

QbD based simple, robust and accurate RP-HPLC method for the estimation of gliclazide and its related impurity A in its pure form.

CAAs & CMPs

BBD was employed to study the interactions between input variables such as Flow rate (mL/min), Injection Volume (microlitre) and buffer strength (mM) in order to optimize the responses such as retention time and peak area.

DoE

Experimental design, data analysis, and desirability function calculations were performed by using Design- Expert trial version 10.0.0. (Stat-Ease Inc., Minneapolis).

Using multivariate regression analysis, a fitted full quadratic model was obtained for the average response Y, given by the following equation:

$$Y = \beta_0 + \beta_1 X_1 + \beta_2 X_2 + \beta_3 X_3 + \beta_{11} X_1^2 + \beta_{22} X_2^2 + \beta_{33} X_3^2 + \beta_{12} X_1 X_2 + \beta_{13} X_1 X_3 + \beta_{23} X_2 X_3$$

where, Y = selected response;β_0 = arithmetic mean response; and 1, 2 and 3 = regression coefficients of the factors X_1, X_2 and X_3, respectively.

Through the experimental design, a total of 17 distinct compositions with the aim of optimizing both the drug's retention time and GI-A were formulated. These various compositions are detailed in Table 6.9. To understand the impact of the chosen independent variables on the observed responses, response surface analysis was employed. This analysis allowed us to establish mathematical relationships, revealing that the coefficients in the second-order polynomial equations for both drug retention time (RT) and GI-A were of a quadratic nature and included interaction terms. We further examined response surface plots to gain insights into how these parameters influenced selected responses, such as RT1 and RT2.

$$RT_1 = 5.79 - 1.645A + 0.346B + 0.525C + 0.893AB + 0.213AC - 0.815BC + 1.296A^2 + 1.736B^2 + 1.272C^2$$

$$RT_2 = 3.82 + 1.685A + 0.486B + 0.971C + 1.018AB + 0.306AC + 0.855BC + 1.885A^2 + 1.061B^2 + 1.2795C^2$$

Table 6.9. Optimized method parameters for Box-Behnken experimental design.

S. No	Input Variables			Output Responses	
	A: Flow Rate (ml/min)	B: Injection Volume (µl)	C: Buffer Strength (mM)	RT_1 (Min)	RT_2 (Min)
1	1	20	25	5.799	3.819
2	1.25	22.5	25	8.462	6.112
3	1	22.5	30	8.664	6.994
4	1.25	20	30	7.621	5.234
5	1	20	25	3.819	3.819

Contd...

6	1.25	17.5	25	5.764	3.152
7	1	17.5	20	7.321	3.614
8	1	20	25	5.799	3.819
9	1	17.5	30	9.82	7.683
10	0.75	22.5	25	10.112	8.341
11	0.75	30	30	10.342	10.256
12	0.75	20	20	9.538	8.12
13	1	20	25	5.799	3.819
14	1	20	25	5.799	3.819
15	1.25	20	20	5.967	4.324
16	1	22.5	20	9.425	6.345
17	0.75	17.5	25	10.986	10.986

Optimized conditions

Column : Inertsil ODS column (250 mmX4.6 mm, 5μm)
Temperature : Ambient (25°C)
Mobile phase : O-phosphoric acid buffer(25mM): Acetonitrile (50:50 v/v)
Detection : 235nm
Flow rate : 1ml/min
Inj. volume : 20μl

Table 6.10. The predicted and observed response values of Drug and GI-A.

Independent variable	**Optimized level**	
A: Flow Rate (ml/min)	1	
B: Injection Volume (μl)	20	
C: Buffer Strength (mM)	25	
Dependent variable	**Predicted**	**Observed**
RT_1	5.321	5.799
RT_2	3.142	3.819
Desirability	1	0.96

Table 6.11. Optimized analytical regression parameters of Drug and GI- A.

Parameter	**Drug**	**GI - A**
Adjusted R^2	0.9923	0.9901
Predicted R^2	0.9465	0.9308
DF	9	9
F value	231.89	179.13
Prob>F	0.043	0.043
R2 value	0.9966	0.9956
Suggested model	Quadratic	Quadratic

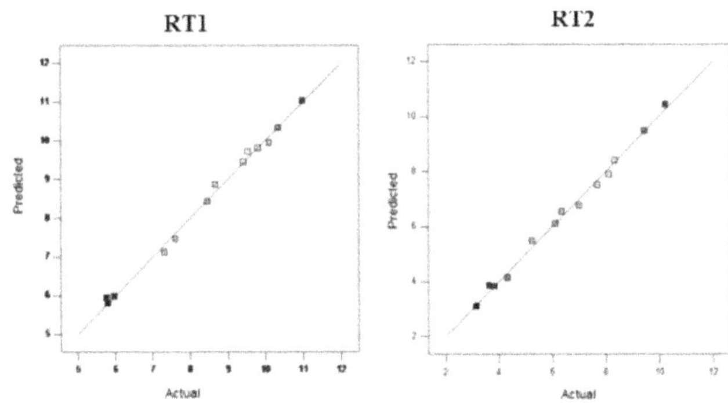

Fig. 6.18. & 6.19 Predicted & actual value of RT of gliclazide and GI-A.

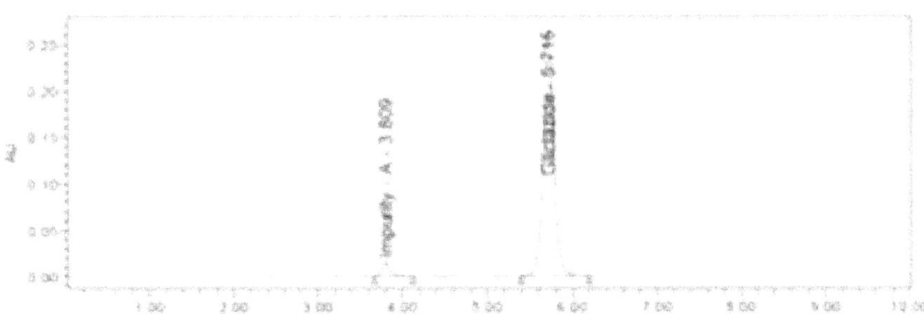

Fig. 6.20. Representative Chromatogram of Gliclazide and GI-A.

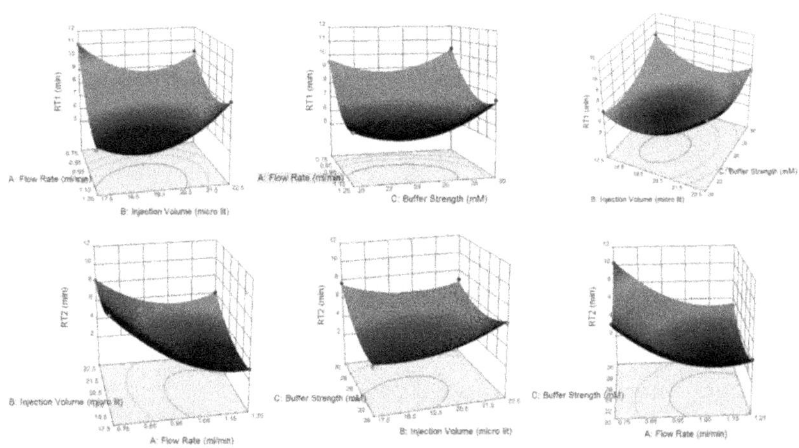

Fig. 6.21. 3D-response surface plots showing the influence of independent variables on retention time of GI (RT1) and GI-A (RT2).

Table. 6.12 Chromatographic conditions & validation parameters for GI & GI-A.

Chrom. Conditions / Validation Parameters	GI	GI-A
Retention time (min)	5.799	3.189
Asymmetry factor	1.05	1.25
Theoretical plates	12655	8921
Linearity (μg/ml)	25-150	25-150
Regression Coefficient (R^2)	0.999	0.999
Method precision (% RSD)	0.5	0.1
Accuracy (% recovery)		
50% Level	99.4	99.4
100% Level	100.9	100.9
150% Level	99.6	99.6
LOD (μg/ml)	0.0066	0.0075
LOQ (μg/ml)	0.0202	0.0228

***

Practical Examples of AQbD applied to HPLC Method Development

Simultaneous Estimation of Saxagliptin and Dapagliflozin

Drug Profile

Saxagliptin is an orally active hypoglycaemic (anti-diabetic drug) of the new dipeptidyl peptidase-4 (DPP-4) inhibitor used for treatment of type 2 diabetes mellitus. chemically, known as (1 s, 3 s, 5 s) - 2 - [(2 s) - 2 - a m i n o - 2 - (3 – hydroxyl - tricyclo [3.3.1.1] dec-1-yl) acetyl]-2-azabicyclo [3.1.0] hexane-3 carbonitrile, It is used as monotherapy or in combination with other drugs. Dapagliflozin is chemically described as (1s)-1,5-anhydro-1-C-[4-chloro-3-[(4-ethoxy phenyl) methyl]phenyl]-D-glucitol. It belongs to a new class of oral antidiabetic drugs called sodium glucose cotransporter 2 (SGLT2) inhibitors

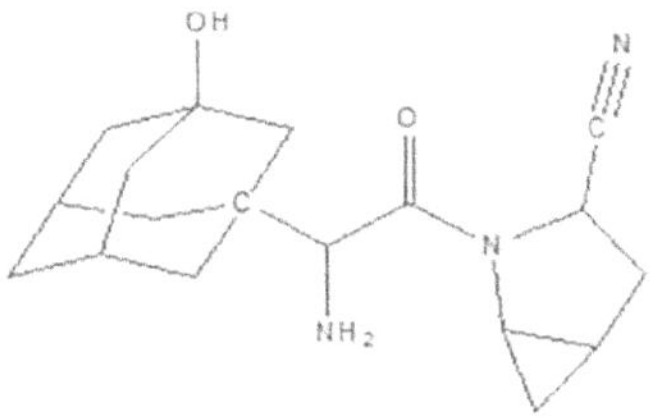

Fig. 6.22. Structure of Saxagliptin.

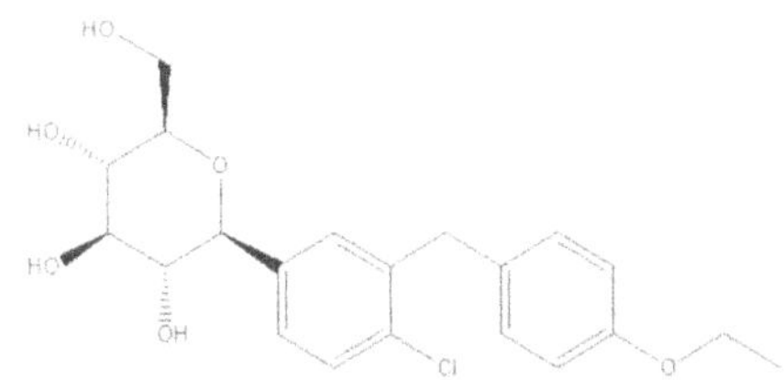

Fig. 6.23. Dapagliflozin Structure.

Literature

A few analytical methods were reported for determination of SAXA and DAPA alone and with other drugs. SAXA alone by Stability indicating RP HPLC and RP-LC-PDA methods, with other drugs like vildagliptin, spectrophotometric and spectrofluorimetric methods, with metformin hydrochloride, RP-HPLC in binary mixtures was estimated. DAPA alone by UV spectrophotometry and RP HPLC method, with other drugs like metformin hydrochloride, UV spectrophotometric method and first derivative photometric method in a synthetic mixture was estimated.

ATP

A simple, sensitive, precise, accurate and robust high performance liquid chromatographic method has been developed for simultaneous estimation of SAXA and DAPA in pharmaceutical formulation.

CAAs & CMPs

Three independent factors; mobile phase composition, flow rate and column temperature were used to design mathematical models.

DoE

CCD was used to study the response surface methodology and to study in depth the effects of these independent factors. Desirability function was used to simultaneously optimize the retention time and resolution of SAXA and DAPA. The optimized and predicted data from contour diagram consisted of acetonitrile and ortho phosphoric acid (0.1%) in the ratio of 50:50 respectively, at a flow rate of 0.98 ml/min and column temperature 31.4°C.

Table 6.13 Experimental plan of CCD showing factors with levels.

Factors	Code	Range levels Low (-1)	Range levels High (+1)	Responses	Code	Range levels Low (-1)	Range levels High (+1)
Proportion of organic phase (%)	X_1	45	55	**RT of SAXA**	Y_1	-	-
Flowrate of MP (ml/min)	X_2	0.9	1.1	**RT of DAPA**	Y_2	-	-
Column temperature (°C)	X_3	28	32	**Resolution**	Y_3	-	-

Table 6.14 Coded values for factor level and observed responses in CCD for 20 analytical trials.

Run	Type	X_1	X_2	X_3	Y_1	Y_2	Y_3
1	Factorial	45	0.9	28	3.204	3.876	3.5
2	Axial	41.591	1	30	2.889	3.575	3.7
3	Factorial	45	1.1	32	2.582	3.17	3.8
4	Axial	58.409	1	30	2.687	3.297	3.8
5	Centre	50	1	30	2.771	3.405	3.6
6	Centre	50	1	30	2.772	3.407	3.6
7	Centre	50	1	30	2.771	3.406	3.6
8	Axial	50	1	26.6364	2.769	3.746	4.8

Contd...

9	Centre	50	1	30	2.772	3.407	3.6
10	Factorial	55	1.1	32	2.491	3.05	4.2
11	Axial	50	1.16818	30	2.395	2.948	3.7
12	Centre	50	1	30	2.77	3.406	3.6
13	Factorial	55	1.1	28	2.486	3.157	3.8
14	Factorial	55	0.9	28	3.046	3.833	4.1
15	Centre	50	1	30	2.771	3.407	3.6
16	Factorial	45	1.1	28	2.615	3.517	4.7
17	Axial	50	0.831821	30	3.33	4.107	3.8
18	Factorial	55	0.9	32	3.029	3.716	4.3
19	Axial	50	1	33.3636	2.792	3.42	4.3
20	Factorial	45	0.9	32	3.17	3.903	4.2

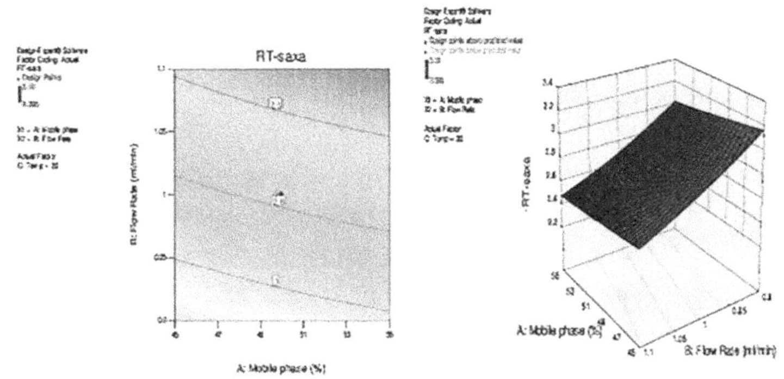

(A) (B)

Fig 6.24. 2D (A) and 3D (B) contour plots showing the effect of mobile phase ratio (X_1) and flow rate (X_2) on retention time of SAXA (Y_1).

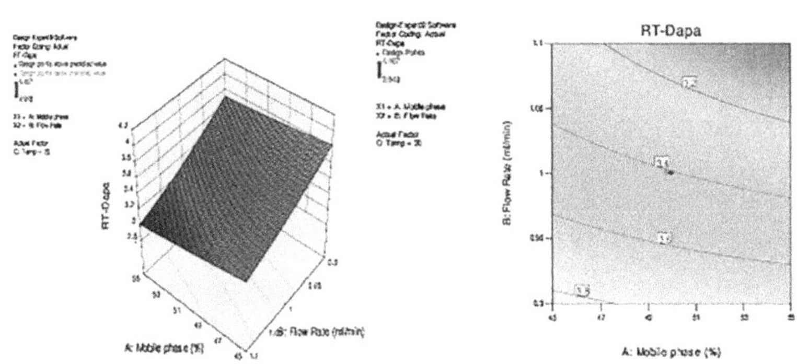

(A) (B)

Fig. 6.25. 2D (A) and 3D (B) contour plots showing the effect of mobile phase ratio (X_1) and flow rate (X_2) on retention time of DAPA (Y_2).

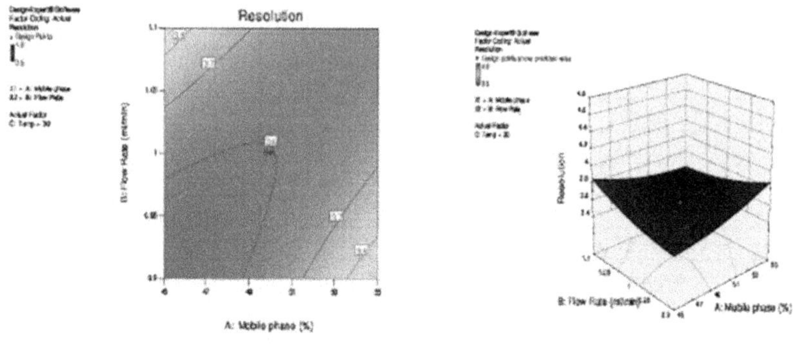

(A) (B)

Fig. 6.26. 2D (A) and 3D (B) contour plots showing the effect of mobile phase ratio (X_1) and flow rate (X_2) on resolution (Y_3).

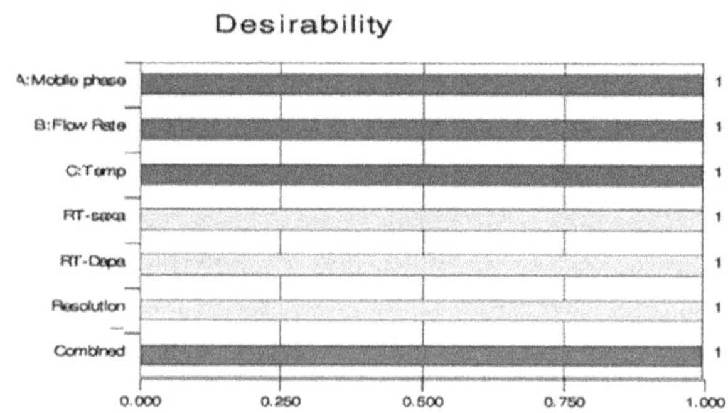

Fig. 6.27. Desirability function representation basis unity=1.

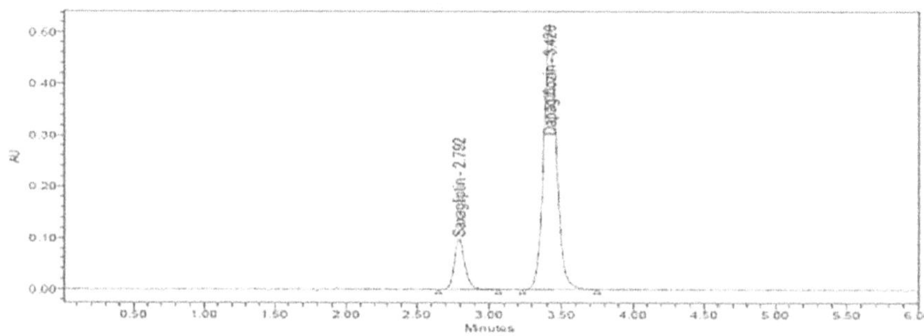

	Peak Name	RT	Area	% Area	USP Plate Count	USP Resolution	Asym @ 10
1	Saxagliptin	2.792	513372	14.21	7381		1.3
2	Dapagliflozin	3.420	3098582	85.79	7626	4.3	1.2

Fig. 6.28. Optimized RP-HPLC chromatogram for SAXA and DAPA at 210 nm.

Table 6.15 ANOVA regression analysis for models and responses.

Response	$\bar{X}$	SD	% CV	Press value	R^2	Adj. R^2	Pred. R^2	Adq precision	F	p
SAXA Rt (Y_1)	2.81	0.014	0.5	0.015	0.9983	0.9968	0.9873	96.445	666.4	0.0001
DAPA Rt (Y_2)	3.49	0.052	1.48	0.23	0.9845	0.9705	0.8653	29.953	70.44	0.0001
Resolution (Y_3)	3.91	0.24	6.05	4.89	0.8003	0.6205	-0.745	6.118	4.45	0.0144

$\bar{X}$ Mean **SD** Standard deviation, **CV** Coefficient of variations, **R^2** Coefficient of Regression, **F** Fischer's ratio

Table 6.16 Validation results for SAXA and DAPA.

Parameters	SAXA	DAPA
System suitability parameters		
No. of theoretical plates	4613.66±96.70	4599±85.082
(Mean ± SD*)	2.0	1.8
% RSD		
Resolution (Mean ± SD*)	3.266±0.057	
% RSD	1.7	
Tailing factor (Mean ± SD*)	1.44±0.005	1.60±0.015
% RSD	0.3	0.9
Linearity		
Range	12.5-75	25-150
Slope	11316	38865
Intercept	3931.8	5685.8
Correlation coefficient	0.999	0.999
Accuracy		
Recovery studies	99.91±1.10	98.92±0.7997
% RSD	1.10	0.87
Precision (% RSD)		
Repeatability	0.27	0.4
Intermediate precision	0.3	0.6
LOD (µg/ml)	0.13	0.09
LOQ (µg/ml)	0.39	0.27

***

CHAPTER 7

AQbD for GC Method Development

7.1 Introduction

Gas chromatography (GC) stands out as a distinctive and adaptable method. Initially, it found its application in the testing of gases and vapours originating from highly volatile substances. The pioneering work of Martin and Synge, followed by James and Martin, in the realm of gas-liquid chromatography (GLC), marked a pivotal moment that transformed chemical separations and analyses. In its capacity as an analytical tool, GC serves multiple purposes, enabling the direct separation and analysis of gaseous samples, liquid solutions, and volatile solids. Should the sample in question prove non-volatile, the techniques of derivatization or pyrolysis can come to the rescue.

What sets GC apart from other chromatographic techniques is its utilization of a gaseous mobile phase, which enables the separation of components into vaporous states. This unique feature makes it particularly effective in segregating and detecting low-molecular-weight compounds present in the gas phase. The sample introduced into the system can either be in a gaseous or liquid state, with vaporization occurring at the injection port. The mobile phase responsible for gas chromatography is a carrier gas, typically helium, chosen for its low molecular weight and chemical inertness. It is applicable to the qualitative and quantitative analysis of flavor and aroma components, food products, natural products, a variety of transformation products and contaminants such as environmental pollutants, pesticides, fumigants, natural toxins, veterinary drugs, packaging materials etc. It has been used as an indispensable technique for the characterization of complex mixtures of geometric isomers when combined with other analytical techniques like spectroscopy.

A gas chromatograph (GC), as illustrated in Fig. 7.1, is an analytical technique employed for quantifying the composition of diverse components within a given sample. The analytical procedure developed by a gas chromatograph is referred to as gas chromatography. It comprises essential components such as a cylinder containing the carrier gas, flow meters, regulators, a precisely temperature-controlled enclosure (comprising an injection port, column, and detector), as well as a recording system.

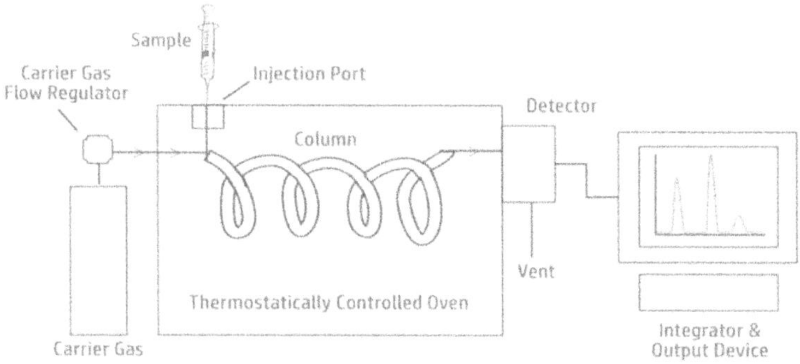

Fig. 7.1. Layout of a gas chromatograph.

7.2 Principle of GC

It is based on the distribution of the analyte (sample) between a mobile phase The injected sample solution is introduced into the instrument and carried by a gas stream into a separation tube referred to as the "column" where the separation process takes place. Helium or nitrogen serves as the carrier gas in this context. Within the column, the different components of the sample are effectively separated from one another. Subsequently, as these components exit the column, the detector quantifies their amounts.

When measuring the concentration of a sample with an unknown content, a standard sample with a known concentration is likewise introduced into the instrument. By comparing the retention time (appearance time) and the area of the peak obtained from the standard sample to those of the test sample, the concentration of the test sample can be calculated.

7.3 Classical Approach for GC Method Development

When developing a method for gas chromatography, three important points to be considered are (1) Instrumentation, (2) Column selection and (3) Parameter optimization for rapid, high-quality separations. To analyse a new type of sample, the first thing to be considered is the volatility of the sample i.e., the boiling point range of analyte (low B.P. range <50°C (highly volatile), medium B.P. range 50- 300°C (medium volatile) and high B.P. > 250°C (low volatile)).

Detector Choice

In the realm of GC instrumentation, careful consideration must be given to selecting an appropriate detector for determining the compounds within the sample. While the most commonly employed universal detectors include the

FID and MS, there are also alternative detector options to contemplate for specific needs, such as the ECD, TCD, FPD, or more advanced detectors.

Column Dimensions

Optimal column dimensions selection hinges on several factors: (1) The type of detector employed, which dictates the column's inner diameter (ID). (2) The number of compounds requiring analysis, influencing the column's length. (3) The volatility of the sample plays a role in determining the necessary film thickness. However, the most favourable outcome is typically achieved with the shortest column and the thinnest film that the sample's characteristics permit.

Column Phase

In the process of choosing the column phase, it's essential to take into account the composition of the sample, whether it predominantly exhibits non-polar, moderately polar, or highly polar characteristics. While a single general-purpose column exists, suitable for a wide range of standard samples, it is the 30 m BPX5 column with a 0.25 mm inner diameter and a standard film thickness of 0.25 μm. Utilizing this column enables the analysis of up to 80% of standard sample types.

Examples:

for non-polar compounds - 100% methyl Polysiloxane phase;
for medium polar compounds - 5% phenyl polysiloxane phase;
for strongly polar compounds - Polyethylene Glycol (wax) phase

Optimizing parameters for rapid and high-quality separations

Carrier Gas and flowrate

The initial decision to be considered involves choosing the carrier gas and adjusting its flow rate.

Examples:

N_2 -10 to 15 cm/sec;
He - 30 to 35 cm/sec;
H_2 - 40 to 45 cm/sec

Van Deemter equation can be used to determine the optimum average gas velocity.

$$\mathbf{HETP = A + B/u + Cu}$$

where HETP = Height equivalent to a theoretical plate; A = Eddy diffusion; B = Longitudinal diffusion; C = Resistance to mass transfer; u = flowrate of carrier gas.

GC method development involves the scheme depicted in the Table 7.1

Table 7.1. Scheme for GC method development.

Collection and identification of drug(s)
↓
Literature
↓
Define a Separation goal
↓
Experimental work
↓
Analytical method development
↓
Need for special GC procedure, Sample pre-treatment etc
↓
Selection of Chromatographic conditions viz., Carrier gas, injector, column, detector, temperature programming etc
↓
Selection of GC method, Preliminary run, estimate best separation conditions
↓
Optimization of separation Conditions
↓
Check for problems or requirements for special procedures
↓
Recovery of purified material, qualitative and quantitative estimation
↓
Optimizations of results
↓
Method development report
↓
Validation of developed method
↓
Use of developed method for regular analysis

7.4 AQbD Elements for GC Method Development

Creation of Knowledge Space

An analytical and pharmaceutical professional must be well versed with all the literature and tools that are a fundamental part of research and development. Method development starts with conducting literature survey to have the knowledge on physicochemical characteristics of analyte (molecular structure, dissociation constant), selecting chromatographic conditions like column (type of stationary phase, column length, internal diameter, and film thickness) and carrier gas (type and flowrate) for developing an approach to analytical method, preparing sample, and optimizing the method followed by its validation. Temperatures have to be carefully programmed including the initial temperature, final temperature, initial and final hold, ramp rate along with controlling injector and detector temperature.

Analytical Target Profile

Generation of new ATP due to the change in procedure along with partial requalification may be undertaken for attaining reliable results. ATP defines the goal of the GC method development process, and is the indicator of method performance. It involves the determination of amount of drug in API or in formulation, accurately and precisely by employing a simple, sensitive and economical analytical method. It can also be used for determination of drug in the presence of impurities i.e., stability indicating assay method.

Analytical Method Performance Characteristics

The quantitative and qualitative variables that influence method performance and the method outcomes should be identified. AMPCs are the validation parameters/ characteristics that are normally evaluated during GC method validation. The characteristics such as accuracy, precision, specificity, linearity, range, detection limit, quantitation limit, robustness, ruggedness can be determined as per ICH Q2 R1 guidelines.

Selection of Analytical Techniques

with reference to ATP defined in the step 2, GC technique is selected to meet the goals. Gas chromatography is an important tool of analytical techniques for identification and characterization of active ingredients present in a sample. Selection of GC depends upon the sample volatility, thermal stability, solubility, composition of analyte (functional groups, polarity), melting point, boiling point and aggregation state. Non-volatile compounds are subjected to derivatization or pyrolyze a sample before entering into a column for separation and quantitation. Analytical gas chromatography using head space method has been developed by QbD approach which has become an important concept for the pharmaceutical industry to find out and measure the CAAs and its design space.

Identification of Critical Analytical Attributes (CAAs)

After the selection of technique, detailed assessment of the risks associated with method parameters, viz., Type of carrier gas, its flow rate, run time, type of column and its dimensions, particle size, column temperature, injection volume, injector splitting ratio, type of detector etc. are focused. To control the

"Variability" of materials and method, CAAs and CMPs are identified through Risk Management process. For GC technique, typical CAAs are Retention time, NTP, Resolution, peak area, asymmetric factor. It helps to have better understanding of method & its performance thus helping Life Cycle Management of the method (LCM).

Risk Assessment

The next step may involve the application of risk identification and risk assessment tools including the Ishikawa diagram and failure mode effect analysis (FMEA) respectively. The risk that a GC method is vulnerable against during its operation needs to be listed out and assigned a rank. The risks that show a direct impact on the GC method need to be documented that may serve as a reference through the GC method development.

It identifies the critical method variables, the parameters which have impact on ATP. Commonly used risk assessment tools for GC technique are Ishikawa (fishbone) diagram (Fig. 7.2.) and failure mode and effects analysis (FMEA) as they help to identify and classify main sources of hazards associated with the method.

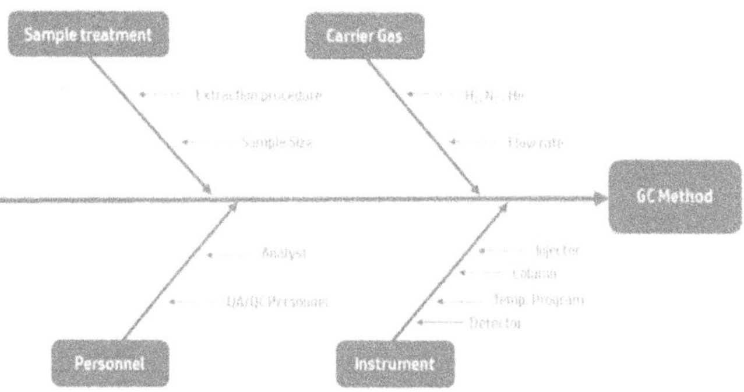

Fig. 7.2. Ishikawa (fishbone) diagram - Risk assessment tools for GC technique.

Design of Experiments (DoE)

An appropriate DOE has to be utilized for optimization of variables and establishing scientific knowledge and understanding. Application of DOE in the GC method development step needs a thorough understanding of the science of selecting input variables and corresponding output responses. The experiments employ four primary types of scientific designs: factorial designs, mixture designs, D-optimal designs, and CCDs. During the runs, the impact of various factors on the responses is assessed, and the outcomes are analyzed using specialized software tools like Design Expert, Minitab, or Microsoft

Excel. These software platforms facilitate data analysis and interpretation, aiding in the understanding of the experimental results in a rigorous and systematic manner.

MODR

As per the requirement of ICH Q8 guidelines, MODR can be established in the GC method development phase with the ultimate aim of increasing the robustness while decreasing the cost. MODR, formed as result of output from DOE, is an operating range for the input variables that are critical in generating a result that continually meets the goals as set by ATP. Flexibility is provided by MODR with respect to input method parameters so as to meet the appropriate criteria for method performance and suitable response for method without resubmitting to FDA. Suggestions by FDA include the simultaneous conductance of MODR and GC method validation. After it is defined, the required method controls are appropriately set and method validation is done with.

Furthermore, the MODR is generated that contains a combination of all set of GC method condition variables that have had their predefined GC method objectives met. Optimization of method parameters is undertaken with the optimized method parameters lying somewhere around the MODR. Many trials of different columns, flow rates, column temperature, etc., are employed for optimization in GC. The outcomes undergo documentation and the best possible and suitable results are subjected to statistical evaluation.

Control strategy

The control strategy in QbD of GC is an essential concept as it assures the performance of GC method. Risk assessment helps to identify different risk factors to be considered during the implementation of control strategy. For an analytical technique such as GC, control strategy is the control of input factors required to meet both system suitability requirements in a traditional sense and other needs associated with performance.

Continuous Method Monitoring

The GC method has to be validated in the operable region for the purpose of method performance which should be subjected to control strategy for continual improvement The continuous monitoring allows an analyst to detect, identify & address any abnormal or OOT performance of analytical method.

***

7.5 Practical Examples of AQbD applied to GC Method Development

Identification & Estimation of Essential Oils in Herbal Formulation

Essential oils

Essential oils are natural, complex, lipophilic compounds, volatile in nature with characteristic pleasant aroma. They are obtained from plant parts such as fruits, flowers, seeds, buds, leaves, bark, wood, twigs or roots and are known to possess a number of medicinal properties like antimicrobial, antioxidant, antifungal, analgesic, anti-inflammatory activity.

Herbal Formulation

A blend of essential oils possessing synergistic carminative properties was formulated in oily base. Ajowan oil, cardamom oil, caraway oil, coriander and fennel oil were selected for development of formulation.

Ajowan oil is extracted from the crushed seeds of ajowan, botanically known as Trachyspermum capsicum, through the steam distillation process. This light yellow colored liquid has a strong characteristic aroma. It is also popular as an aromatherapy oil due to its unique pungent and spicy aroma.

Cardamom essential oil is retrieved from the Cardamom seeds (Elaichi Seeds – Elettaria cardamomum) through a process called Steam Distillation. It has a typical fragrance that comforts your mind and it has a detoxifying effect on your skin. It is widely used in both Skin Care and Hair Care products due to its therapeutic properties.

Caraway essential oil is purely extracted from carum carvi with the help of steam distillation method. It might improve digestion and relieve spasms in the stomach and intestine.

Coriander essential oil Its aroma is green, sharp and slightly pungent. Coriander is considered anti-inflammatory and sedative. It's indicated for stress, anxiety and insomnia. Used as a massage oil to ease arthritis pain and migraine headaches.

Fennel oil is extracted from the seeds of Foeniculum vulgare. Fennel oil is commonly used to treat disorders of the digestive system.

Peppermint essential oil can be extracted from the leaves of the peppermint plant (Mentha piperita) and is used for a variety of purposes. It has a sharp odour that is cool and refreshing, and the taste is similar. The main chemical components of peppermint oil are menthol and menthone.

Each oil was characterized making use of a marker compounds like linalool for coriander oil, cineol for cardamom oil, anethol for fennel oil, carvone for caraway oil, thymol for ajowan oil and menthol for peppermint oil. Marker compounds were characterized using mass spectroscopy.

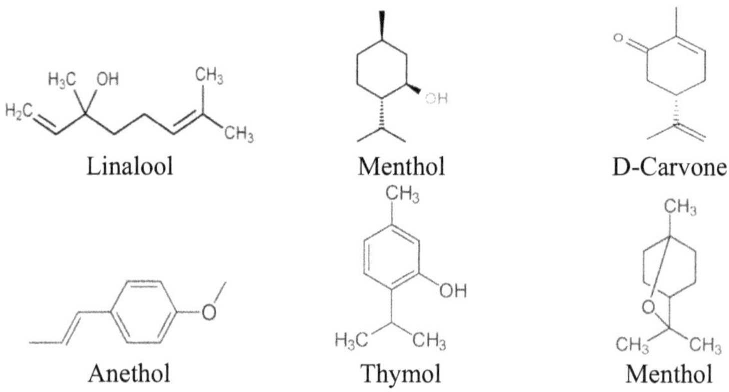

Fig. 7.3. Chemical structures of marker compounds.

ATP

It involves the development of a validated GC head space method based on QbD for routine quality control purpose.

CAAs

Parameters like gas flow rate, detector temperature, split ratio and head-space oven temperature, Needle temperature, transfer line temperature, thermostat time, headspace carrier pressure were selected. Among all the chromatographic parameters gas flow, head space oven temperature and head space thermostat time were identified as CAAs of the method which could alter the two critical system suitability parameter resolution (Rs_1) between D-carvone- anethol and resolution (Rs_2) between thymol and cineol peak.

DoE

An experimental design is an experimental set-up to simultaneously evaluate several factors at a given numbers of levels in a predefined number of experiments. The experimental design along with statistical analysis of data was performed by Design-Expert 8.0 software. A two-level full factorial design (2^3) is selected to determine the main effects and all interactions between the factors. The design comprised with 21 robustness experiment trials with parameters.

Minimum ±10% variation was considered from the actual chromatographic condition of those three variables and the design set as a standard set of gas flow 1.0 ml/minutes to 1.4 ml/minutes, thermostat time from 27 to 33 min and thermostat oven temperature from 77 °C to 94°C. This led a total 20 chromatographic conditions including 4 duplicate centre points (Table 7.2.).

Table 7.2. Robustness experiment.

GC Parameters	-ve Control condition	Control condition	+ve Control condition	No. of Experi-ments
Carrier gas flow (N_2) (ml/min)	1	1.2	1.4	3
Detector temperature (°C)	250	270	290	3
Injector temperature (°C)	210	220	240	3
Split ratio	1:1	5:1	10:1	3
Oven temperature (°C)	75	85	95	3
Needle temperature (°C)	90	95	100	3
Transfer line temperature (°C)	90	100	110	3
Thermostat time (min)	20	30	40	3

Table 7.3. DoE experiment Study design.

Std.	Run	Factor-1 Flow/Min	Factor-2 Oven temperature (°C)	Factor-3 Thermostat time (min)
13	1	1.00	94	33
8	2	1.40	94	27
20	3	1.20	85	30
12	4	1.40	77	33
6	5	1.00	94	27
10	6	1.00	77	33
11	7	1.40	77	33
14	8	1.00	94	33
19	9	1.20	85.5	30
2	10	1.00	77	27
17	11	1.20	85.5	30

Contd...

15	12	1.40	94	33
7	13	1.40	94	27
3	14	1.40	77	27
9	15	1.00	77	33
1	16	1.00	77	27
16	17	1.40	94	33
18	18	1.20	85	30
5	19	1.00	94	27
4	20	1.40	77	27

Table 7.4. Result of system suitability parameter in DoE experiment.

Std.	Run	Factor-1 Flow/Min	Factor-2 Oven temperature (°C)	Factor-3 Thermostat time (min)	Rs_1	Rs_2
13	1	1.00	94	33	5.6	5.1
8	2	1.40	94	27	3.7	3.2
20	3	1.20	85	30	4.8	4.2
12	4	1.40	77	33	3.8	3.5
6	5	1.00	94	27	6.1	5.2
10	6	1.00	77	33	5.9	5.4
11	7	1.40	77	33	3.8	3.2
14	8	1.00	94	33	6.2	5.2
19	9	1.20	85.5	30	5.2	4.4
2	10	1.00	77	27	6.2	5.3
17	11	1.20	85.5	30	4.9	4.3
15	12	1.40	94	33	3.9	3.8
7	13	1.40	94	27	4.1	3.6
3	14	1.40	77	27	4.1	3.6
9	15	1.00	77	33	5.8	5.6
1	16	1.00	77	27	5.8	5.4
16	17	1.40	94	33	3.8	3.2
18	18	1.20	85	30	4.9	4.4
5	19	1.00	94	27	5.6	5.8
4	20	1.40	77	27	3.9	2.9

Rs_1 Resolution between D-carvone- Anethol; Rs_2 Resolution between Thymol – Cineol peak.

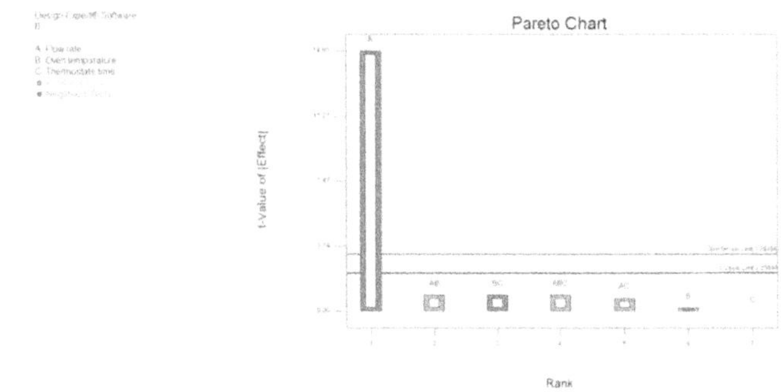

Fig. 7.4. Pareto chart of resolution between D-carvone and Anethol.

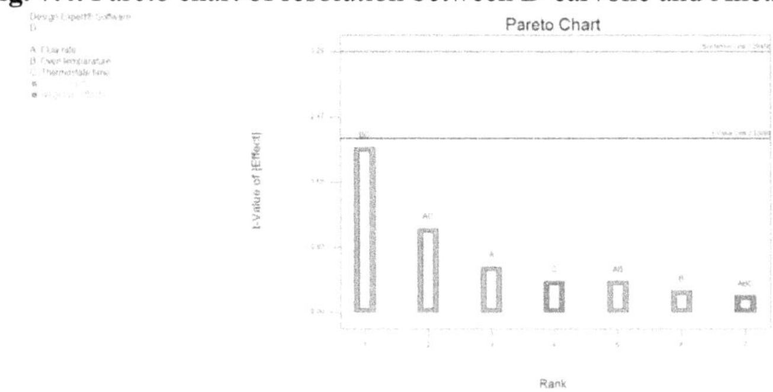

Fig. 7.5. Pareto chart of resolution between Thymol and Cineol.

The 1st pareto chart (Fig. 7.4.) demonstrate resolution (Rs_1) between D-carvone and Anethol was affected due to dual as well as mixed interaction between the three variables. A positive effect was found due to interaction between flow rates with oven temperature or flow rate with thermostat temperature and even due to mixed interaction between three variables but individually has no independent effect on this system suitability parameter. Hence negative effect was found which has demonstrated in the pareto chart in the blue histogram. Interaction between oven temperatures with thermostat temperature also showed negative effect in the chart.

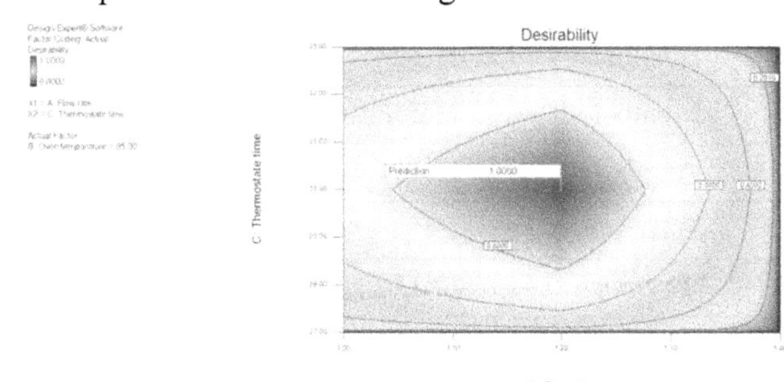

Fig. 7.6. Counter desirability graph on CQA of Flow rate vs Thermostat time.

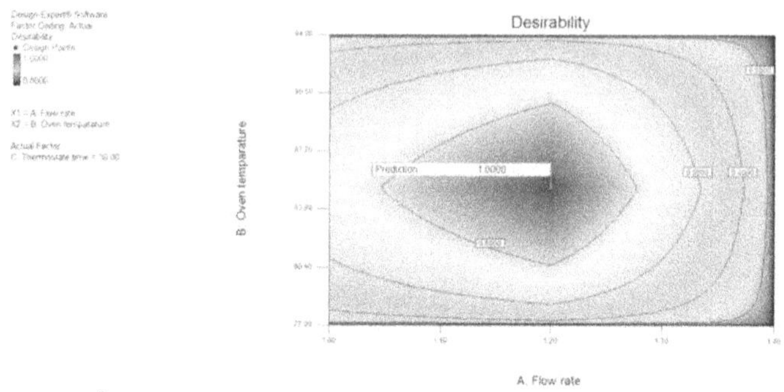

Fig. 7.7. Counter desirability graph on CQA of oven Flow rate vs oven temperature.

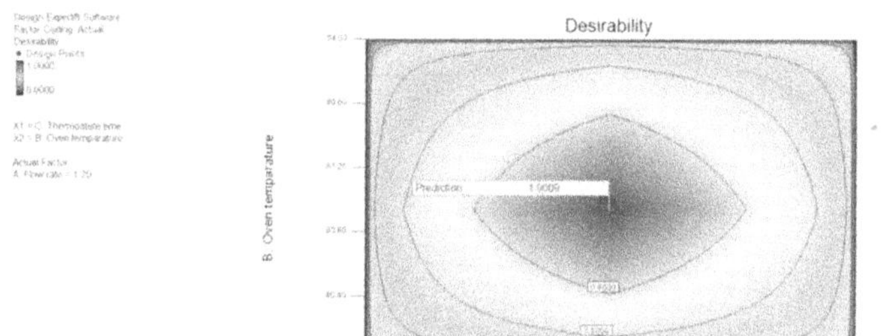

Fig. 7.8. Counter desirability graph on CQA of Thermostat time vs oven temperature.

Table 7.5. The RT of the marker and percentage present in each Essential oil in assay.

Essential oil	Marker compound	RT of the pure marker peak in standard solution (Min)	RT of marker peak in individual oil (Min)	Assay (% of marker present in oil)
Coriander	Linalool	11.82	11.84	69%
Peppermint	Menthol	13.53	13.53	67%
Fennel	Anethol	16.11	16.08	75%
Caraway	D-Carvone	15.54	15.52	55%
Ajowan	Thymol	17.15	17.15	53%
Cardamom	Cineol	17.66	17.66	55%

Table 7.6. System suitability parameter of the standard of blend of marker compounds.

Essential oil	Plate count	Tailing	Resolution
Linalool	32382	1.3	NA
Menthol	23006	0.99	17.3
D-Carvone	21768	1.0	21.1
Anethol	19109	1.1	4.8
Thymol	17090	1.2	7.4
Cineol	13003	1.3	4.4

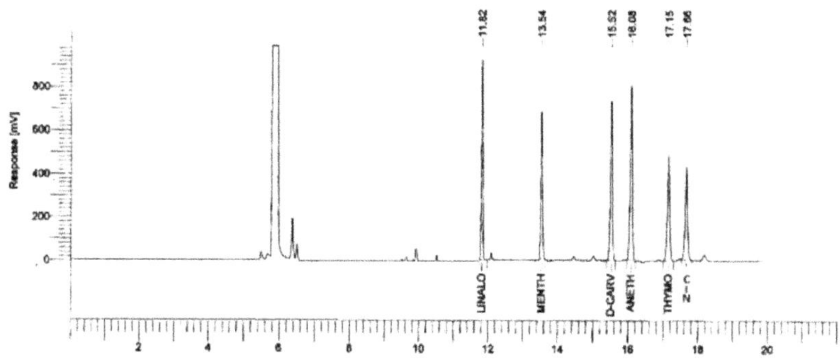

Fig. 7.9. Typical chromatogram of system suitability solution of standard.

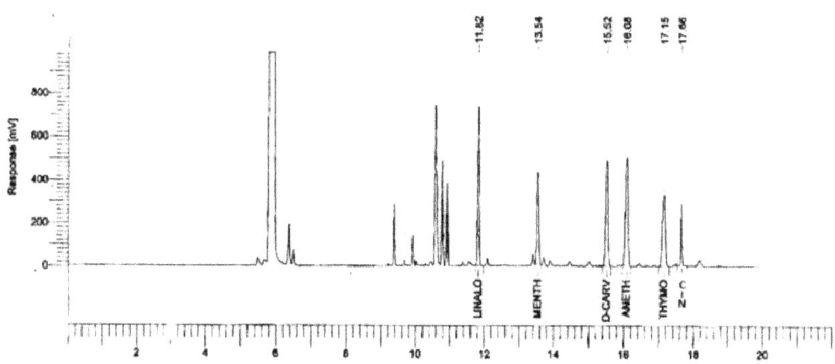

Fig. 7.10. Typical chromatogram of blend sample solution in precision.

Optimized Conditions:

Gas chromatography fitted with flame ionization detector equipped with Headspace auto sampler analyzer.

Column : DB-624 Capillary column with 30 m length, 0.32 mm ID & 1.8 μm

Carrier Gas : Nitrogen

Flow rate : 1.2 ml/min

Oven Temp : Initial: 60°C (hold for 2 min) ramp at 15°C/ min to 180°C (hold for 10 min) 240°C (Final) ramp at a rate of 15°C/ min

Detector temp. : 270°C

Head-space temp.: 85°C, Needle temp.: 95°C, Transfer line temp.: 100°C

Split ratio : 5:1

Total run time : 20 min

Table 7.7. Summary of Validation parameters.

Validation Parameters	Coriander Linolool	Caraway D-Carvone	Fennel Anethol	Ajowan Thymol	Cardamom Cineol
Linearity *(ppm)*			250 - 750		
Regression Coefficient *(R^2)*	0.9992	0.9992	0.9997	0.9997	0.9996
Slope	5145	7638.9	6469.1	8046.5	3308.6
Interday precision *(% RSD)*	1.5	1.8	1.9	1.4	1.9
Intraday precision *(% RSD)*	1.3	1.1	1.2	1.4	1.4
Accuracy *(% recovery)*					
50%	99.5±1.1	99.9±1.1	99.7±1.2	100.3±0.8	99.2±0.8
100%	100.4±1.0	100.3±1.1	99.2±1.0	99.2±0.4	100.1±0.8
150%	99.6±1.1	99.7±1.0	100.4±1.0	99.8±0.8	99.8±1.2
LOD, µg/ml *by S/N ratio*	3	2	2.2	1.5	4
LOQ, µg/ml *by S/N ratio*	35	25	25	18	50

***

Practical Examples of AQbD Applied to GC Method Development

Quantitation of Alkyl Camphor Sulfonates as Potential Genotoxic Impurities

Alkyl sulfonates

Alkyl sulfonates are generated by the esterification reaction of sulfonic acid with residual alcohols used in the manufacturing process of APIs such as methanol, ethanol and isopropanol. They are known as alkylating agents which can induce genetic mutations or chromosomal aberrations. Therefore, they should be strictly controlled with tight acceptance criteria if produced or introduced during production of APIs due to their potentially genotoxic behavior. According to the ICH M7 guideline regarding mutagenic impurities, PGIs should be controlled below the Threshold of Toxicological Concern (TTC) in the absence of appropriate limits based on toxicity data. The limits of PGIs in APIs derived from the TTC can be calculated based on the expected maximum daily dose. The TTC value for PGIs in APIs is set at 1.5 g/day, corresponding to a 10-5 lifetime risk of cancer.

Camphorsulfonic acid

Camphorsulfonic acid (CSA) is the 2nd most used sulfonic acid salt after methanesulfonic acid. Alkyl camphorsulfonates are potential genotoxic impurities and present structurally alerting properties like other sulfonic acid alkyl esters. The three alkyl camphorsulfonates, methyl camphorsulfonate (MCS), ethyl camphorsulfonate (ECS) and isopropyl camphorsulfonate (ICS), can be produced from the reaction of camphorsulfonic acid and alcohols in API manufacturing processes (Fig. 7.11). These can behave as alkylation reagents and have a possibility of alkylating DNA bases (on N-7 of guanosine and N-3 of adenine). These substances have the possibility of causing genetic mutations and present carcinogenic behaviors at even small exposure levels, and therefore must be accurately quantitated and controlled below the TTC.

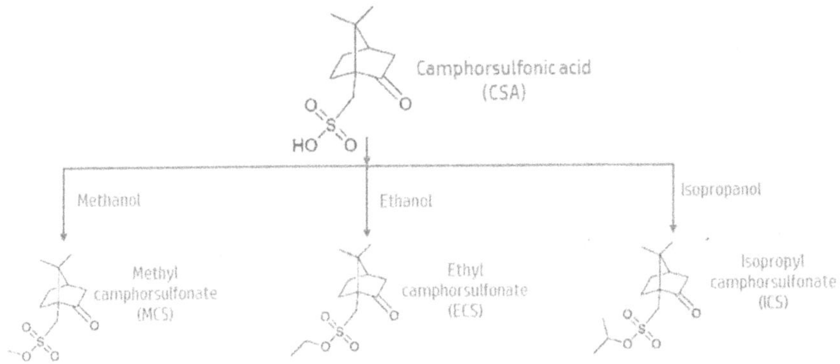

Fig. 7.11. Synthetic route & structures of MCS, ECS and ICS.

ATP

In order to control the alkyl camphor sulfonates as PGIs, it is essential to develop a highly sensitive, reproducible and stable GC analytical method based on AQbD principles.

CAAs & CMPs

The peak height of each analyte and the resolution between adjacent peaks were selected as the critical method attributes (CMAs) since the most critical analytical target profiles (ATPs) in the analysis of PGIs is detection sensitivity and specificity due to their low specification limits. A risk assessment was performed in order to determine the CMPs expected to have the greatest impacts on the CAAs. Through the risk assessment, the flow rate of carrier gas, inlet temperature, detector temperature, column oven temperature and sample injection volume were chosen as the CMPs.

DoE

Fusion QbD Professional 9.8.1.135 (S-matrix, Eureka, CA, USA) was used to create the Design of Experiment (DoE) for the method screening and optimization study.

Screening

An experimental plan was created in Software using a two-level resolution V type including three center points. A total of 19 experiments were performed. The Design of Experiments (DoE) and the experimental results of each CMA are tabulated in Table 7.8. The Analysis of Variance (ANOVA) statistical test was performed in order to determine the statistical significance of each response, shown in Table 7.9. The p-values of the responses for each of the PGIs were found to be below 0.05 and, thus, were proven to have statistical significance.

Table 7.8. Design of Experiment for screening & Response corresponding DoE.

Run	Method Parameters for Screening					Responses				
	X_1	X_2	X_3	X_4	X_5	R_1	R_2	R_3	R_4	R_5
1	1.5	170	340	330	2.2	2.06	1.75	0.46	14.34	6.74
2	1.5	230	340	330	1.8	4.15	4.26	0.59	4.28	1.98
3	1.5	170	180	330	1.8	1.57	1.32	1.14	14.08	6.61
4	2.5	170	340	270	2.2	2.75	2.25	0.83	13.46	6.19
5	2.5	170	180	330	2.2	2.72	2.19	2.00	12.92	5.95
6	2.5	170	180	270	1.8	2.32	1.89	1.68	13.31	6.21
7	2.5	230	180	330	1.8	5.28	5.39	3.57	3.93	1.97
8	2.5	230	340	270	1.8	5.43	5.67	1.37	4.05	1.94
9	2.0	200	280	300	2.0	4.20	3.93	3.09	8.08	3.94
10	2.0	200	280	300	2.0	4.23	3.96	3.14	8.15	3.97
11	2.5	230	340	330	2.2	6.39	6.60	1.64	3.91	1.87
12	1.5	230	340	270	2.2	4.48	4.67	0.65	4.03	1.84
13	2.5	230	180	270	2.2	5.89	5.90	3.85	3.73	1.87
14	1.5	230	180	270	1.8	3.60	3.72	2.01	4.05	2.02
15	1.5	230	180	330	2.2	4.45	4.60	2.47	4.04	2.02
16	2.0	200	280	300	2.0	4.27	4.00	3.12	8.28	4.03
17	1.5	170	340	270	1.8	1.68	1.40	0.38	14.61	6.85
18	1.5	170	180	270	2.2	1.92	1.65	1.42	14.04	6.65
19	2.5	170	340	330	1.8	2.28	1.84	0.72	13.56	6.20

X_1: Flow rate (mL/min); X_2: Oven temperature (°C); X_3: Inlet temperature (°C); X_4: Detector temperature (°C); X_5: Inject volume (µl); R_1: peak height of MCS; R_2: peak height of ECS; R_3: peak height of ICS; R_4: resolution between MCS and ECS; R_5: resolution between ECS and ICS.

Table 7.9. ANOVA regression analysis for models and responses of Screening.

Response	R^2	Adjust. R^2	SS	df	MS	F	p
MCS Height	0.9995	0.9987	38.8914	10	3.8891	1334	<0.0001
ECS Height	0.9998	0.9995	51.1069	10	5.1107	3658	<0.0001
ECS Resolution	0.9999	0.9998	385.4958	7	55.0708	15098	<0.0001
ICS Height	0.9999	0.9997	14.8934	12	1.2411	3349	<0.0001
ICS Resolution	0.9997	0.9995	81.2602	6	13.5434	5475.84	<0.0001

The model term ranking Pareto charts represent the effects and interactions of each of the parameters based on the CMAs established by the model term effect and the cumulative percentage. The model term ranking Pareto charts are shown in Fig 7.12. The Pareto charts show that the column oven temperature and/or the flow rate had the greatest effect on the CMAs. The selected responses were shown to not be affected or partially affected by the detector temperature and injection volume. As a result, the column oven temperature, flow rate of the carrier gas and inlet temperature were selected as the CMPs for the method optimization study.

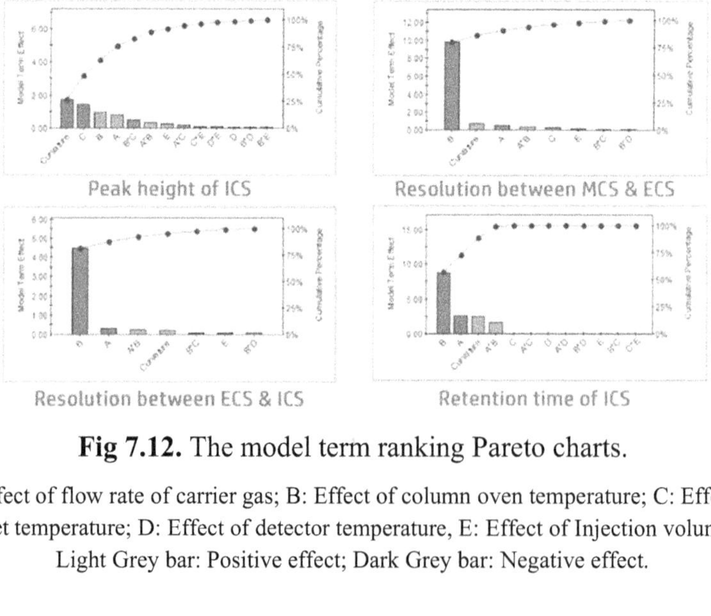

Fig 7.12. The model term ranking Pareto charts.

A: Effect of flow rate of carrier gas; B: Effect of column oven temperature; C: Effect of inlet temperature; D: Effect of detector temperature, E: Effect of Injection volume; Light Grey bar: Positive effect; Dark Grey bar: Negative effect.

Optimization

The experiments were designed using a response surface-central composite full type including three center points by a DoE. The DoE and the experimental results of each CMA are tabulated in Table 7.10. The models created were statistically validated using general regression statistics and the ANOVA statistical test. As shown in Table 7.11., the p-values for each of the responses are less than 0.0001, which is substantially smaller than the acceptance criteria of 0.05. The response surface methodology (RSM) analysis was reviewed using 3D response surface plots to identify underlying interactions between selected parameters (Fig. 7.13).

Table 7.10. Design of Experiment for Optimization & Response corresponding DoE.

Run	Parameters for Optimization			Responses					
	X_1	X_2	X_3	R_1	R_2	R_3	R_4	R_5	R_6
1	2	220	280	3.22	4.11	2.68	4.91	2.43	2.95
2	2	200	300	2.74	3.35	2.23	8.21	3.96	4.60
3	2.2	220	300	3.53	4.58	2.67	5.16	2.53	2.75
4	1.8	180	300	1.75	1.98	3.19	12.32	4.92	8.46
5	1.8	200	280	2.46	3.04	2.06	8.37	4.04	4.96
6	2.2	180	260	1.99	2.24	1.68	11.81	5.50	7.58
7	2	200	260	2.69	3.31	2.43	8.47	4.09	4.61
8	2	180	280	1.84	2.12	2.04	12.09	6.36	8.10
9	1.8	220	300	3.09	4.03	2.07	5.46	2.65	3.17
10	2	200	280	2.60	3.21	2.15	8.27	4.00	4.60
11	2	200	280	2.75	3.34	2.25	8.60	4.11	4.60
12	2	200	280	2.69	3.28	2.29	8.36	4.10	4.60
13	2.2	180	300	1.98	2.25	1.46	12.01	5.54	7.57
14	1.8	220	260	2.90	3.74	2.18	5.22	2.58	3.17
15	2.2	200	280	2.71	3.24	2.38	8.05	3.86	4.03
16	2.2	220	260	3.73	4.70	3.23	5.55	2.72	2.76
17	1.8	180	260	1.74	1.97	3.94	12.23	4.84	8.46

X_1: Flow rate (mL/min); X_2: Oven temperature (°C); X_3: Inlet temperature (°C); R_1: peak height of MCS; R_2: peak height of ECS; R_3: peak height of ICS; R_4: resolution between MCS and ECS; R_5: resolution between ECS and ICS; R_6: retention time of ICS.

Table 7.11. ANOVA regression analysis for models and responses of Optimization.

Response	R^2	Adjusted R^2	SS	df	MS	F	p
R1	0.9954	0.9908	5.7025	8	0.7128	215	<0.0001
R2	0.9934	0.9868	11.9727	8	1.4966	150	<0.0001
R3	0.9923	0.9824	5.7238	9	0.636	100	<0.0001
R4	0.9943	0.9935	117.0834	2	58.5417	1224	<0.0001
R5	0.9971	0.9948	23.4002	7	3.3429	4.4	<0.0001
R6	1.0000	1.0000	9076.33	8	1134.54	672190	<0.0001

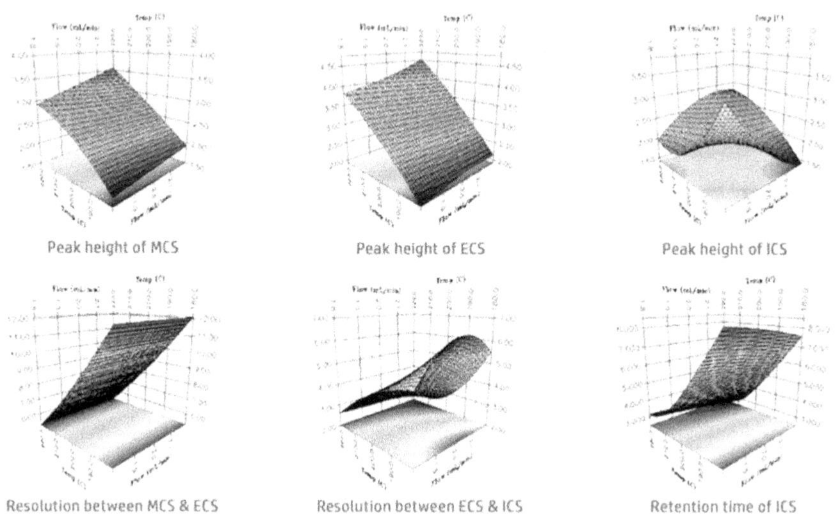

Fig. 7.13. 3D response surface plots for each response as a function of Flow rate & Column oven temperature at 280 °C.

Design Space

The method operable design region (MODR) and proven acceptable ranges (PARs) are shown in Fig. 7.14. The optimal region was set by superimposing all responses of interest. The acceptance criteria for each of the responses were set to satisfy the purpose of the ATP. The acceptance criteria of all peak heights were set to 2 or greater, in order to ensure sufficient sensitivity in order to detect trace amounts of each of the PGIs. To ensure that each peak is sufficiently separated, and inter-peak interference is minimized, the acceptance criteria for the degree of separation were set at 7 or greater for MCS and ECS and 3 or greater for

ECS and ICS. The retention time of the last eluted peak, ICS, was set to 7 min or less in order to shorten the analysis time. The shaded contour areas in Fig. 7.14 indicate the unacceptable area and the unshaded areas indicate acceptable areas. The unshaded area depicts the parameter values that can be represented as a design space with analytical method flexibility. The PAR was defined up to the set center point of the parameter range within a predefined MODR based on a linear combination of parameters. The resolution between ECS and ICS and the peak height of ICS had the most influence on establishing the MODR and PAR.

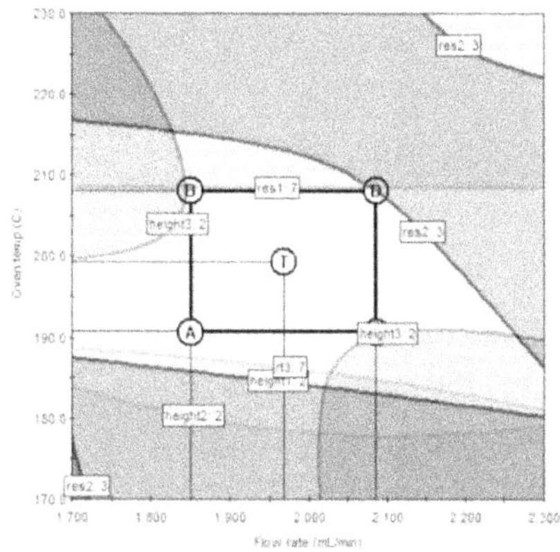

Fig.7.14. Method operable design region and proven acceptable ranges.

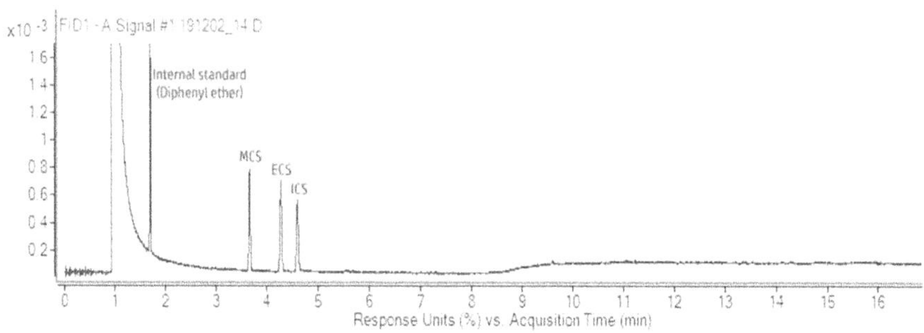

Fig. 7.15. GC-FID Chromatogram of Standard.

Optimized Conditions:

Column : HP-1 capillary column 25m x 0.32mm i.d.; 0.52μm film thickness

Column oven temp. : 200°C (hold for 8 min), ramp at 70°C/min to 260°C, hold for 8 min.

Injection heater temp.: 280°C

Detector heater temp.: 300°C

Carrier gas : Helium

Flow rate	: 2.0 mL/min Total flow set at 25 mL/min
Split ratio	: 10:1
Air flow rate	: 400 mL/min,
H2 fuel flow rate	: 30 mL/min (Helium as the make-up gas)
Injection volume	: 2.0 µL using a 5 µL auto liquid sampler syringe.
Total run time	: 16.9 min

Table 7.12. Summary of Validation results.

Validation Parameters		MCS	ECS	ICS
Specificity – Resolution		--	9.51	4.53
Precision (% RSD ≤ 10.0)	10 ppm	1.14	2.50	5.58
	30 ppm	7.79	6.97	6.64
	150 ppm	2.27	3.22	8.83
Accuracy (% recovery)	10 ppm	95.3	102.6	96.4
	120 ppm	101.3	100.7	101.2
	150 ppm	100.4	99.9	103.2
	180 ppm	99.3	98.8	102.9
LOD (ppm)		1.5	1.5	1.9
LOQ (ppm)		4.9	5.1	6.4
Linearity (ppm)			QL – 180	
Range (ppm)			30 - 150	
Regression Coefficient (R^2)		0.99953	0.99988	0.99983
Slope		0.00501	0.00544	0.00494
y-intercept		0.01200	0.00192	0.01838

***

Practical Examples of AQbD applied to GC Method Development

Analysis of Essential Oils from *Salvia Officinalis*

Essential oils

Essential oils are complex mixtures, constituted by terpenoid hydrocarbons, oxygenated terpenes and sesquiterpenes. They originate from the plant secondary metabolism and are responsible for their characteristic aroma. Essential oils are amongst the most complex samples an analyst can face in terms of the number of compounds involved.

Sage essential oil

Sage essential oil was isolated from 50 g dried vegetal product immersed in 600 mL bidistilled water by hydrodistillation in Clevenger-type apparatus for 4 hours, up to the point at which the oil contained in the herbaceous matrix was exhausted. The obtained volume (in mL) of essential oil was reported at 100 g vegetal product.

Fig. 7.16. Salvia officinalis.

ATP

To develop a rapid, sensitive, robust and economical analytical GC-MS method for chemical composition determination of essential oils obtained from leaves of Salvia officinalis using QbD-oriented systematic analytical approach. The studies were carried out in two phases: screening for identifying the CMVs and optimization of chromatographic conditions.

CAAs & CMPs

The CQAs for a GC-MS method are operators, sample preparations, mobile phase (nature of gas and flow), and the instrumental system (injector type and injection mode, column type and dimensions, oven temperature program, detector type and parameters).

Risk Assessment

Ishikawa fishbone diagram (Fig. 7.16.) is used for risk identification and assessment.

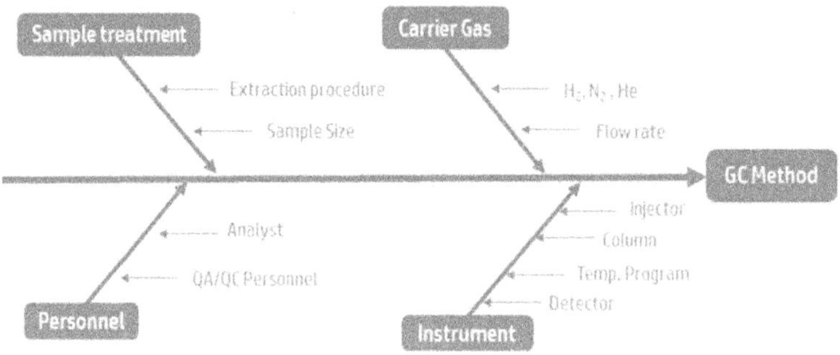

Fig. 7.17. Ishikawa fishbone diagram.

DoE

From the factors influencing the analytical performance of a generic GC method, presented in Fig. 7.16, the factors that can improve the quality of GC separation, component identification and quantitation were studied. A standardized experimental design was developed, encompassing various parameters such as 2 injection volumes, 2 split ratios, 2 flow rates, and 3 oven temperature programs.

Table 7.13. Parameters for GC Method - Experimental design.

Parameter	Description
Injection Volume	0.1 µL and 1 µL
Split ratio	100:1 and 50:1
Flow rate	0.7 and 1 1 mL/min
Temp. Program	40 - 280°C (10°C/min) 40 - 80°C (10°C/min), 80 - 260°C (5°C/min), 260 - 280°C (10°C/min) 40 - 80°C (10°C/min), 80 - 260°C (2°C/min), 260 - 280°C (10°C/min)

This led to the creation of 24 distinct chromatographic conditions (obtained by combining the different factors). The evaluation of these 24 conditions followed a two-tiered approach. Initially, they were assessed for the number of separated peaks, retention times, and analysis time, resulting in 3 optimal chromatographic conditions (formed by specific combinations of 1 injection volume, 1 split ratio, 1 flow rate, and 3 oven temperature programs). In the second phase, these 3 conditions underwent a more stringent evaluation, considering factors such as peak symmetry, peak area (affecting method sensitivity), and identification quality (with a minimum of 80% accuracy). The final method was chosen based on these attributes, ensuring its reliability and suitability for long-term use in product analysis.

Optimized conditions

The final conditions for separating sage essential oils are as follows:

1 μL of oil is injected into a split/splitless injector at a temperature of 250°C. The separation is carried out using a capillary column DP-5MS (30 m × 0.25 mm, 0.25μm film thickness) with helium (1 mL/min) as the mobile phase. The oven temperature is increased at a rate of 10°C/min, starting from 40°C and ending at 280°C. The separated compounds are then transferred to the MS detector, which operates at 280°C. The parameters for the MS detector are set as follows: source temperature at 230°C, quadrupole temperature at 150°C, mass range from 15 to 450 AMU, and the mode of acquisition is set to SCAN.

Under these conditions, the analysis time required is less than 25 minutes. For a visual representation of the chromatographic results, please refer to Fig. 7.18, which displays a chromatogram of a sage essential oil sample.

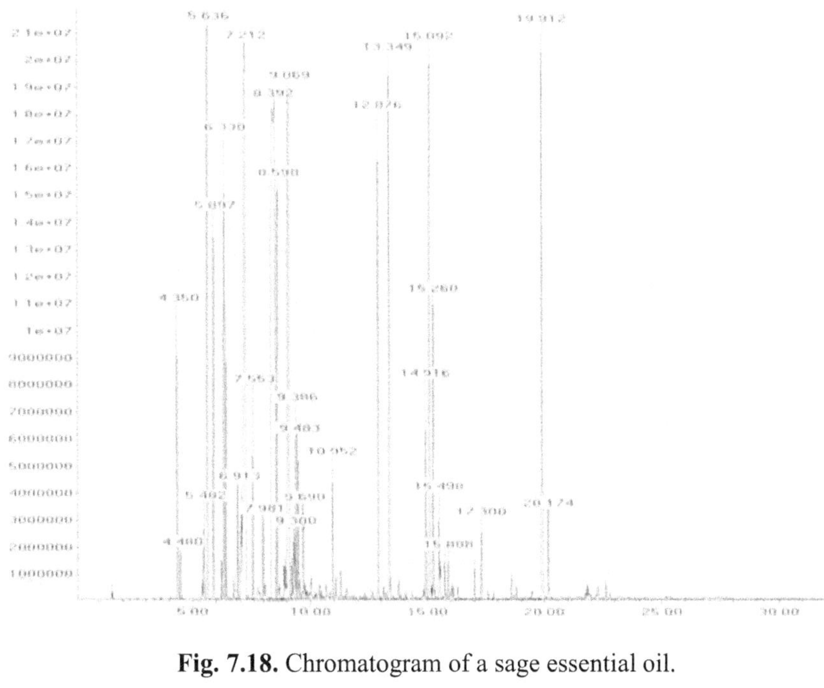

Fig. 7.18. Chromatogram of a sage essential oil.

Table 7.14. The main identified compounds of Salvia Officinalis.

S. No.	Name	Rt	Area %	Quality (%)
1	β- Thujone	8.39	19.1	98
2	1,8 - Cineole	7.21	10.9	99
3	Camphor	9.07	8.68	98
4	Viridifloral	15.10	7.44	99
5	α- Pinene	5.63	6.39	96
6	13-Epimanool	19.92	5.59	90
7	α- Humulene	13.35	5.38	98
8	α- Thujone	8.60	4.23	98
9	Trans – Caryophylene	12.88	3.57	99
10	β- Pinene	6.33	2.93	97
11	Camphene	5.90	2.75	97
12	Decahydro-Naphthalene	15.26	2.04	83
13	Caryophyllene oxide	14.91	1.8	94
14	Myrcene	6.42	1.56	95
15	Cis - Salvene	4.35	1.41	97
16	γ- Terpinene	7.55	1.21	97
17	Borneol 1	9.38	1.14	97
18	Terpinen-4-ol	9.48	1.03	98
19	Para-Cymene	7.05	0.99	97
20	(+)-m-Mentha-1,8-diene	9.68	0.91	87
21	Sabinyl acetate	10.94	0.83	84
22	α- Terpinene	6.91	0.74	98
23	Isocamphane	15.49	0.72	88
24	α- Thujene	5.48	0.64	94
25	5,7-Dimethoxy-1-napthol	20.17	0.64	90
26	Caryophylla-4(12).8(13)-dien-5-β-ol	15.53	0.51	87
27	Terpinolene	7.98	0.5	98
	Other 34 compounds		5.51	

***

Practical Examples of AQbD applied to GC Method Development

Quantitation of 19 Alkyl Halides as Potential Genotoxic Impurities

Alkyl halides

Alkyl halides, also known as haloalkanes or halogenoalkanes, are chemical compounds formed from alkanes containing one or more halogen atoms, such as chlorine, bromine, fluorine, or iodine. These compounds are mainly used in alkylation reactions via nucleophilic substitutions as starting materials or reagents in synthetic processes of active pharmaceutical ingredients (APIs) because of their good reactivity, ease of use, reasonable prices, and commercial availability. Alkyl halides are considered potential genotoxic impurities (PGIs) because they can possibly alkylate DNA bases (on N-7 of guanine and N-3 of adenine).

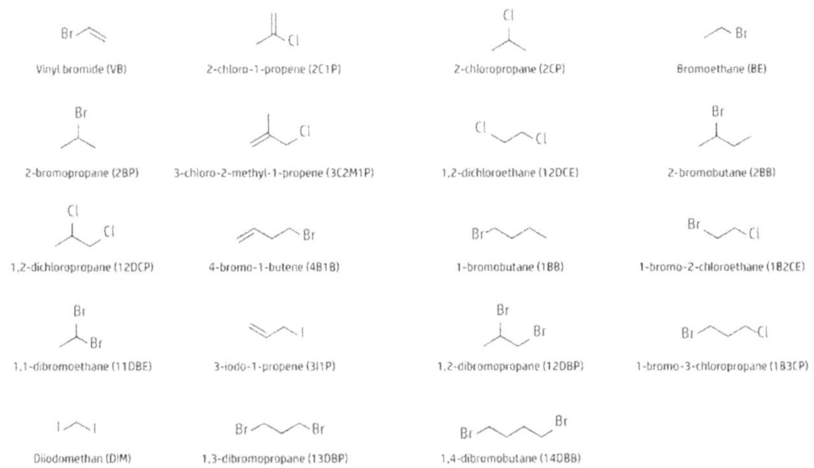

Fig. 7.19. Alkyl halides considered to be potential genotoxic impurities (PGIs).

Alkyl halides are potentially formed during API manufacturing processes during undesired chemical reactions or are carried over to APIs when used as starting materials or reagents. For these reasons, alkyl halides should be considered significant PGIs when developing manufacturing processes and designating quality control strategies for APIs to manage genotoxic impurities.

ATP

The analytical method development using the analytical QbD approach and GC–MS focused on high sensitivity, specificity, and reproducibility for the selected 19 alkyl halides.

CAAs & CMPs

The peak area & resolution of each peak were selected as the CMAs due to the most important ATPs in the analytical method for PGIs being detection sensitivity and specificity.

The potential CMPs selected were the initial oven temperature, oven temperature hold time, oven temperature ramping rate, column flow rate, sample injection volume, final oven temperature, type of carrier gas, sample injector temperature, detector temperature, type of column, sample injection route, type of detector, and type of diluent.

Risk Assessment

The peak area & resolution of each peak were selected as the CMAs due to the most important ATPs in the analytical method for PGIs being detection sensitivity and specificity. Fishbone diagram and the initial risk assessment based on a cause and effect (C&E) analysis was used to select CMPs.

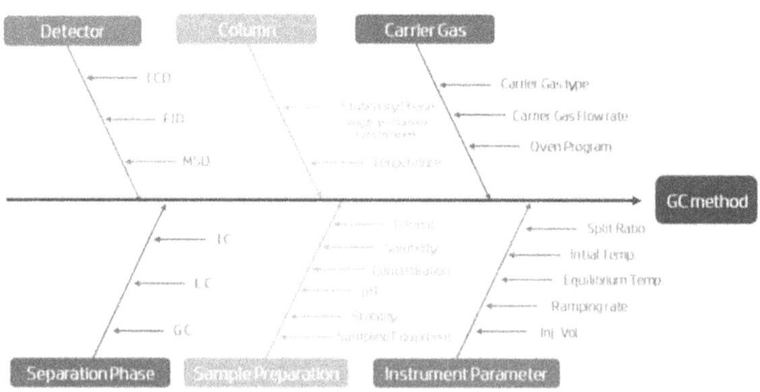

Fig. 7.20. Fishbone diagram to select CMPs.

DoE

A two-level-full factorial design with four center points was designed and tested with the CMPs that are expected to have critical effects on the selected response, resolution, and peak area.

Screening: The DoE & regression analysis of variance analysis (ANOVA) was evaluated to check the appropriate model fitting (Table 7.15. & Table 7.16). The model terms ranking the Pareto charts are summarized in Fig. 7.21 & 7.22. The flow rate of the carrier gas and the initial temperature of the oven were selected as the CMPs for the method optimization study.

Table 7.15. DoE for Screening.

Method-A					Method-B				
Run	X_1	X_2	X_3	X_4	Run	X_1	X_2	X_3	X_4
A-1	2.0	35	2.5	225	B-1	2.5	40	2.0	225
A-2	2.0	65	2.5	225	B-2	2.5	90	2.0	225
A-3	0.3	35	2.0	225	B-3	1.0	40	1.5	225
A-4	2.0	35	2.5	215	B-4	2.5	40	2.0	215
A-5	2.0	35	2.0	225	B-5	2.5	40	1.5	225
A-6	2.0	35	2.0	215	B-6	2.5	40	1.5	215
A-7	0.3	35	2.5	225	B-7	1.0	40	2.0	225
A-8	2.0	65	2.5	215	B-8	2.5	90	2.0	215
A-9	1.2	50	2.3	220	B-9	1.8	65	1.8	220
A-10	1.2	50	2.3	220	B-10	1.8	65	1.8	220
A-11	1.2	50	2.3	220	B-11	1.8	65	1.8	220
A-12	0.3	65	2.5	215	B-12	1.0	90	2.0	215
A-13	2.0	65	2.0	215	B-13	2.5	90	1.5	215
A-14	0.3	65	2.5	225	B-14	1.0	90	2.0	225
A-15	0.3	65	2.0	215	B-15	1.0	90	1.5	215
A-16	0.3	65	2.0	225	B-16	1.0	90	1.5	225
A-17	2.0	65	2.0	225	B-17	2.5	90	1.5	225
A-18	1.2	50	2.3	220	B-18	1.8	65	1.8	220
A-19	0.3	35	2.5	215	B-19	1.0	40	2.0	215
A-20	0.3	35	2.0	215	B-20	1.0	40	1.5	215

X_1: the flow rate of the carrier; X_2: initial oven temp.; X_3: oven temp. ramping rate; X_4: sample injector temp;

Table 7.16. Screening Statistics results.

Response		SS	df	MS	F	p
VB	Peak Area	363545	4	90886	123.65	<0.01
2C1P	Resolution	2.31	9	0.25	115.00	<0.01
	Peak Area	28372838	1	28372838	134.66	<0.01
2CP	Resolution	2.50	6	0.41	723.67	<0.01
	Peak Area	1617766	2	808883	55.08	<0.01
BE	Resolution	25.01	7	3.57	382.44	<0.01
	Peak Area	5578546	1	5578546	171.11	<0.01
2BP	Resolution	449.97	3	149.99	839.29	<0.01
	Peak Area	174573	2	87286	58.73	<0.01
3C2M1P	Resolution	60.00	5	12.00	675.49	<0.01
	Peak Area	313435	1	313435	133.11	<0.01
12DCE	Resolution	370.90	8	46.36	207.03	<0.01
	Peak Area	336637	6	56106	185.06	<0.01
2BB	Resolution	127.72	7	18.24	114.85	<0.01
	Peak Area	1122779	2	561389	56.16	<0.01
12DCP	Resolution	144.53	5	28.90	159.55	<0.01
	Peak Area	252402	1	252402	176.19	<0.01
4B1B	Resolution	10.91	3	3.63	66.17	<0.01
	Peak Area	0.0003	4	<0.0001	36.66	<0.01
3I1P	Peak Area	7891128	5	1578225	35.95	<0.01
1BB	Resolution	57.83	4	14.45	39.10	<0.01
	Peak Area	703483	1	703483	84.49	<0.01
1B2CE	Resolution	44.15	3	14.71	58.83	<0.01
	Peak Area	135246	2	67623	38.70	<0.01
11DBE	Resolution	26.54	3	8.8497	62.24	<0.01
	Peak Area	109070	2	54535	240.22	<0.01
12DBP	Resolution	5359	3	1786	176.64	<0.01
	Peak Area	1562157	5	312431	47.35	<0.01
DIM	Resolution	308.94	6	51	133.18	<0.01
	Peak Area	1205161	3	401720	19.31	<0.01
13DBP	Resolution	1.63	3	0.54	79.58	<0.01
	Peak Area	<0.0001	9	<0.0001	20.92	<0.01
14DBB	Resolution	3483	2	1741	153.26	<0.01
	Peak Area	12128	7	1732	8.42	<0.01

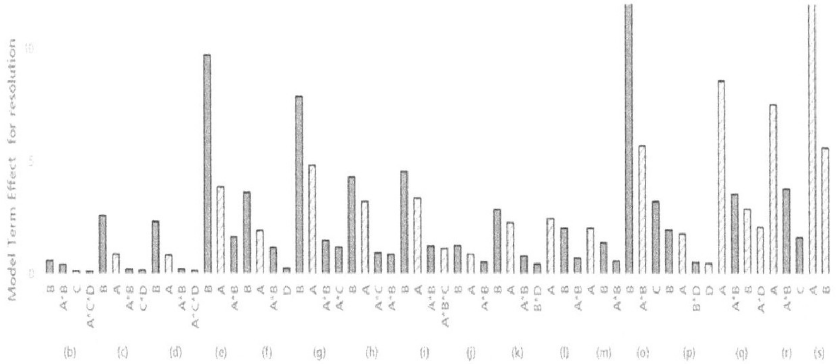

Fig. 7.21. Pareto charts for resolution.

A: initial oven temp., B: the flow rate of the carrier, C: oven temp. ramping rate D: sample injector temp; (a) VB, (b) 2C1P, (c) 2CP, (d) BE, (e) 2BP, (f) 3C2M1P, (g) 12DCE, (h) 2BB, (i) 12DCP, (j) 4B1B, (k) 1BB, (l) 1B2CE, (m) 11DBE, (n) 3I1P, (o) 12DBP, (p) 1B3CP, (q) DIM, (r) 13DBP, (s) 14DBB.

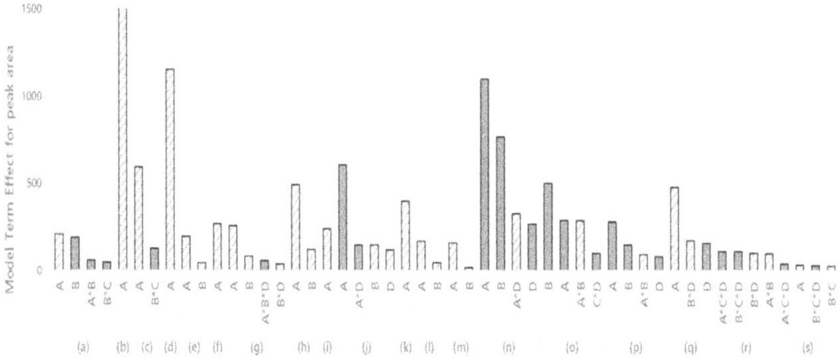

Fig. 7.22. Pareto chart for peak area.

A: initial oven temp., B: the flow rate of the carrier, C: oven temp. ramping rate D: sample injector temp; (a) VB, (b) 2C1P, (c) 2CP, (d) BE, (e) 2BP, (f) 3C2M1P, (g) 12DCE, (h) 2BB, (i) 12DCP, (j) 4B1B, (k) 1BB, (l) 1B2CE, (m) 11DBE, (n) 3I1P, (o) 12DBP, (p) 1B3CP, (q) DIM, (r) 13DBP, (s) 14DBB.

Optimization: The response surface methodology (RSM), which is based on standard orthogonal arrays that contain three levels for each experiment variable, was employed for the method optimization study. Based on the results obtained from the method screening, the flow rate of the carrier gas in the column and the initial temperature of the column were selected as the CMPs for method optimization studies. The DoE is tabulated in Table 7.17. The regression ANOVA statistics result (Table 7.18) was shown to be significant with a p-value and F-ratio for all responses.

Table 7.17. DoE for Optimization.

Method-A			Method-B		
Run	Flow rate	Initial Temp.	Run	Flow rate	Initial Temp.
A-1	1.7	45	B-1	1.8	90
A-2	1.7	40	B-2	1.8	65
A-3	2.0	40	B-3	2.5	65
A-4	2.0	45	B-4	2.5	90
A-5	1.3	35	B-5	1.0	40
A-6	1.3	40	B-6	1.0	65
A-7	1.7	40	B-7	1.8	65
A-8	2.0	35	B-8	2.5	10
A-9	1.7	40	B-9	1.8	65
A-10	1.7	40	B-10	1.8	65
A-11	1.7	35	B-11	1.8	40
A-12	1.3	45	B-12	1.0	90

Table 7.18. Screening Statistics results.

Response		SS	df	MS	F	p
VB	Peak Area	39784	3	13261.43	10.4579	<0.01
2C1P	Resolution	0.3267	1	0.3267	26.6667	<0.01
	Peak Area	5078587	3	1692862	10.3662	<0.01
2CP	Resolution	3.1395	4	0.7849	16.018	<0.01
	Peak Area	658727	3	219575	14.451	<0.01
BE	Resolution	1.1267	1	1.1267	29.9778	<0.01
	Peak Area	125017	3	41672	13.1523	<0.01
2BP	Resolution	27.9528	3	9.3176	29.3893	<0.01
	Peak Area	<0.01	3	<0.01	41.9238	<0.01
3C2M1P	Resolution	5.5787	3	1.8596	14.2526	<0.01
	Peak Area	49069	3	16356	32.7338	<0.01
12DCE	Resolution	38.805	3	12.935	4.3709	0.042
	Peak Area	21604	2	10802	16.9309	<0.01
2BB	Resolution	7.935	1	7.935	13.79	<0.01
	Peak Area	370632	3	123544	97.5273	<0.01
12DCP	Resolution	17.2294	3	5.7431	10.4585	<0.01
	Peak Area	42511	3	14170	23.6012	<0.01
4B1B	Resolution	0.8388	2	0.4194	13.9608	<0.01
	Peak Area	113294	3	37764	13.383	<0.01
3I1P	Peak Area	5270439.51	4	1317609	56.0824	<0.01
1BB	Resolution	2.1687	2	1.0844	7.0698	0.014
	Peak Area	171839	3	57279	52.615	<0.01
1B2CE	Resolution	1.5	1	1.5	5.1546	0.047
	Peak Area	23564.55	1	23564	48.6432	<0.01

Contd...

Response		SS	df	MS	F	p
11DBE	Resolution	1.9267	1	1.9267	6.0397	0.034
	Peak Area	4647.75	3	1549	4.2898	0.044
12DBP	Resolution	1631.06	3	543.6883	52.3332	<0.01
	Peak Area	6255223.87	4	1563805	12.6797	<0.01
1B3CP	Resolution	3.1758	2	1.5879	11.8351	<0.01
	Peak Area	496361.17	2	248180	12.5135	<0.01
DIM	Resolution	53.0399	2	26.5199	10.9916	<0.01
	Peak Area	1008620.08	1	1008620	8.8133	0.014
13DBP	Resolution	0.0158	2	0.0079	52.7139	<0.01
	Peak Area	150401.39	2	75200	4.538	0.048
14DBB	Resolution	2185.18	3	728.3925	12.1323	<0.01
	Peak Area	172456.65	2	86228	8.2038	<0.01

RSM analysis

3D response surface plots of 8 PGIs with relatively low resolutions and peak areas were selected. The effects of the flow rate and oven temperature on the resolution of PGI are shown in Fig. 7.23 and the effects of the flow rate and oven temperature on the peak area are shown in Fig. 7.24.

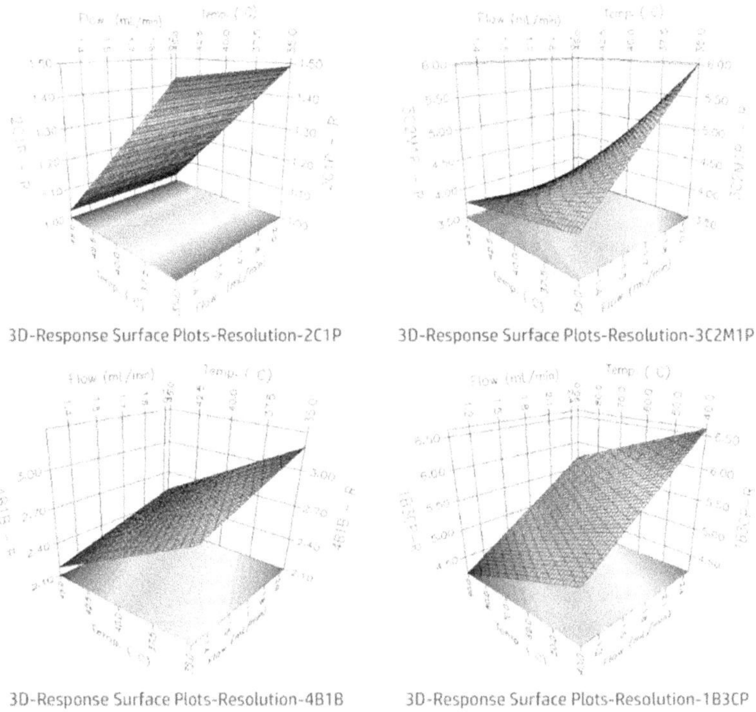

Fig. 7.23. The 3D response surface plots for the resolution.

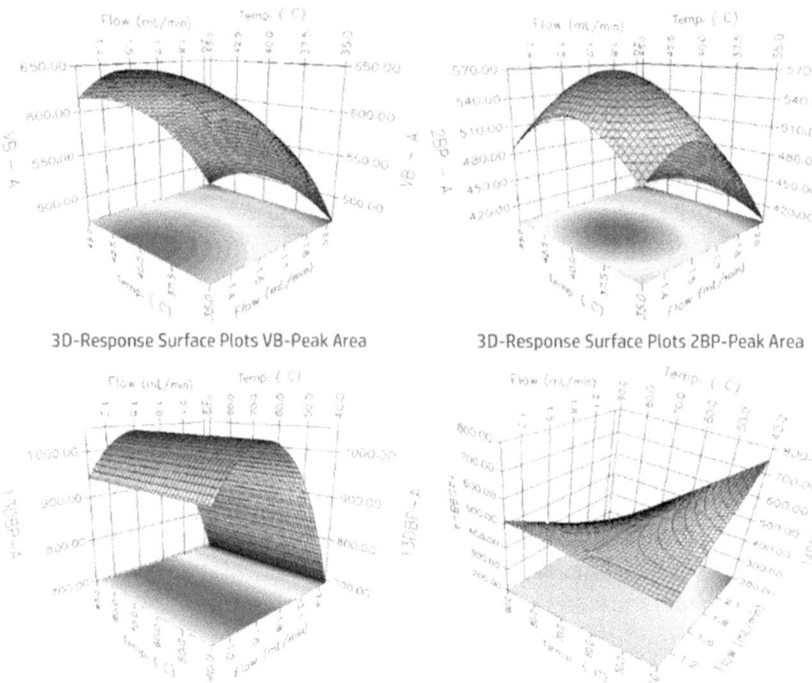

3D-Response Surface Plots VB-Peak Area   3D-Response Surface Plots 2BP-Peak Area

3D-Response Surface Plots 13DBP-Peak Area   3D-Response Surface Plots 14DBB-Peak Area

Fig. 7.24. The 3D response surface plots for the Peak area.

MODR

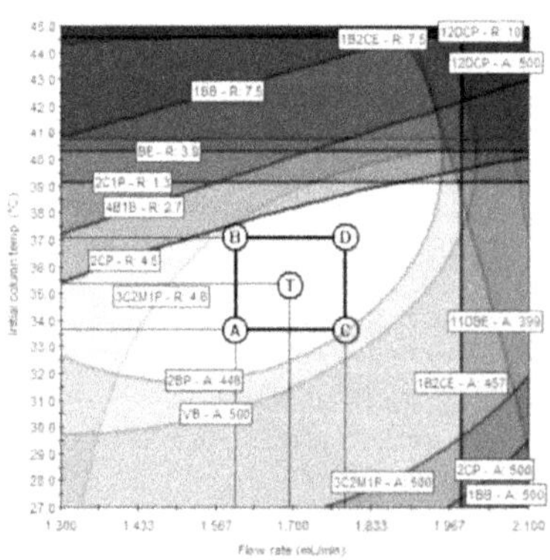

Fig. 7.25. MODR & PARs for Method-A.

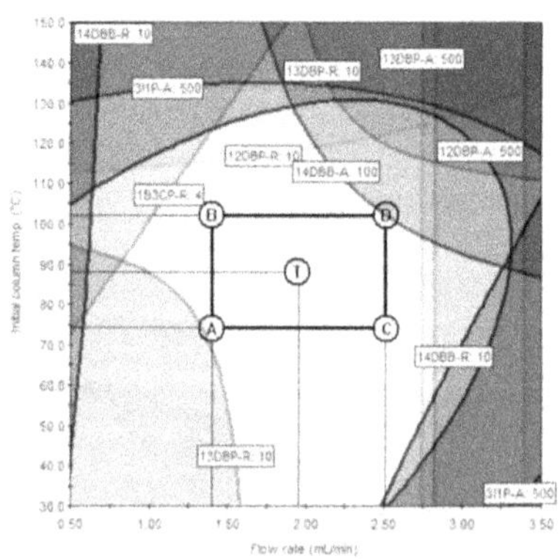

Fig. 7.26. MODR & PARs for Method-B.

For the set acceptance criteria (10 for resolution and 500 for the peak area), the shaded contour represents the unacceptable region, while the unshaded represents the acceptable region. In the final optimization study, the unshaded region may represent the design space for the variables being studied in terms of the graphed response. The MODR in Fig. 7.25 and 7.26 show the regions for acceptable results for all responses, simultaneously.

Optimized Conditions:

Gas chromatography fitted with MSD; FID equipped with Headspace auto sampler analyzer.

Column : VF-624ms (60m x 0.25mm i.d., 1.4 μm film thickness)

Carrier Gas : Helium

Flow rate : 1.7~2.0 mL/min

Oven Temp : Method-A: Initial: 35°C, ramp at 3°C/min to 124°C (hold for 10 min)

Method-B: Initial: 90°C, ramp at 2°C/min to 100°C, ramp at 5°C/min to 130°C, ramp at 10°C/min to 160°C.

Inj. Heater temp. : 280°C

Split ratio : 2:1

Injection volume : 1000μL

Total run time : 20 min

Table 7.19. Summary of Validation parameters.

Name	Specificity	Sensitivity (ppm)		Linearity	Accuracy (%)			Precision (%RSD)	
	Rs	DL	QL	R^2; m; C	Low	Mid	High	Repeatability	QL Level
Acc.	≥1.5	≤ 0.3	≤ 1.0	≥ 0.995; -; -	≥ 85%	≥ 85%	≥ 85%	≤ 10	≤ 10
VB	-	0.09	0.29	0.9989 137.91 15.699	90.84	97.90	92.57	4.01	4.35
2C1P	1.5	0.01	0.03	0.9990 1215.68 109.155	87.97	97.64	92.75	5.45	3.35
2CP	5.4	0.03	0.10	0.9993 402.58 29.440	86.79	93.95	90.08	4.51	3.47
BE	4.6	0.01	0.04	0.9997 304.53 37.785	90.72	95.23	89.52	3.69	2.11
2BP	17.4	0.05	0.16	0.9997 170.84 4.359	90.73	96.36	91.21	2.99	1.80
3C2M1P	5.2	0.03	0.09	0.9994 298.47 1.804	95.29	98.51	93.85	1.94	1.80

Contd...

Name	Speci ficity	Sensitivity (ppm)		Linearity	Accuracy (%)			Precision (%RSD)	
	Rs	DL	QL	R^2; m; C	Low	Mid	High	Repeat-ability	QL Level
Acc.	≥1.5	≤ 0.3	≤ 1.0	≥ 0.995; -; -	≥ 85%	≥ 85%	≥ 85%	≤ 10	≤ 10
12DCE	18.4	0.04	0.13	0.9996 212.38 13.247	99.58	99.16	93.33	3.20	6.43
2BB	12.6	0.01	0.04	0.9996 529.32 8.433	100.64	103.81	98.26	2.07	1.61
12DCP	12.2	0.04	0.14	0.9975 192.29 24.495	98.07	97.78	90.49	3.33	3.31
4B1B	2.8	0.02	0.06	0.9996 347.26 58.163	97.93	97.02	91.62	2.91	1.34
1BB	8.2	0.02	0.05	0.9994 304.80 38.029	98.91	99.47	93.24	2.04	1.93
1B2CE	8.3	0.05	0.16	0.9998 153.73 6.450	100.21	96.61	92.26	4.48	4.31
11DBE	5.9	0.05	0.18	0.9993 158.29 2.456	101.25	99.50	95.67	3.42	3.81
3I1P	-	0.07	0.25	0.9997 619.84 19.912	96.77	92.01	96.52	3.36	2.28
12DBP	27.8	0.07	0.25	0.9988 321.55 15.625	94.64	93.67	93.67	6.60	3.97
1B3CP	5.3	0.10	0.33	0.9988 122.00 4.4667	95.70	97.30	95.51	5.41	1.82
DIM	20.6	0.07	0.24	0.9991 318.22 5.9208	98.81	100.12	98.83	4.54	1.01
13DBP	11.7	0.11	0.38	0.9999 100.11 0.7792	101.14	102.47	99.88	2.93	1.68
14DBB	63.4	0.07	0.29	0.9993 55.283 3.3083	96.09	97.97	93.34	3.38	2.95

***

CHAPTER 8

AQbD for HPTLC Method Development

8.1 Introduction

Applying QbD technique to analytical methods would aid in building quality in the method right from scratch. It should not be inferred that AQbD necessarily means less testing. This technique basically arms us with a sound strategy to manage variability and ensures robust analytics. The primary purpose of AQbD is ensuring that a reliable analytical testing method has been developed. Reliability of an analytical method is demonstrated by its robustness and ruggedness. Processes, for example, have been defined as robust if they have the ability to tolerate the expected variability of raw materials, operating conditions, process equipment, environmental conditions, and human factors. Robustness testing involves estimating the influence of a small change in any of the variables on the entire operation. Ruggedness indicates whether the process is reproducible under various test conditions. The factors that tend to have an effect on ruggedness of an operation are instruments and differences in their calibrations, method of handling, changes in the laboratory conditions etc. Mostly the QbD technique is applied to the broad arena of product development. This necessitates a discussion of application of Qbd to analytical techniques. The time has come to make the traditional analytical method obsolete and embrace the data driven and scientific approach of AQbD. The key concepts and activities associated with successful implementation of AQbD have been discussed earlier in a step-wise manner. (See chapter 2)

8.2 Principle of HPTLC

High-Performance Thin-Layer Chromatography (HPTLC) is a chromatographic technique used to separate, identify, and quantify components in a mixture. It is an extension of traditional thin-layer chromatography (TLC) that offers higher resolution and improved sensitivity. HPTLC is a planar chromatography method that involves the migration of solutes on a thin layer of adsorbent material. HPTLC method development involves designing an optimized procedure to achieve the best separation and detection of analytes in a given sample.

High-performance thin-layer chromatography (HPTLC) is employed widely in pharmaceutical industries for process development, identification, and detection of adulterants in herbal products; identification of pesticide content and mycotoxins; and in quality control of herbs and health food.

HPTLC has been reported to offer several advantages over the most widely used HPLC technique because of its high throughput (multiple samples can be analyzed simultaneously), economy in use of mobile phase, and cost effectiveness.

It is based on the use of special layers made from narrowly distributed fine particles of ~5 μm. It is actually not a special technique because all fundamental parameters, theoretical considerations, and practical aspects of classical TLC still apply. HPTLC is not very different from TLC in terms of the underlying principle. Briefly, you apply the sample on a TLC plate and run the sample by dipping the plate in a particular solvent system. The compounds in the sample will then separate based on their polarities. The difference lies in how the experiment is performed, in that HPTLC uses a computer system connected to an auto-sampler and a scanner (and occasionally an Automatic Developing Chamber and a Chromatogram Immersion Device).

The auto-sampler spots the specified amount of your sample on the plates, after which the plates can be developed in a glass chamber or an automatic developing chamber. Once the chromatogram run is complete, the plates are dipped in the derivatization agent either manually or using a chromatogram immersion device. Alternatively, the derivatization agent can be sprayed on the plate using a Derivatizer. Finally, the compounds are quantified by scanning the plate using a scanner. An HPTLC auto-sampler however, is a precision instrument that applies a specified amount of sample by spraying it using nitrogen gas. Also, a computer system connected to the auto-sampler is used to feed data about the amount of sample to be applied and the number, width, and position of the bands of the samples.

Nowadays, HPTLC has become a routine analytical technique due to its advantages of reliability in quantitation, analysis at microgram and even in nanogram levels and cost effectiveness. This method is advantageous since large number of samples can be simultaneously subjected to analysis. The amount of solvent required in comparison to HPLC is very less. This reduces the time and cost of analysis and possibilities of pollution of the environment. HPTLC also facilitates repeated detection (scanning) of the chromatogram with same or different parameters. Simultaneous assay of several components in a multicomponent formulation is also possible.

8.3 Classical Approach for HPTLC Method Development

The classical approach for HPTLC method development involves the scheme depicted in the Fig.8.1.

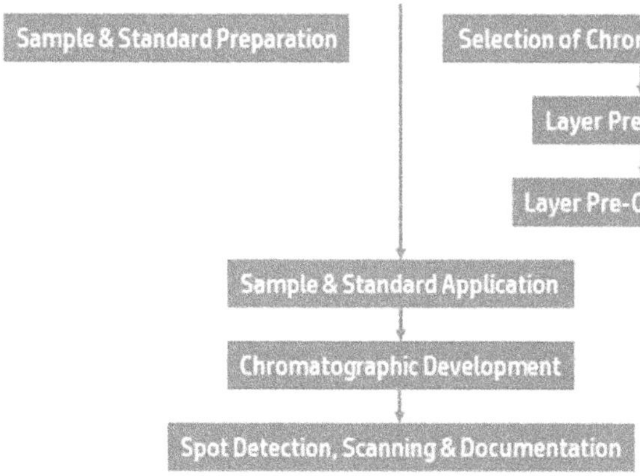

Fig. 8.1. Schematic Procedure for HPTLC Method Development.

The steps involved in HPTLC method development are

Define the Objective: Determine the purpose of the analysis, such as identifying and quantifying specific compounds or assessing the purity of a sample.

Selection of Stationary Phase: Choose a suitable HPTLC plate coated with a specific stationary phase that best suits the analytes of interest. Different stationary phases have varying affinities for different compounds, affecting separation efficiency.

Selection of Mobile Phase: The mobile phase is the solvent or a mixture of solvents that helps carry the analytes along the stationary phase. Select appropriate mobile phases based on the polarity and interactions of the analytes with the stationary phase. You may need to perform some initial trial runs with different mobile phases to find the most suitable one.

Sample Preparation: Prepare the samples by dissolving the analytes in a suitable solvent. The sample should be clear, free from impurities, and appropriately concentrated for application on the HPTLC plate.

Application Technique: Apply the samples on the HPTLC plate using a suitable application technique, such as band or spot application. The application volume should be consistent across all samples.

Development of the Plate: Place the HPTLC plate in a development chamber with the mobile phase. Allow the solvent to migrate up the plate until it reaches a specific distance or height. Ensure that the plate is developed under controlled conditions to obtain reproducible results.

Drying and Detection: After development, dry the HPTLC plate to remove any residual solvent. Detect the separated analytes using various detection methods, such as UV absorption, fluorescence, or chemical reagents.

Data Analysis: Measure the distance travelled by each spot or band and calculate the Rf (Retention factor) values. Rf values are used to identify the compounds by comparing them with known standards. Quantification can be done by comparing the peak areas or intensities of the spots to a calibration curve.

Optimization: If the separation is not satisfactory or the peaks are not well-defined, adjust the mobile phase composition, sample concentration, or other parameters and repeat the process until the desired separation is achieved.

Validation: Once the method is optimized, validate the method according to applicable guidelines to ensure its reliability, accuracy, precision, and robustness.

8.4 AQbD Elements for HPTLC Method Development

Creation of Knowledge Space

Method development demands primary knowledge about the physicochemical characteristics of sample, nature of the sample, such as structure, polarity, volatility, stability and solubility. It involves considerable trial and error procedures. Steps involved in HPTLC method development are selection of stationary and mobile phase, application of sample, development, derivatization, documentation of plate, labelling, quantitative evaluation of chromatogram, and documentation of work performed. Instrument installation and operation qualification (IQ/OQ) and good laboratory practice/good manufacturing practice (GLP/GMP) requirements in regulated laboratories are met by many of the latest TLC instruments, such as sample applicators, developing chambers and densitometers.

Analytical Target Profile

The initial stage in the application of AQbD is known as the Analytical Target Profile (ATP). It establishes the primary objective of the HPTLC method development process and serves as a metric for method effectiveness. It entails accurately and precisely quantifying the quantity of a drug in either the API or the formulation, using a straightforward, sensitive, and cost-effective analytical approach. Additionally, it can be utilized for the determination of a drug's quantity in the presence of impurities (SIAM) as well as for assessing the drug release amount in in-vitro dissolution studies.

Analytical Method Performance Characteristics

It is the responsibility of the analyst to identify parameters that are relevant to the performance of the given analytical procedure, as well as to design proper validation protocols including acceptance criteria and to perform an appropriate evaluation. The efficient development and validation of analytical methods are critical elements in the development of pharmaceuticals. Success in these areas can be attributed to several important factors, which in turn will contribute to regulatory compliance. Validation requirements for HPTLC method are highly diversified, depending on the actual type of test, as planar chromatography can be used in a wide range of applications. AMPCs are the validation parameters/ characteristics that are normally evaluated during HPTLC method validation. The characteristics such as accuracy, precision, specificity, linearity, range, detection limit, quantitation limit, robustness, ruggedness can be determined as per ICH Q2 R1 guidelines.

Selection of Analytical Technique

HPTLC is superior to other analytical techniques in terms of total cost and time for analysis. It is an offline process in which various stages are carried out independently. Important features of HPTLC include the ability to analyze crude samples containing multi-components, application of large number of sample and a series of standards using the spray-on technique, choice of solvents for the HPTLC development is wide as the mobile phases are fully evaporated before the detection step, processing of standards and samples identically on the same plate leading to better accuracy and precision of quantification, different and universal selective detection methods, and in situ spectra recording in sequence to obtain positive identification of fractions, storage of total sample on layer without time constrains. In addition, HPTLC method may help to minimizes exposure risk of toxic organic effluents and significantly reduces its disposal problems, consequently, reducing environment pollution. Therefore, it can be considered as an environment friendly method.

Identification of Critical Analytical Attributes (CAAs)

After the selection of technique, detailed assessment of the risks associated with method parameters, viz., Plate dimensions, SP and coating thickness, MP composition, saturation time, development time & distance, sample volume (spot), drying time, visualization technique, band length etc. are focused. To control the "Variability" of materials and method, Critical Analytical Attributes

(CAA) and Critical method parameters (CMP) are identified through Risk Management process. For HPTLC technique, typical CAAs are Retardation factor, theoretical plates, resolution, peak area, asymmetric factor, Peak Height, Capacity factor. It helps to have better understanding of method & its performance thus helping Life Cycle Management of the method (LCM).

Risk Assessment

Studies on risk assessment were conducted to determine the CMPs that have elevated risks based on their significance and potential to impact CAAs. Additionally, these risk assessments shed light on the anticipated interactions among the CMPs and CPPs, allowing for the estimation of any potential future failures.

The initial phase of the risk assessment involved a systematic compilation of all conceivable factors that could influence the method. These factors were then structured hierarchically, typically using an Ishikawa or "fishbone" diagram. Subsequently, prioritization studies were carried out to select the CMPs/CPPs with the highest risk, employing the Failure Modes and Effects Analysis (FMEA) risk assessment technique. The FMEA results in Risk Priority Numbers (RPN) for each combination of occurrence probability, severity of failure mode, and likelihood of detection, providing a basis for ranking the risks.

Design of Experiments (DoE)

DoE methodology assesses the interaction between factors, provides global knowledge, delivers high-quality information at every point of the experimental domain and requires fewer experiments than classical approach. The most commonly used screening designs in HPTLC method development are PBD, D-optimal design and Taguchi design. The optimization designs preferred are BBD and CCD.

MODR

MODR of any analytical method, also termed as Analytical Design Space (ADS), or Proven Acceptable Range (PAR), is the multidimensional combination and interaction of input variables that have been demonstrated to provide assurance of quality. Before validating a MODR, confirmatory validation runs should be performed to rectify the empirical model resulting from a DoE exercise.

It permits the flexibility in various input method parameters to provide the expected method performance criteria and method response without resubmission to FDA. It is based on a science, risk based and multivariate approach to evaluate effects of various factors on method performance.

Control strategy

Development of QbD analytical methods does not end with the DS. A control strategy of the method has to be implemented to assure that the method will perform as intended on a routine basis. It is obtained from the procedure understanding gained from modeling the design space. An analytical adaptation of control strategy is defined as the controls on input factors to a method that ensure the method meets both traditional system suitability criteria and wider performance-related goals. Here, elements from the DS can be used to select responses that have to be monitored at each analytical run. These responses that will be implemented in the control strategy are known as system-suitability tests or validity tests.

Continuous Method Monitoring

AQbD principles in development of a robust and cost-effective analytical method are applicable throughout the lifecycle of the product, to facilitate the regulatory flexibility in analytical method. It means the freedom to change method parameters within a method's design space, referred to as the method operable design region. It helps to identify & address any abnormal results of the analytical method.

***

Practical Examples of AQbD Applied to HPTLC Method Development

Estimation of Mangiferin in Bio-analytical Samples

Drug Profile

Mangiferin, a polyphenolic C-glucosyl xanthone, exists as a principal phytoconstituent in the leaves and stem bark of Mangifera indica belonging to family Anacardiaceae. Chemically, 2-C - β- D - gluco-pyranosyl - 1, 3,6,7-tetrahydroxy xanthone exhibits moderate aqueous solubility, i.e., 1.44 mg/mL and low lipophilicity (log P) of −0.59. It has antioxidant activity for scavenging free radicals and protection against ROS-induced oxidative stress.

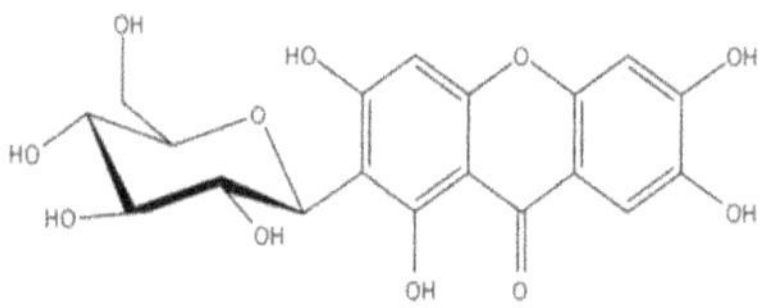

Fig. 8.2. Mangiferin Structure.

Literature

Numerous techniques have been reportedfor the quantification of Mangiferin. These methods encompass UV-vis spectroscopy, spectrofluorimetry, thin-layer chromatography (TLC), high-performance liquid chromatography (HPLC), high-performance thin-layer chromatography (HPTLC), liquid chromatography -mass spectrometry (LC-MS), and tandem mass spectrometry (LC-MS-MS). These techniques have been employed for Mangiferin quantification in both the bulk drug and various bioanalytical samples such as rat plasma, urine, and aqueous humor. Nevertheless, none of these methods have been deemed highly satisfactory due to their reliance on intricate mixtures of aqueous and organic solvents, as well as the complexity of monitoring the chromatographic conditions.

ATP

Table 8.1. enlists the ATP elements setup for developing an efficient thin-layer densitometric method with enhanced chromatographic separation of mangiferin.

Table 8.1. ATP for Bioanalytical Thin-Layer Densitometry Method of Mangiferin.

ATP Element	Target
Mangiferin	Active ingredient/antioxidant
Method type	Liquid densitometry
Instrument requirement	HPTLC system equipped with a scanner
Sample characteristic	Liquid
Biological sample preparation	Handling, weighing, sampling, admixing with solvents

CAAs & CMPs

To meet the ATP, various CAAs were earmarked, namely Rf, peak height, capacity factor, theoretical plates and separation number.

Table 8.2. CAAs for Bioanalytical Thin-Layer Densitometry Method of Mangiferin.

CAAs	Target
Retention/retardation factor (Rf)	Optimum (between 0.5 and 0.7)
Peak height	High
Capacity factor	High
Theoretical plates	High
Separation number	High

DoE

Screening

D-optimal design was employed for selecting the combination of the ratios of different solvents as the mobile phase mixture and an 11-factor 12-run Plackett–Burman design was employed for screening studies for identifying the CMPs influencing the method CAAs.

Table 8.3. Screening Design Matrix as per the D-Optimal Response Surface Design.

Run	Ethyl acetate	Acetic acid	Formic acid	Water
1	6	1	1	2
2	6	1	2	1
3	6	2	1	1
4	7	1	1	1
5	8	0	1	1

Contd...

Run	Ethyl acetate	Acetic acid	Formic acid	Water
6	6.5	0.5	1	2
7	6	2	1	1
8	7	0	2	1
9	6.25	1.25	1.25	1.25
10	6	0	3	1
11	7	0	1	2
12	7	0	2	1
13	7.5	0	1	1.5
14	6.5	0	1.5	2
15	6	1	2	1
16	6	0.5	1.5	2
17	7	1	1	1
18	6	0	3	1
19	6.25	0.25	2.25	1.25
20	6	0	2	2

Table 8.4. Screening Design Matrix as per the PBD Design (11-Factor 12-Run).

Run	MP	ST	VL	DP	SS	SD	ST	MD	AP	SP	PD
1	1	1	1	-1	-1	-1	1	-1	1	1	-1
2	-1	1	1	1	-1	-1	-1	1	-1	1	1
3	-1	1	-1	1	1	-1	1	1	1	-1	-1
4	1	1	-1	1	1	1	-1	-1	-1	1	-1
5	1	1	-1	-1	-1	1	-1	1	1	-1	1
6	-1	-1	-1	-1	-1	-1	-1	-1	-1	-1	-1
7	-1	1	1	-1	1	1	1	-1	-1	-1	1
8	-1	-1	-1	1	1	-1	1	-1	1	1	1
9	1	-1	-1	-1	1	1	1	1	-1	1	1
10	1	-1	1	1	1	1	1	1	-1	-1	-1
11	1	-1	1	1	1	-1	-1	-1	1	-1	1
12	-1	-1	1	-1	1	1	-1	1	1	1	-1

MP: Mobile phase ratio; ST: Saturation time; VL: Volume loaded; DP: Developmental phase; SS: Scan speed; SD: Slit dimension; DT: Distance between tracks; MD: Migration distance; AP: Application position; SP: Stationary Phase; PD: Plate dimension

Method Variables & Process Parameters at their respective Low & High Levels		
Name of the factors	**Levels**	
	Low (-1)	**High (-1)**
Mobile phase ratio	6 : 1.5 : 1.5 : 1	8 : 0.5 : 0.5 : 1
Saturation time (min)	2	4
Volume loaded (μL)	2	6
Developmental phase (mL)	10	15
Scanning speed (mm/sec)	10	15
Slit dimension (mm)	5	6
Distance between tracks (mm)	5	10
Migration distance (mm)	70	80
Application position (mm)	5	10
Stationary phase	Si-coated Al-based 60	Si-coated Al-based 60 F_{254}
Plate dimension (cm)	10 × 10	20 × 10

Selection of primary parameters

Based on the observations, chromatographic solution using ethyl acetate : acetic acid : formic acid : water in the ratio of 7 : 1 : 1 : 1 was identified to meet the desired objectives for the CAAs. The 3D response surface plot for the CAAs, Rf and peak height illustrated in Fig. 8.3.

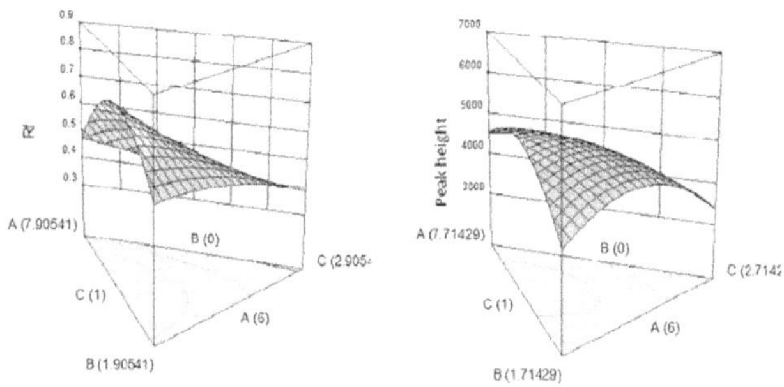

Fig. 8.3. 3D response surface plot using D-optimal design depicting the influence of the mobile phase ratio on CAAs, where (A) ethyl acetate, (B) acetic acid, (C) formic acid and (D) water.

Selection of secondary parameters

Factor screening studies were carried out for selecting secondary parameters using the Plackett–Burman design. The first-order polynomial models for estimating the main effect(s) was performed by analysis of coefficients as per the following equation, where β1 to βn represent the coefficients of the model terms, and β0 represents the intercept term.

$$Y = \beta_0 + \beta_1X_1 + \beta_2X_2 + \beta_3X_3 + \beta_4X_4 + \beta_5X_5 + \beta_6X_6 + \beta_7X_7$$

The evaluation of polynomial equations generated for each CAA selected during screening studies indicated the absence of any significant interaction effect(s) among the factors. Based on the critical observations on the highly influential factors obtained from the Pareto charts, the volume loaded and plate dimension were finally selected as the CMPs for optimizing the method performance.

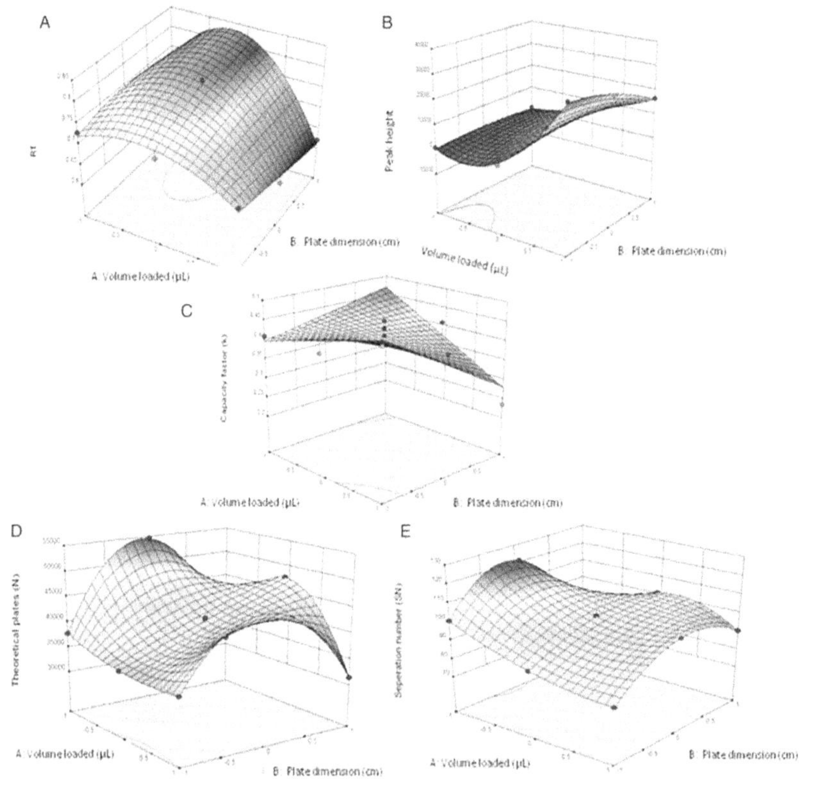

Fig. 8.4. 3D response surface plot depicting the interactions among chosen CMPs on CAAs, i.e., (A) Rf, (B) peak height, (C) capacity factor, (D) theoretical plates and (E) separation number.

Optimization:

Face-centered cubic design was selected for optimization of method parameters. The table 8.5. is the design matrix as per the FCCD employed for method optimization.

Table 8.5. Design Matrix as per the Face-Centered Cubic Design for Method Optimization.

Run	Coded factor levels	
	Factor 1	Factor 2
1	1	-1
2	1	1
3	0	0
4	0	0
5	0	0
6	-1	1
7	0	-1
8	-1	-1
9	1	0
10	0	0
11	0	1
12	-1	0
13	0	0

Translation of coded levels in actual units			
Coded level	**-1**	**0**	**1**
Volume loaded (µl)	**2**	**4**	**6**
Plate dimension (cm)	10 × 10	15 × 10	20 × 10

The coefficient analysis was performed by analyzing the quadratic polynomial model equations generated as per the following equation for each CAA. Table 8.6. illustrates the coefficients of the polynomial model equations.

$$Y = \beta_0 + \beta_1 X_1 + \beta_2 X_2 + \beta_3 X_1^2 + \beta_4 X_2^2 + \beta_5 X_1 X_2 + \beta_6 X_1^2 X_2 + \beta_7 X_1 X_2^2$$

Table 8.6. Values of the Coefficients of the Polynomial Equations and R^2 for CAAs.

Coefficient code	Polynomial coefficient values for response variables				
	Rf	Peak height	Capacity factor	Theoretical plates	Separation number
β_0	+0.80	+5732.17	+0.41	+43677.94	+103.02
β_1	−0.045	+11693.45	−0.025	−1882.10	−3.52
β_2	+3.333E−003	−1678.52	−0.033	+539.50	−0.95
β_3	−0.015	−3656.53	−0.069	+812.70	+9.88
β_4	−0.11	+8150.01	-	+1159.59	+1.42
β_5	−0.013	−1930.49	-	−8235.63	−15.78
R^2	0.8960	0.9571	0.9777	0.9422	0.9747

Response surface analysis was carried out employing 3D response surface plots and 2D contour plots for each of the CAAs (Fig. 8.4).

MODR

The numerical optimization suggested CMPs with volume loaded (i.e., 5.9 μL) and plate dimension (i.e., 10 × 13.503 cm) as the optimized solution, exhibiting a desirability value of 1 and values of the CAAs, i.e., Rf of 0.65, peak height of 26876.2, capacity factor of 0.4127, theoretical plates of 41811.3 and separation number of 96.9. The obtained optimal solution was demarcated in the analytical design space employing the graphical optimization method.

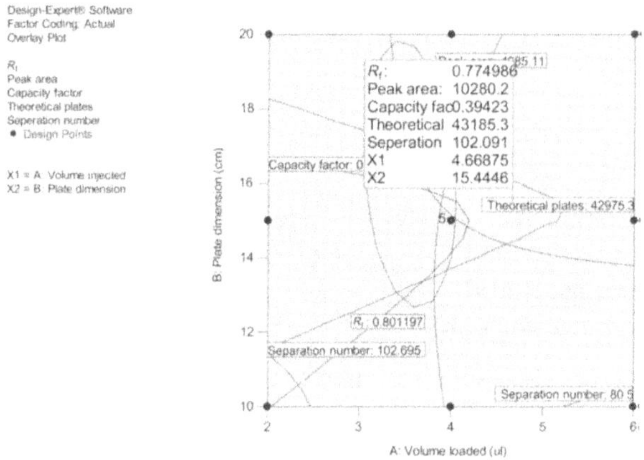

Fig. 8.5. Overlay contour plot depicting the optimal analytical design space region.

Optimized Chromatographic conditions:

Stationary Phase : Precoated silica gel aluminum TLC plate 60 (10x10 cm, 100 μm thickness)

Chamber : Flat bottom and twin-trough TLC developing chamber

Applicator : Hamilton syringe (100 mL) with slit dimensions of 6 mm× 0.30 mm, Scanning speed of 20 mm/s & Data resolution of 100 μm/step

Sample application : Position - 10 mm from the bottom and 10mm from the side edges 10mm as the distance between tracks, with each band of length 6mm.

Mobile Phase : Ethyl acetate: Acetic acid: Formic acid: Water (7:1:1:1)

Detection : UV detection at 262 nm

Mangiferin Rf : 0.68 ± 0.02.

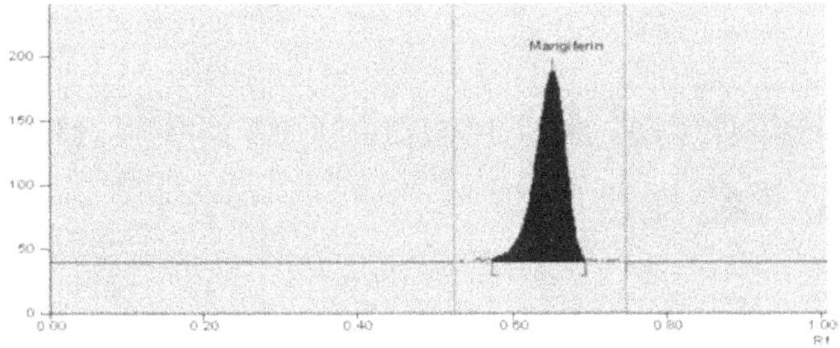

Fig. 8.6. Representative densitogram of Mangiferin obtained employing chromatographic conditions from design space.

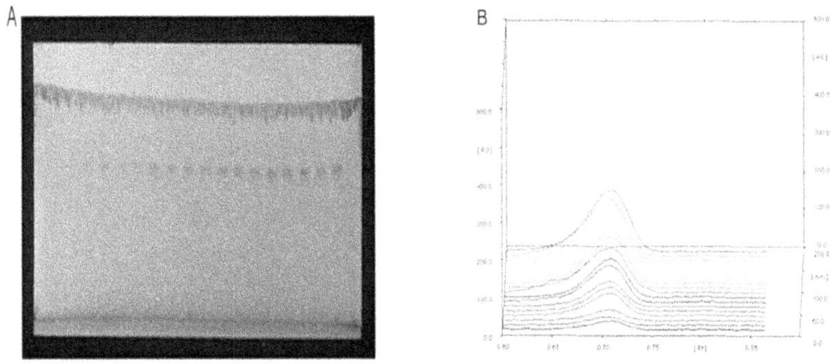

Fig. 8.7. HPTLC densitometry chromatogram profiles (A) calibration bands on aluminum-based silica plate and (B) corresponding 3D densitogram tracks.

Table 8.7. Summary of Validation parameters.

Parameter		Value
Linearity range (ng/band)		50–800
Regressed equation		y = 3.046x + 1,066
Correlation coefficient		0.996 ± 0.0012
Slope ± SD		3.046 ± 0.557
Accuracy (% recovery)	50%	96.75
	100%	97.34
	150%	99.47
Precision (% RSD)		< 2 %
Robustness (% RSD)		< 2 %
Ruggedness (% RSD)		< 2 %
LOD		12.06 ng/mL
LOQ		36.55 ng/mL

***

Practical Examples of AQbD Applied to HPTLC Method Development

Estimation of Anagliptin in Bulk and In-house Tablets

Drug Profile

Anagliptin, N - [2 - [[2 - [(2S) - 2-Cyano pyrrolidin-1-yl]-2-oxo ethyl] amino]-2 methyl propyl]-2-methyl pyrazolo [1,5-a] pyrimidine-6-carboxamide, is an orally available, potent, selective dipeptidyl peptidase 4 inhibitor, with hypoglycemic activity, under investigation for the treatment of LDL Cholesterol, Coronary Disease, Diabetes Mellitus. Compared to vildagliptin, it has longer lasting inhibition of DPP-4 activity.

Its physico-chemical properties are:

Water Solubility : 0.179 mg/mL

pKa *(Strongest Acidic)* : 13.3

pKa *(Strongest Basic)* : 8.29

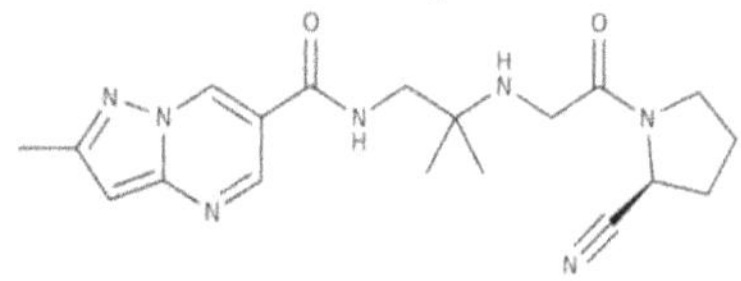

Fig. 8.8. Anagliptin Structure.

Literature

Literature revealed that UV-spectrophotometry method was reported and no HPTLC method has been reported for the estimation of AGP in tablets.

ATP

The ATP of this method is systematic QbD based development of Normal phase-HPTLC method for qualitative and quantitative estimation (Assay) of anagliptin in bulk and in-house tablets and it must have the application in routine analysis of drug in tablets. ATP for HPTLC method of AGP is illustrated in Table. 8.8.

Table 8.8. ATP for HPTLC Method of anagliptin.

ATP Element	Target
Target Sample	Bulk drug and drug product
Type of stationary phase	Normal phase

Contd...

ATP Element	Target
Stock standard preparation	Stock solution prepared using bulk drug in methanol
Sample preparation	Sample solutions were also prepared in methanol
Purpose of method	For assay of AGP

CAAs

In order to meet the desired ATP, Peak-area, Peak-height and retention factor were identified as CAAs.

Risk Assessment

Risk assessment studies were performed to identify the CMPs, which possess high risk based on their criticality and influence to affect the CAAs. All the possible factors that could influence method were organized hierarchically using an Ishikawa diagram (Fig. 8.9.).

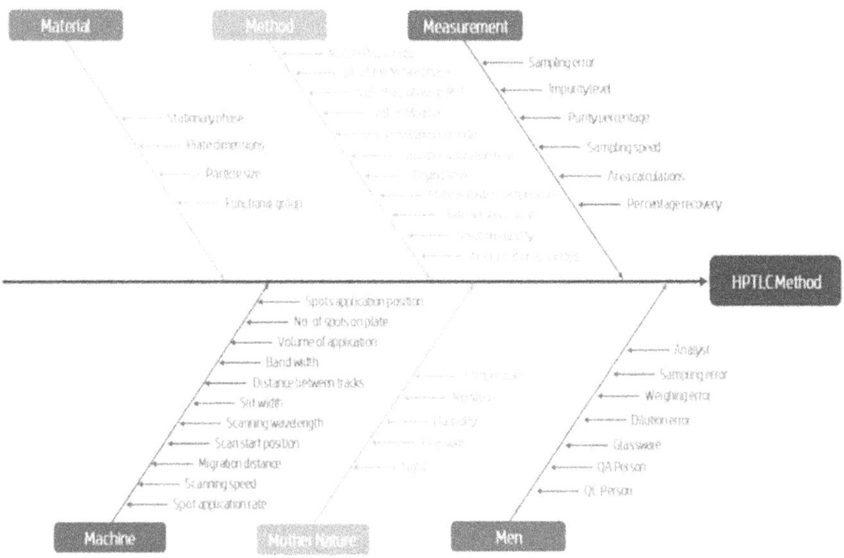

Fig. 8.9. Ishikawa fish-bone diagram showing the CAAs of HPTLC method.

DoE

Factor screening was done by using Taguchi design. For this, seven factors were considered and eight plates were developed and scanned. Factor screening helps to identify CMPs which critically affecting CAAs. Table 8.10. shows the design matrix enlisting the studied factors and the decrypted translation of their respective low and high levels.

Table 8.9. Taguchi design matrix for screening of factors.

Run	MPR	DD	RH	ST	AT	T.Sp	T.Sc
1	+	+	+	-	-	+	+
2	-	-	+	+	-	+	-
3	-	+	-	-	+	+	-
4	+	-	-	+	+	+	+
5	-	-	+	-	+	-	+
6	+	-	-	-	-	-	-
7	-	+	-	+	-	-	+
8	+	+	+	+	+	-	-

MPR: MP ratio (v/v); DD: Development distance; RH: Relative humidity; ST: Saturation time, AT: Activation time; T.Sp: Time from spotting to chromatography; T.Sc: Time from chromatography to scanning

Method Variables & Process Parameters at their respective Low & High Levels

Factors	Levels	
	Low (-)	High (+)
MP ratio DCM: MeOH(v/v)	9.1: 0.9	9.3: 0.7
Development distance	7.5	8.5
Relative humidity	55	65
Saturation time	15	25
Activation time	8	12
Time from spotting to chromatography	10	30
Time from chromatography to scanning	10	30

Further, prioritization studies were carried out for selecting the CMPs/CPPs with high risk by FMEA risk assessment technique (Table 8.9.).

Table 8.10. FMEA risk assessment technique.

Factors	S	O	D	RPN
Mobile phase ratio	5	5	5	125
Mobile phase volume	2	2	1	4
Development distance	3	2	2	12
Relative humidity	2	3	3	18
Saturation time	4	3	5	60
Activation time	4	2	3	30
Time from spotting to chromatography	3	3	4	36
Time from chromatography to scanning	3	3	4	36
Plate size	2	1	1	2

S: Severity; O: Occurrence probability; D: Detectability;
RPN: risk priority numbers = S x O x D

From FMEA study, five factors identified such as mobile phase ratio, development distance, and relative humidity, duration of saturation and activation time of prewashed plates which were associated with high risk.

Screening studies were pushed forward for method optimization by Central composite design with $\alpha = 1$ for selection of CMPs affecting method performance based on preliminary risk assessment and factor. Here, mobile phase ratio and saturation time were taken as CMPs for evaluating CAAs, namely retention factor (Rf), Peak-area and Peak-height. CMPs are studied at five levels, that is, low, intermediate, high, extremely high and extremely low. Table 8.10. summarizes a design matrix consisting of 13 experimental runs as per CCD including a total of nine experimental runs together with five runs of centre point (0, 0).

Table 8.11. CCD matrix for optimisation of method parameters.

Run	MP ratio	Saturation time
1	0	0
2	+α	0
3	-α	0
4	+1	+1
5	+1	-1
6	-1	-1
7	0	-α
8	0	+α
9	-1	+1
10	0	0
11	0	0
12	0	0
13	0	0

Method Variables & Process Parameters at their respective Low & High Levels

Factors	Levels				
	-α	**-1**	**0**	**+1**	**+ α**
MP ratio DCM : MeOH (v/v)	9.06:0.94	9.1: 0.9	9.2: 0.8	9.3: 0.7	9.34: 0.66
Saturation time	12.93	15	20	25	27.07

The experimental data underwent validation through ANOVA, in conjunction with the F-test. Only the coefficients that demonstrated significance (with P-values less than 0.05) in the ANOVA analysis were taken into account when formulating the polynomial equation. Additionally, various parameters such as lack of fit, coefficient of correlation (r2), and the predicted error sum of squares (PRESS) were assessed to ensure the suitability of the model fitting.

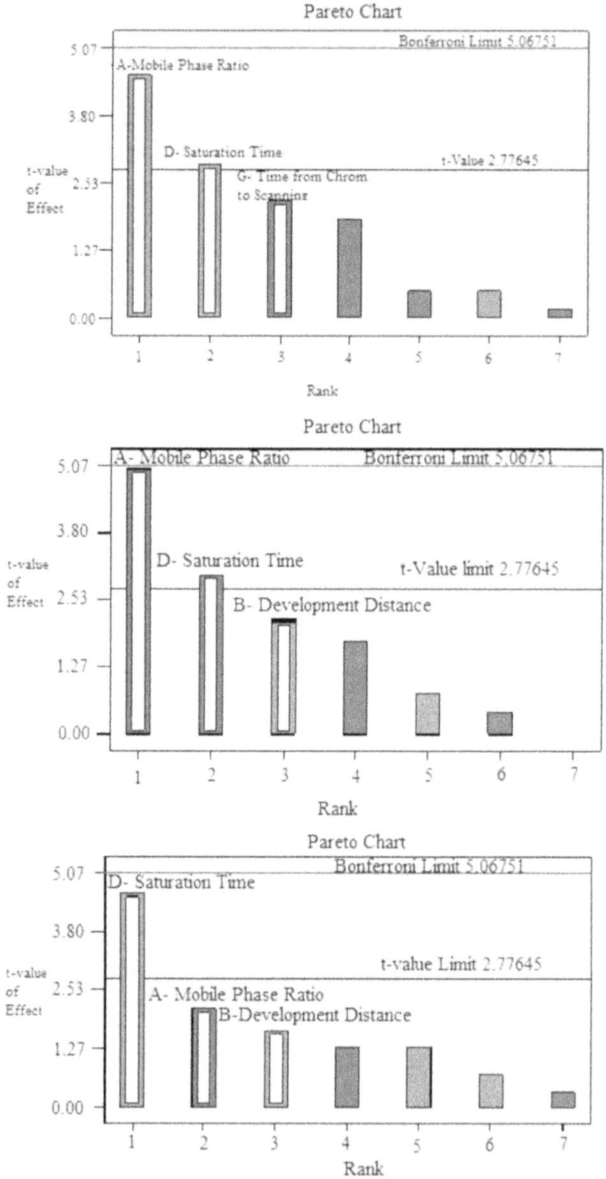

Fig. 8.10. Pareto charts depicting the influence of CMPs on method CAAs for HPTLC method of Anagliptin during screening.

Table 8.12. Results of ANOVA for measured responses.

Source	Sum Sq	Df	MS	F-value	P-Value	Model Significance
Rf						
Model	0.010	2	0.005231	170.19	<0.0001	Significant
Residual	0.000307	10	0.0000307	-	-	-
Total	0.011	12	-	-	-	-
Area						
Model	2225.91	2	1112.95	4.48	0.0409	Significant
Residual	2487.02	10	248.70	-	-	-
Total	4712.92	12	-	-	-	-
Height						
Model	200.88	2	100.44	17.30	0.0006	Significant
Residual	58.05	10	5.80	-	-	-
Total	258.92	12	-	-	-	-

Response surface analysis involved the utilization of 2D-contour plots and 3D-response surfaces. Additionally, model diagnostic plots, including the normal probability plot, run plot, residual plot, and histogram plot, were employed to assess the extent to which the collected data fit the model.

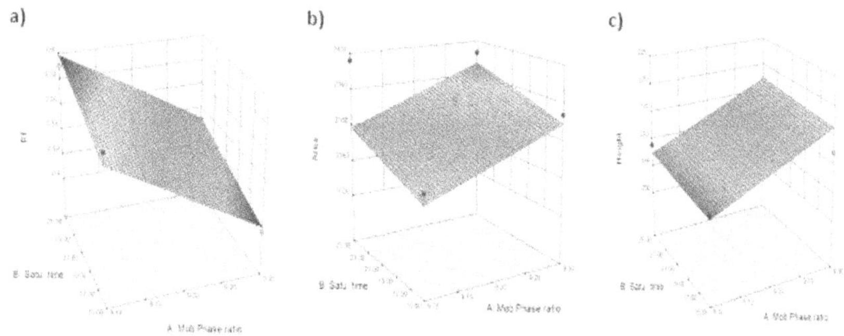

Fig. 8.11. 3D surface plots showing (a) influence of mobile phase ratio (X_1) and chamber saturation time (X_2) on Rf value (Y_1) of AGP, (b) influence of mobile phase ratio (X_1) and chamber saturation time (X_2) on Peak-area (Y_2) of AGP and (c) influence of mobile phase ratio (X_1) and chamber saturation time (X_2) on Peak-height (Y_3) of AGP.

The examination of response surface plots provided insights into the impact of parameters on the response. These plots revealed that saturation time had a lesser effect on Rf value and peak area compared to the mobile phase ratio. On the other hand, both the mobile phase ratio and saturation time had a similar influence on peak height. Specifically, as the dichloromethane content in the mobile phase increased, the Rf value of AGP decreased, whereas an increase in saturation time led to an increase in the Rf value, as depicted in Fig. 8.11 (a). Furthermore, Fig. 8.11 (b) and 8.11 (c) demonstrated that both peak area and peak height increased with higher saturation time and a greater dichloromethane content in the mobile phase.

Taguchi design was employed for screening of CMPs. The first-order polynomial equation for response variables was generated and analyzed. The below equation shows the coefficients β_1 to β_7 represent the model terms, and the coefficient β_0 representing the intercept term, Y represents response while X_1–X_7 are factors.

$$\mathbf{Y = \beta_0 + \beta_1 X_1 + \beta_2 X_2 + \beta_3 X_3 + \beta_4 X_4 + \beta_5 X_5 + \beta_6 X_6 + \beta_7 X_7}$$

The polynomial equation obtained in the initial screening phase indicates the absence of any notable interaction effects among the factors. Figure 3 illustrates Pareto charts that depict the impact of Critical Method Parameters (CMPs) on Critical Analytical Attributes (CAAs). In the screening process, it was determined that the factors, namely, mobile phase ratio and saturation time, had statistically significant influences on CAAs (with a significance level of $p < 0.05$). Consequently, only these factors were taken into account during the optimization phase.

Method development as per the experimental design and statistical analysis

Experimental runs of design were executed in random order to minimize bias. Polynomial equations were obtained for Rf, Peak-area and Peak - height using Design Expert software:

$$\mathbf{Y_1 = +\,0.55 - 0.033\ X_1 + 0.014\ X_2}$$

$$\mathbf{Y_2 = +\,2364.08 + 14.14\ X_1 + 8.85\ X_2}$$

$$\mathbf{Y_3 = +\,211.92 + 4.98\ X_1 + 0.52\ X_2}$$

where Y1 (Rf value), Y2 (Area) and Y3 (Height) are responses, X1 (Mobile phase ratio), and X2 (Chamber saturation time) are the factors.

A numerical optimization technique by desirability approach was used to obtain optimum conditions for the HPTLC method of AGP. It suggested the optimized conditions having mobile phase composition with dichloromethane: methanol (8.2: 0.8 v/v) and chamber saturation time of 20 minutes with desirability of 0.990. The typical chromatogram of AGP is shown in Fig. 8.12.

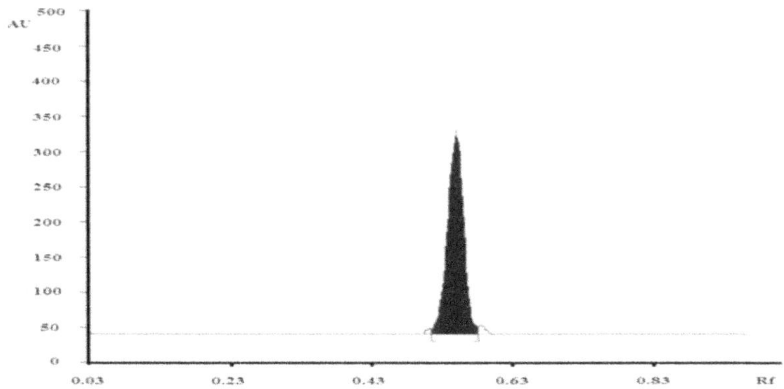

Fig. 8.12. Typical densitogram of AGP (Rf 0.55 ± 0.03) in DCM: MeOH (8.2 :0.8 v/v).

Optimised conditions

A Camag HPTLC system containing Camag Linomat 5 sample applicator, Hamilton syringe (100μL), Camag TLC Scanner-3 with winCATS software version 1.3.0

Stationary phase	: Aluminium backed Silica gel F254 plates
Prewashing of plates	: methanol
Activation of plates	: 110°C for 5 min
Mobile phase	: Dichloromethane: methanol (9.2: 0.8 v/v)
Development technique	: Linear Ascending development (20x10 cm twin trough glass chamber)
Chamber saturation	: 20 min
Development distance	: 8 cm
Densitometry scanning	: 248 nm

The method was validated by establishing linearity, accuracy, inter-day and intra-day precision, LOD & LOQ of measurement with sample application. Proposed method was used for the assay of AGP in in-house tablets. The peak at Rf for AGP was observed in the densitogram of the drug samples extracted from Tablets. There was no interference observed from the excipients used in the formulation of in-house Anagliptin tablets. The drug content ± SD was found to be 99.41 ± 1.24 for Anagliptin.

Table 8.13. Summary of Validation parameters.

Parameter		Value
Specificity		No interference
Linearity range (ng/band)		100–600
Regressed equation		Y = 5.252 X + 767.9
Correlation coefficient		0.999
Accuracy (% recovery)	80%	98.61
	100%	98.823
	120%	99.462
Precision- repeatability (% RSD)		1.02
Intermediate precision (% RSD)		1.34
Robustness (% RSD)		< 2
LOD (ng/mL)		8.74
LOQ (ng/mL)		26.51

***

Practical Examples of AQbD Applied to HPTLC Method Development

Determination of Apremilast based on Failure Mode Effect Analysis (FMEA)

Drug Profile

Apremilast, N-{2-[(1S)-1-(3-ethoxy-4-methoxy phenyl) - 2 - methane sulfonyl ethyl] - 1,3 - dioxo-2,3-dihydro - 1H - iso indol - 4-yl} acetamide, is a phosphor-diesterase 4 (PDE4) inhibitor used to treat various types of symptoms resulting from certain inflammatory autoimmune diseases. Apremilast is a non-steroidal medication used for the treatment of inflammatory conditions such as psoriasis and psoriatic arthritis.

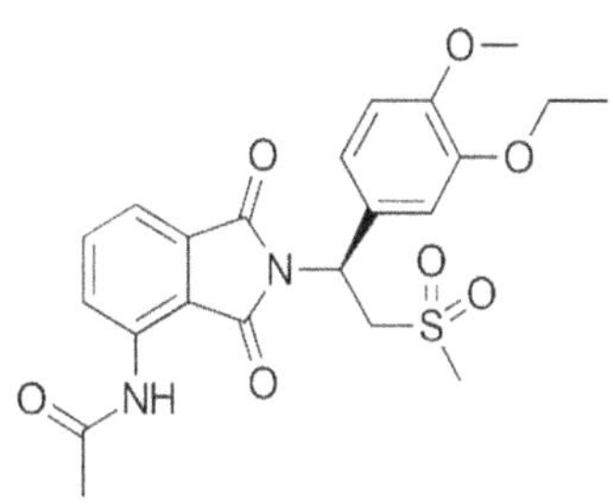

Fig. 8.13. Apremilast Structure.

Its physico-chemical properties are water solubility 0.034 mg/mL; pKa 12.58.

Literature

Literature survey reveals that 5 stability indicating HPLC and 4 UV-Visible spectrophotometry methods, 1 stability indicating HPTLC Method by conventional approach, and 1 HPTLC by application of box-behnken design (without stability study) for estimation of Apremilast are available.

No stability indicating HPTLC method was found using quality by design approach for estimation of Apremilast.

ATP

The ATP is to develop a stability-indicating HPTLC method. This method should effectively separate all degradation product spots observed under various stress conditions with a resolution greater than 1.5 between the peaks, along with a tailing factor ranging from 0.9 to 1.2.

CAAs & CMPs

Various failure modes were studied for their effect on results, such as separation of degradants spots (resolution). Methanol, ethyl acetate and toluene combination was selected as effective solvent system to separate the degradants spots. The effect of saturation time, volume of mobile phase, solvent front, slit dimension, band width, wavelength for detection on the resolution were investigated. Identified failure modes are listed in Ishikawa diagram (Fig. 8.14) for the risk assessment. Each identified failure mode was analysed for its occurrence, severity and detectability for development of stability indicating HPTLC method. RPN score verses risk factors for quality risk assessment was depicted in Fig. 8.15.

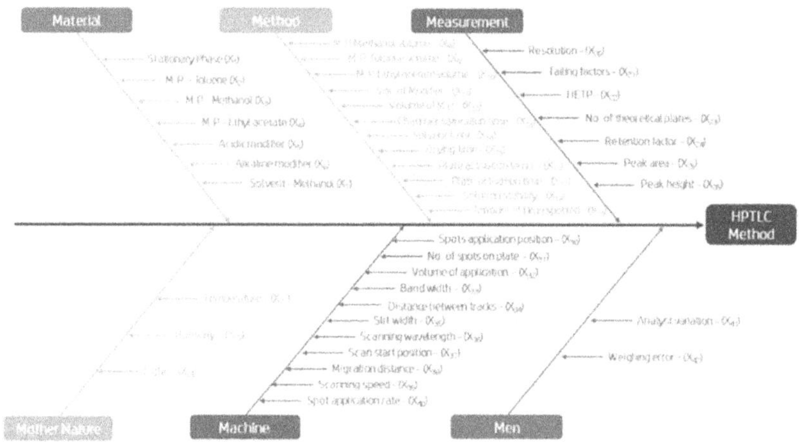

Fig. 8.14. Ishikawa diagram for identification of failure modes in method.

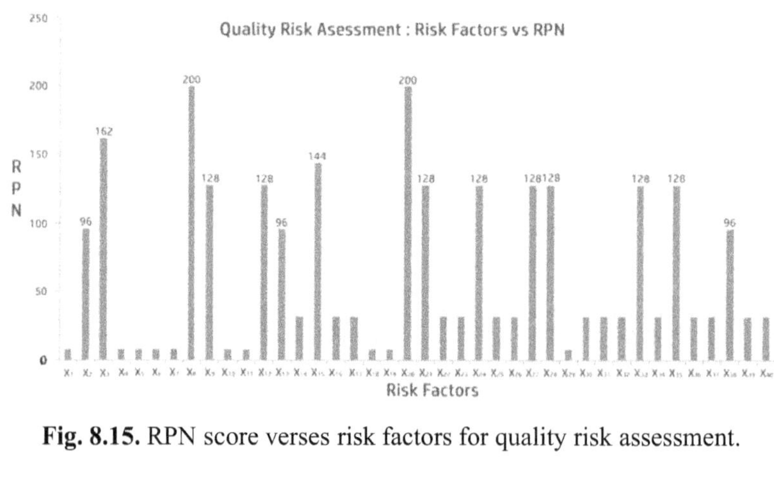

Fig. 8.15. RPN score verses risk factors for quality risk assessment.

Failure modes such as volume of methanol, volume of mobile phase, migration distance, saturation time, band width, detection wavelength and scanning speed, with a high Risk Priority Number (RPN) score were chosen for additional impact analysis as part of the process of developing a robust analytical method.

Temperature and humidity were identified as significant failure modes, yet controlling them directly was not feasible. As a solution, an air conditioning system was implemented to mitigate the impact of temperature and humidity on the outcomes of the analytical method.

Screening by Taguchi OA

A Taguchi OA design was utilized to screen seven potential method variables, each having two levels, and to screen four potential method attributes. Eight experimental runs and corresponding response of Taguchi OA were tabulated in Table 8.13.

Table. 8.14. Experimental runs and response of Taguchi OA,

Std	Factors							Response			
	1	2	3	4	5	6	7	Rs_1	Rs_2	Rs_3	Rs_4
1	1.5	8	4	15	70	240	10	1.724	9.83	10.222	10.25
2	1.5	8	4	45	80	242	20	1.966	8.76	9.642	9.438
3	1.5	10	6	15	70	242	20	1.832	10.3	10.554	10.355
4	1.5	10	6	45	80	240	10	1.911	8.852	9.652	9.127
5	2.5	8	6	15	80	240	20	1.085	10.37	10.75	10.634
6	2.5	8	6	45	70	242	10	0.713	7.35	8.225	8.106
7	2.5	10	4	15	80	242	10	1.13	7.25	8.023	7.892
8	2.5	10	4	45	70	240	20	0.682	10.025	10.503	10.382

Factor 1: Volume of methanol (mL); Factor 2: Volume of mobile phase (mL); Factor 3: Saturation time (min); Factor 4: Migration distance (mm); Factor 5: Detection wavelength (nm); Factor 6: Scanning speed (mm/s); Factor 7: Band length (mm)

The experimental data underwent validation through ANOVA (Table 8.14).

Table 8.15. Results of ANOVA for measured responses – Taguchi OA design.

Source	SS	Df	MS	F- value	P-Value	Model Significance
Resolution 1						
Model	2.02	3	0.67	304.88	<0.0001	Significant
A	1.83	1	1.83	826.89	<0.0001	
D	0.031	1	0.031	14.09	0.0199	
E	0.16	1	0.16	73.66	0.0010	
Residual	$8.837x10^{-3}$	4	$2.209 x10^{-3}$			
Total	2.03	7				

Contd...

Resolution 2						
Model	11.07	3	3.69	480.97	<0.0001	Significant
A	8.64	1	8.64	1125.71	<0.0001	
D	1.83	1	1.83	238.58	0.0001	
E	0.60	1	0.60	78.63	0.0009	
Residual	0.031	4	7.674×10^{-3}			
Total	11.10	7				
Resolution 3						
Model	7.66	3	2.55	129.11	0.0002	Significant
A	5.26	1	5.26	265.86	<0.0001	
D	1.64	1	1.64	83.02	0.0008	
E	0.76	1	0.76	38.45	0.0034	
Residual	0.079	4	0.020			
Total	7.74	7				
Resolution 4						
Model	7.91	3	2.64	88.67	0.0004	Significant
A	6.23	1	6.23	209.50	0.0001	
D	1.07	1	1.07	35.96	0.0039	
E	0.61	1	0.61	20.54	0.0106	
Residual	0.12	4	0.030			
Total	8.03	7				

A-Vol. of MeOH; D-Saturation time; E-Migration distance

Pareto chart analysis of Response 1 to 4 depicted in Fig. 8.16.

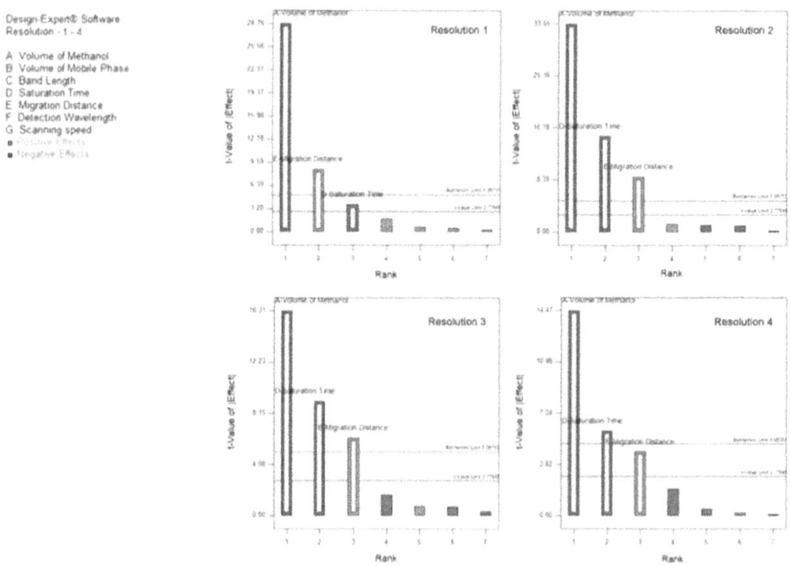

Fig. 8.16. Pareto chart for screening design of resolution 1 to 4.

Response surface modeling by BBD

Through Pareto chart analysis and ANOVA of the screening design, it was determined that the volume of methanol, saturation time, and migration distance had a significant impact on the method variables. Additionally, the resolution between the drug and acid degradation product-1 was identified as a critical method attribute. 17 experimental runs were suggested by design metrics for three levels for all the critical factors (Table 8.15).

The ANOVA table displayed a model F-value of 52.91, suggesting that the quadratic model is the most suitable fitting model (Table 8.16). Probability values below 0.05 indicate the significance of model terms. In this scenario, the volume of methanol, migration distance, and saturation time were identified as significant main effects for the response. Additionally, all quadratic terms related to the volume of methanol and saturation time were deemed significant. Utilizing the analysis of the response surface model and contour plots (Fig. 8.17), the following mathematical model was employed for the purpose of optimizing responses.

$$\mathbf{Y = -2.528 + 3.538 * X_1 + 0.018 * X_2 + 0.020 * X_3 - 1.135 * X_1^2 - 4.166 * 10^{-4} * X_3^2}$$

Table 8.16. Design metrics for Box–Behnken design.

Std	Factor 1	Factor 2	Factor 3	Response Resolution-1
1	1.5	70	30	1.806
2	2.5	70	30	0.715
3	1.5	80	30	1.961
4	2.5	80	30	0.836
5	1.5	75	15	1.728
6	2.5	75	15	0.815
7	1.5	75	45	1.624
8	2.5	75	45	0.733
9	2	70	15	1.498
10	2	80	15	1.705
11	2	70	45	1.318
12	2	80	45	1.558
13	2	75	30	1.636
14	2	75	30	1.593
15	2	75	30	1.568
16	2	75	30	1.653
17	2	75	30	1.549

Factor 1: Volume of methanol, mL; Factor 2: Migration distance, Mm; Factor 3: Saturation time, min

Table 8.17. ANOVA table for BBD.

Source	SS	Df	MS	F-value	P-Value	
Resolution 1						
Model	2.51	5	0.50	145.19	<0.0001	Significant
A	2.02	1	2.02	584.33	<0.0001	
B	0.065	1	0.065	18.90	0.0012	
C	0.033	1	0.033	9.52	0.0104	
A^2	0.34	1	0.34	98.50	<0.0001	
C^2	0.037	1	0.037	10.733	0.0074	
Residual	0.038	11	0.003457			
Lack of Fit	0.028	7	0.004069	1.70	0.3170	Not significant
Pure error	0.009547	4	0.002387			
Cor Total	2.55	16				

A-Vol. of MeOH; B-Migration distance; C-Saturation time

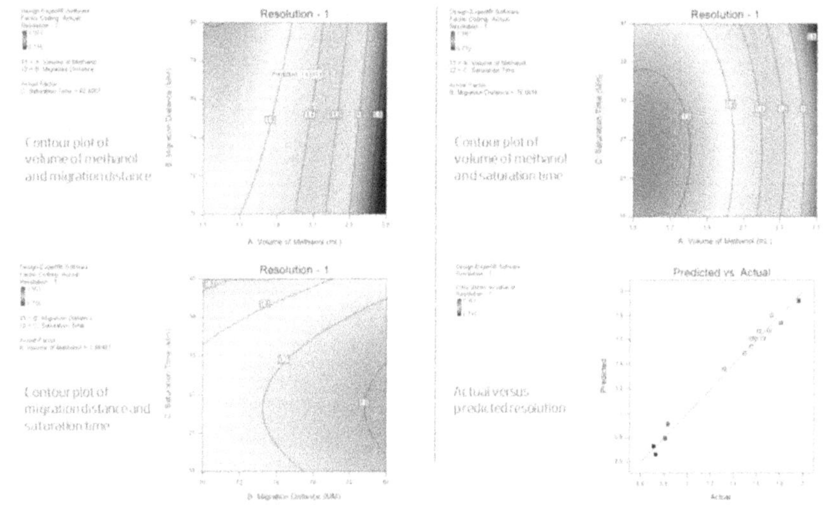

Fig. 8.17. Contour plots and Predicted vs Actual plot.

Validation of the response surface model: Minor fluctuations in the factors within the designated parameter range indicate that the resolution closely aligns with the predicted values. This observation signifies a strong correlation between the predicted and actual results. Consequently, it is reasonable to conclude that the proposed model is robust.

MODR & Control Strategy

The optimal solution that was acquired was marked within the analytical design space using the graphical optimization approach (Fig. 8.18). Based on the design space, the following control strategy (Table 8.18) was put into action to facilitate the development of an analytical method, aiming to achieve a resolution exceeding 1.5.

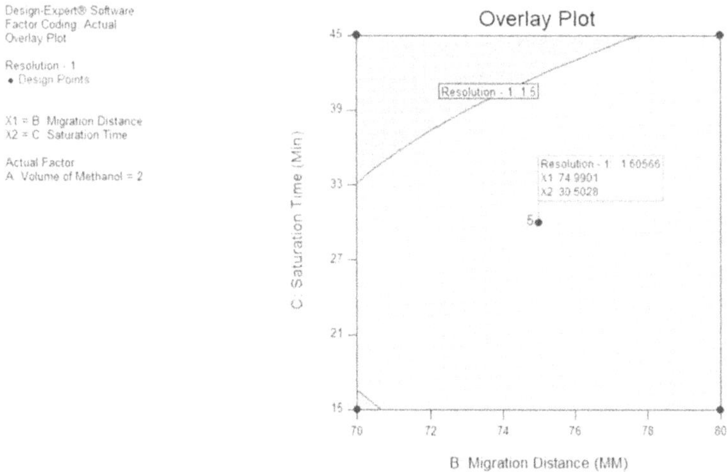

Fig. 8.18. Design space for resolution as per ATP.

Table 8.18. Control strategy.

Method variables	Operating range	Selected condition
Volume of methanol	1.5–2.5 mL	2 mL
Migration distance	70–80 mm	80 mm
Saturation time	15–45 min	30 min
Band length	4–6 mm	6 mm
Detection wavelength	240–242 nm	241 nm
Scanning speed	10–20 mm/s	20 mm/s
Volume of mobile phase	8–10 mL	10 mL

Analysis of force degraded sample: The degradation study data indicates that Apremilast is susceptible to alkaline hydrolysis, while being relatively less susceptible to acid and neutral hydrolysis. Furthermore, it demonstrated stability under oxidative, dry heat, and photolytic stress conditions.

Optimized chromatographic conditions

Stationary phase : Precoated Aluminum TLC plate Silica gel 60 F254 (10x10 cm, 250μm thickness)

Prewashing of plates : methanol

Activation of plates : 50°C for 15 min

Mobile phase : Toluene : Methanol : Ethyl acetate (7:2:1 v/v/v)

Temperature & RH : 25±2°C & 35±5%

Development technique : Linear Ascending development (20x10 cm twin trough glass chamber)

Chamber saturation : 30 min

Development distance : 80 mm

Densitometry scanning : 248 nm

Sample application : Position - 15 mm from the bottom and 10mm from the side edges 11.6mm as the distance between tracks, with each band of length 8mm.

Application rate : 0.1 µl/s.

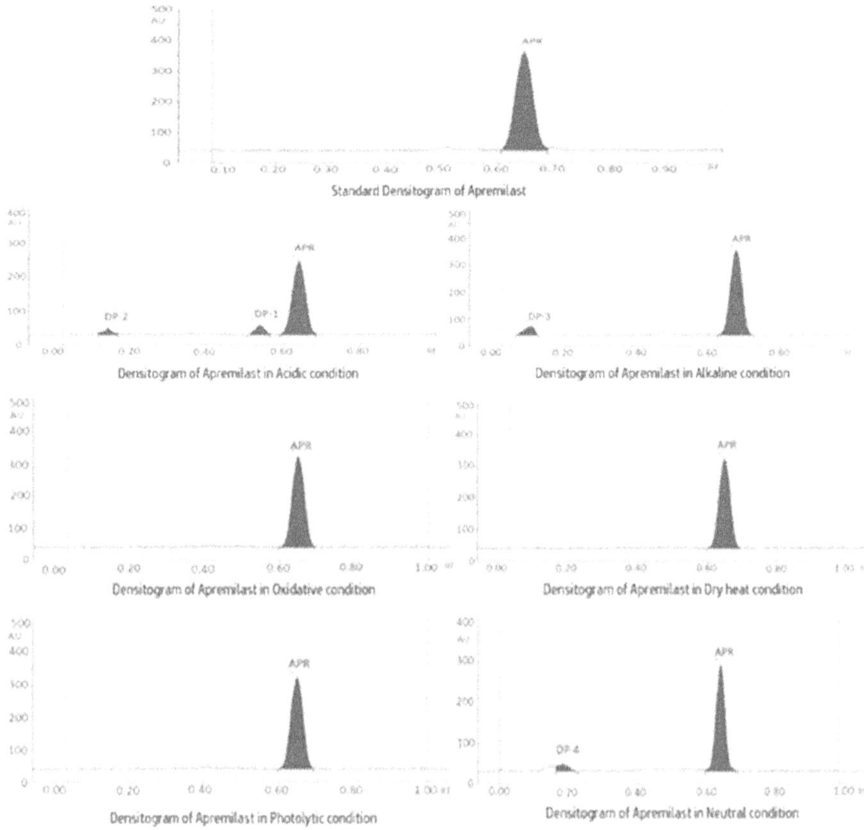

Fig. 8.19. Densitometric chromatograms.

Method validation

The method underwent validation for several parameters, including specificity, linearity, accuracy, inter-day and intra-day precision, repeatability of sample application, and repeatability of sample measurement. Additionally, the detection limit (DL) and quantification limit (QL) were determined.

Table 8.19. Summary of Validation parameters.

Parameter	Value
Linearity range	200–1000 ng/band
Regression equation	y = 6.8696x − 933.66
Regression coefficient (R^2)	0.996
Precision (RSD)	
Repeatability of sample application (n = 7)	0.90%
Repeatability of sample measurement (n = 7)	0.11%
Intermediate precision	
Inter-day precision (n = 3)	0.43–0.74%
Intra-day precision (n = 3)	0.11–0.42%
LOD	4.42 ng
LOQ	13.40 ng
Accuracy (n = 3)	99.71–100.02%

***

Practical Examples of AQbD Applied to HPTLC Method Development

Simultaneous Estimation of Lornoxicam & Eperisone HCl

Drug Profile

Lornoxicam is a commonly prescribed anti-inflammatory medication with the chemical structure of (3E)-6-chloro-3-[hydroxyl (pyridin-2-ylamino) methylene]-2-methyl-2,3-dihydro-4H-thieno-[2,3-e][1,2]- thiazin-4-one 1, 1- dioxide.

Eperisone hydrochloride, on the other hand, is a centrally acting muscle relaxant. Its chemical structure is (2RS)-1-(4-ethylphenyl)-2-methyl-3-piperidin-1-ylpropan-1-one monohydrochloride.

Physico-chemical properties of Lornoxicam and Eperisone

Property	Lornoxicam	Eperisone
Water Solubility, mg/mL	0.0437	0.0437
pKa (Strongest Acidic)	1.82	16.5
pKa (Strongest Basic)	4.22	8.77

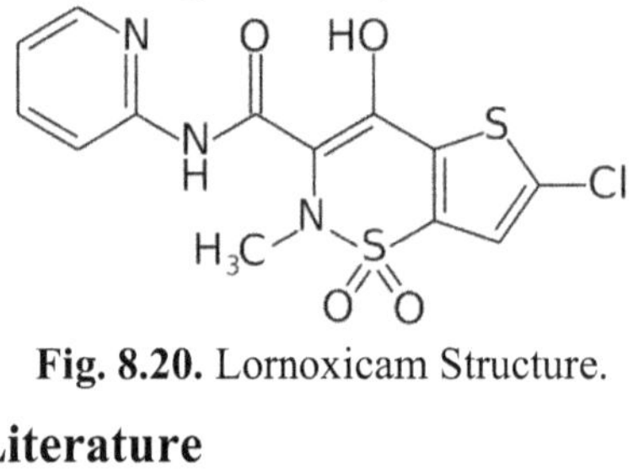

Fig. 8.20. Lornoxicam Structure.

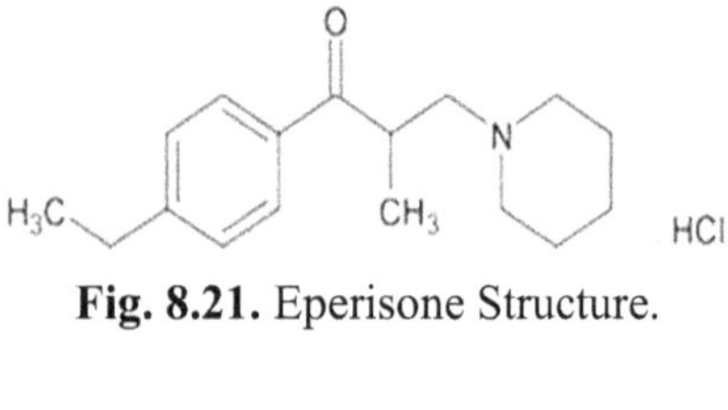

Fig. 8.21. Eperisone Structure.

Literature

Based on the literature review, various analytical methods such as UV-Visible spectroscopy, derivative spectroscopy, and RPHPLC have been documented for the individual quantification of Eperisone and Lornoxicam, both as standalone compounds and in their combinations available in the market. It's noteworthy that, despite these existing methods, no analytical approach has been reported in the literature for the simultaneous estimation of both drugs, utilizing the Quality by Design (QbD) approach. Additionally, there is no documentation of an HPTLC method for the simultaneous estimation of Eperisone and Lornoxicam.

ATP

The desired Analytical Target Profile (ATP) involves the development of an HPTLC method for the simultaneous quantification of Lornoxicam (LOC) and Eperisone (EPR) within a laboratory mixture. The key objectives are to achieve a resolution between the peaks greater than 1.5 and to maintain tailing factors for each peak within the range of 0.9 to 1.1.

Risk Management

In order to meet the Analytical Target Profile (ATP), a valuable tool for quality risk management is the analysis of failure effects and critical effects. This process begins with the identification of potential failure modes when developing an analytical method. Through a combination of experimental trials and existing chromatographic expertise, a range of potential failure modes were successfully identified. These identified failure modes were categorized into six distinct areas: method, machine, manpower, mother nature, material, and measurement. These categories were then structured within an Ishikawa diagram (Fig. 8.22). In order to assess risks, a systematic process was followed. Occurrence (O), severity (S), and detectability (D) scores were assigned to each failure mode. The Risk Priority Number (RPN) was derived by multiplying the scores of severity, occurrence, and detectability (Fig. 8.23).

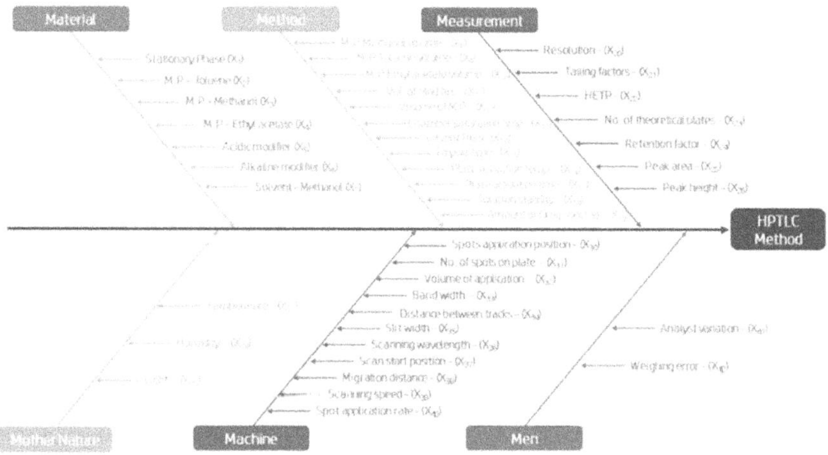

Fig. 8.22. Identified failure modes structured within an Ishikawa diagram.

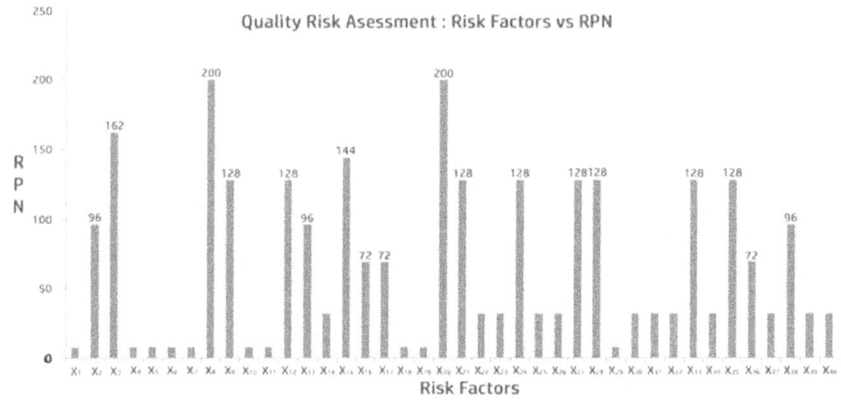

Fig. 8.23. Graph of RPN score versus failure modes.

Plackett–Burman screening design

A total of 11 failure modes were recognized as crucial in the process of developing the HPTLC method.

Table 8.20. Design Metrics for Plackett–Burman Design.

Run	X_1	X_2	X_3	X_4	X_5	X_6	X_7	X_8	X_9	X_{10}	X_{11}	Rs_1
1	3	0.5	8	15	15	8	278	80	10	60	30	3
2	1	0.5	8	45	30	6	280	80	10	60	15	0.9
3	1	0.5	10	45	15	6	278	80	8	70	30	0.7
4	3	0.5	10	15	15	6	280	70	10	70	15	2.5
5	1	0.1	8	45	15	8	280	70	10	70	30	0.5
6	3	0.1	10	45	15	8	280	80	8	60	15	4
7	1	0.5	10	15	30	8	280	70	8	60	30	0.8
8	1	0.1	10	15	30	8	278	80	10	70	15	1.2
9	1	0.1	8	15	15	6	278	70	8	60	15	1.0
10	3	0.1	8	15	30	6	280	80	8	70	30	3.5
11	3	0.1	10	45	30	6	278	70	10	60	30	4.5
12	3	0.5	8	45	30	8	278	70	8	70	15	3.0

X_1: Volume of methanol, mL; X_2: Modifier volume, mL; X_3: Volume of mobile phase, mL; X_4: Chamber Saturation time, min; X_5: Drying time, min; X_6: Band width, nm; X_7: Scanning wavelength, nm; X_8: Migration distance, mm; X_9: Distance between tracks, mm; X_{10}: Plate activation temperature, °C; X_{11}: Plate activation time, min; Rs_1: Response 1: Resolution.

To assess the criticality of these identified failure modes, a Plackett-Berman design based on DoE was chosen, using resolution as the response variable. This design involved twelve experimental runs, as suggested by the design itself. In the laboratory, these twelve experiments were conducted, and the resulting resolutions were input into design analysis software for further evaluation. This analysis employed ANOVA and a Pareto chart to study the impact of each failure mode.

Table 8.21. ANOVA Table for Plackett–Burman Screening Design.

Source	**SS**	**Df**	**MS**	**F-value**	**P-Value**	
Resolution 1						
Model	21.45	4	5.36	28.51	0.0002	Significant
A-Vol. of MeOH	19.76	1	19.76	105.307	<0.0001	
B-Modifier Volume	1.20	1	1.20	6.40	0.0393	
C-Volume of M.P.	0.27	1	0.27	1.44	0.0393	
D-Saturation time	0.21	1	0.21	1.13	0.32222	
Residual	1.32	7	0.19			
Cor Total	22.77	11				

From 11 factors, P-values of volume of mobile phase and acid in mobile phase were found less than 0.05 that indicates only these two failure modes are highly critical for development of HPTLC method and remaining failure modes are non-significant. In Pareto chart, the bar of volume of methanol and the base modifier were only crossing critical significant line and the remaining factors bar were below the significant line.

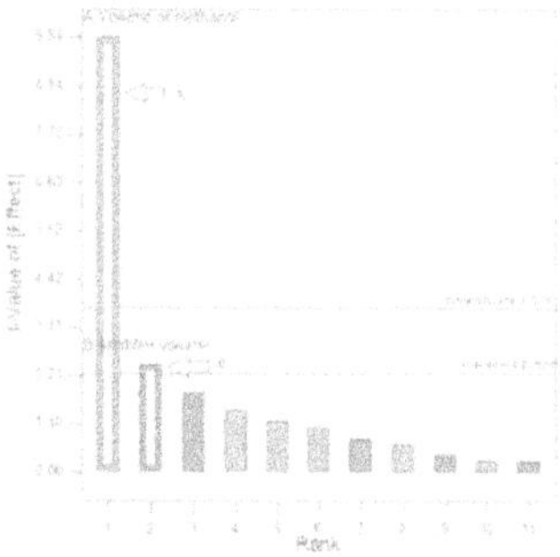

Fig. 8.24. Pareto chart.

Central composite design

A risk analysis of critical failure modes was carried out to establish a connection between critical method parameters and the Critical Quality Attribute (CQA), which in this case is resolution. This analysis was conducted using a center composite design based on the principles of DoE. Thirteen experimental runs were conducted in the laboratory according to the design specifications. The resulting data from these experiments were then input into design analysis software for performing response surface analysis.

Table 8.22. Design Metrics for Central Composite Design.

Std	Run	Space type	X_1	X_2	Resolution
2	1	Factorial	1.000	-1.000	4
12	2	Center	0.000	0.000	2.5
5	3	Axial	-1.400	0.000	0.5
3	4	Factorial	-1.000	1.000	0.5
6	5	Axial	1.500	0.000	4
11	6	Center	0.000	0.000	2.6
10	7	Center	0.000	0.000	2.8
4	8	Factorial	1.000	1.000	3.5
1	9	Factorial	-1.000	-1.000	0.5
8	10	Axial	0.000	1.500	1
13	11	Center	0.000	0.000	2.5
9	12	Center	0.000	0.000	2.9
7	13	Axial	0.000	-1.400	1.5
X_1: volume of methanol, mL; X_2: volume of modifier, mL;					

Table 8.23. ANOVA Table for Central Composite Design.

Source	SS	Df	MS	F-value	P-Value	
Resolution						
Model	19.22	5	3.84	36.47	<0.0001	Significant
A-Vol. of MeOH	16.39	1	16.39	155.54	<0.0001	
B-Modifier Volume	0.12	1	0.12	1.14	0.03203	
AB	0.063	1	0.063	0.59	0.4665	
A^2	0.19	1	0.19	1.76	0.2258	
B^2	2.58	1	2.58	24.46	0.0017	
Residual	0.74	7	0.11			
Lack of Fit	0.61	3	0.20	6.12	0.0563	Not significant
Pure error	0.13	4	0.033			
Cor Total	19.36	12				
Model R^2 Values	R^2: 0.9630			Adj. R^2: 0.9366		Pred. R^2: 0.7650
Adequate precision	18.42					

The proposed equations for full model equation and reduced model equation are:

$$Y = 2.68 + 1.42*X_1 - 0.32*X_2 - 0.013*X_1X_2 - 0.16*X_1^2 - 0.59*X_2^2$$

$$Y = 2.68 + 1.42*X_1 - 0.32*X_2 - 0.59*X_2^2$$

The interaction between the volume of base modifier and the volume of methanol, influencing the resolution of Eperisone and Lornoxicam peaks, was visualized through a 3D contour plot (Fig. 8.25).

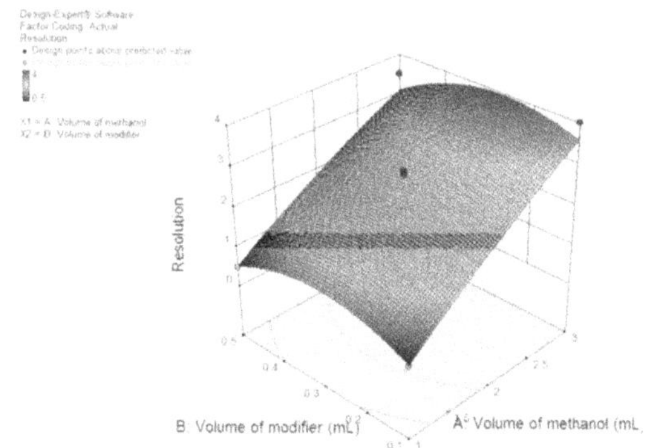

Fig. 8.25. 3D contour plot showing interaction between X_1 and X_2 on Y.

Control strategy and design space

The proposed operational range (Fig.8.26) for the volume of methanol and base modifier in the mobile phase was established as 1.5–3 mL and 0.1–0.3 mL, respectively. The risk assessment for critical failure modes demonstrated minimal impact on resolution loss. Among various control strategy options, a specific point was chosen for the separation of Lornoxicam (LOC) and Eperisone (EPR). This was achieved by employing a mobile phase composed of toluene:ethyl acetate:methanol:triethylamine (5:3.5:1.5:0.2, v/v/v/v) and utilizing a scanning wavelength of 278 nm for the development of the HPTLC method. The chromatogram depicting the standard EPR and LOC is presented in the Fig.8.27.

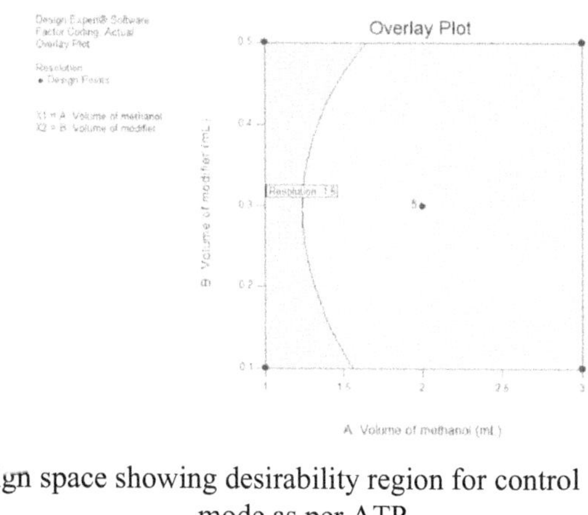

Fig. 8.26. Design space showing desirability region for control of critical failure mode as per ATP.

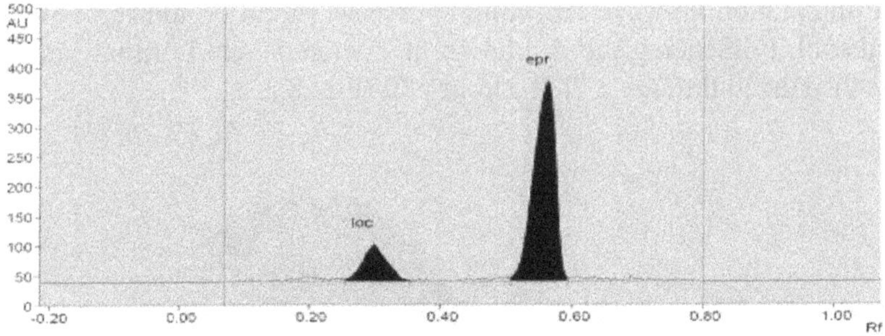

Fig. 8.27. Chromatogram depicting the standard Lornoxicam and Eperisone.

Table 8.24. Summary of Validation parameters.

Parameter	Eperisone	Lornoxicam
Linearity range (ng/band)	50–250	600–3000
Correlation coefficient (R^2)	0.9985	0.9977
Precision (% RSD)	0.93	0.97
Repeatability of sample application	0.95	0.98
Repeatability of measurement		
Intra-day precision (n = 3)	1.19–1.92	1.34–1.88
Inter-day precision (n = 3)	1.11–2.02	1.35–2.11
Accuracy (% recovery)	97.21–100.34	100.91–103.70
LOD (ng/band)	2.09	77.63
LOQ (ng/band)	6.34	235.25

***

CHAPTER 9

AQbD for Bio-Analytical Method Development

9.1 Introduction

The utilization of Quality by Design (QbD) principles in the process of developing analytical methods is centered around the notion of embedding quality within the method during its creation, as opposed to evaluating the method's quality subsequent to development. A key element of QbD involves comprehending the influence of factors and their interplay through a deliberate series of experiments. In the context of applying QbD to High-Performance Liquid Chromatography (HPLC) methods, it becomes crucial to confirm robustness and ruggedness early on in the method development phase. This step is essential to ensure that the method maintains its performance integrity throughout the product's lifecycle.

Utilizing Design of Experiments tools in the process of developing analytical methods proves beneficial for optimizing variables within the method and effectively managing sources of variability. This is achieved by conducting a minimal number of experiments to extract maximal insights, resulting in significant time, cost, and effort savings. The objective of the current chapter is to outline the essential components of DoE and to present the methodology for its application in the development of bio-analytical methods.

9.2 Bio-analytical Method

The advancement of bio-analytical techniques has introduced a dynamic field with abundant prospects for future enhancements. In the pharmaceutical sector, bioanalysis plays a pivotal role by providing quantitative assessments of drugs and their metabolites. The primary aim is to facilitate pharmacokinetics, toxico-kinetics, bioequivalence, and exposure-response studies, including pharmacokinetic/ pharmacodynamic investigations. A range of bioanalytical methods are employed in these studies, encompassing hyphenated techniques, chromatographic methods, and ligand binding assays. The ongoing evolution of this field holds considerable promise for further progress and innovation.

A bioanalytical method encompasses a series of steps encompassing the collection, processing, storage, and analysis of a biological sample in relation to a specific chemical compound. Bioanalytical Method Validation (BMV) refers to the process employed to verify the suitability of a quantitative analytical method for biochemical applications.

Bioanalysis involves the precise measurement of Xenobiotics, such as drugs and their metabolites, as well as biological molecules, under unconventional conditions or concentrations. It also encompasses Biotics, which include macromolecules, proteins, DNA, large molecule drugs, and metabolites within biological systems. Bioanalysis stands as a continually evolving field, and the future presents a wealth of captivating prospects for enhancing multiple aspects such as sensitivity, specificity, accuracy, efficiency, assay throughput, data quality, data management and processing, analysis cost, and environmental sustainability. Some of the commonly used techniques in bioanalytical studies include LC-MS (Liquid Chromatography-Mass Spectrometry), GC-MS (Gas Chromatography-Mass Spectrometry), CE-MS (Capillary Electrophoresis-Mass Spectrometry)

Bioanalysis constitutes a subset of analytical chemistry that focuses on accurately measuring the quantities of drugs and their metabolites within biological systems. In this context, Liquid Chromatography-Mass Spectrometry (LC-MS) emerges as a widely employed technique for quantifying drugs in biological fluids. It holds a prominent position in laboratories, facilitating both quantitative and qualitative analyses of drug substances, drug products, and biological samples.

9.3 LC-MS

LC-MS has significantly contributed to the assessment and interpretation of data related to bioavailability, bioequivalence, and pharmacokinetics.

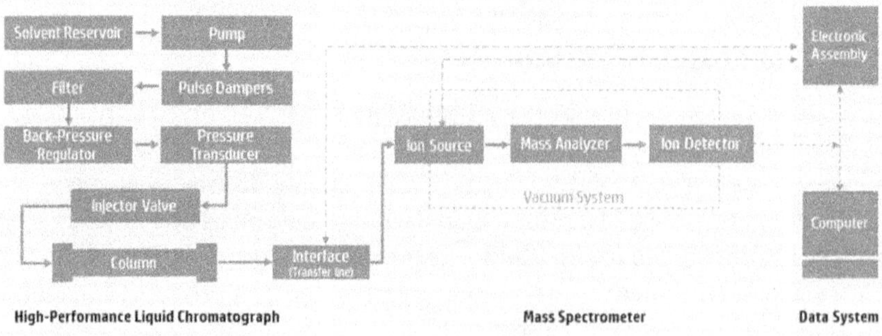

Fig. 9.1. Schematic layout of LC-MS system.

This technique plays a pivotal role across all stages of drug research and quality control, aiding in the determination of biological samples. A typical LC-MS setup comprises essential components such as a liquid chromatograph, an ion source, a mass analyzer, and a detector.

9.4 GC-MS

GC-MS is a method that combines the features of gas-liquid chromatography and mass spectrometry to identify different substances within a test sample. Applications of GC-MS include drug detection, fire investigation, environmental analysis, explosives investigation, and identification of unknown samples. GC-MS can also be used in airport security to detect substances in luggage or on human beings.

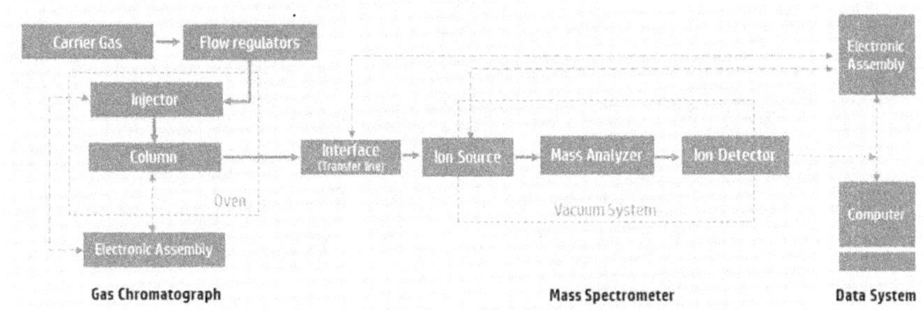

Fig. 9.2. Schematic layout of GC-MS system.

9.5 CE-MS

CE-MS, combining the high efficiency and resolution power of CE, with the high selectivity and sensitivity inherent to MS, is a very attractive analytical technique. However, CE-MS coupling, mostly by means of ESI, was not easy to implement since a closed electrical circuit is necessary not only for the electrophoretic separation but also for an efficient ionization in the source.

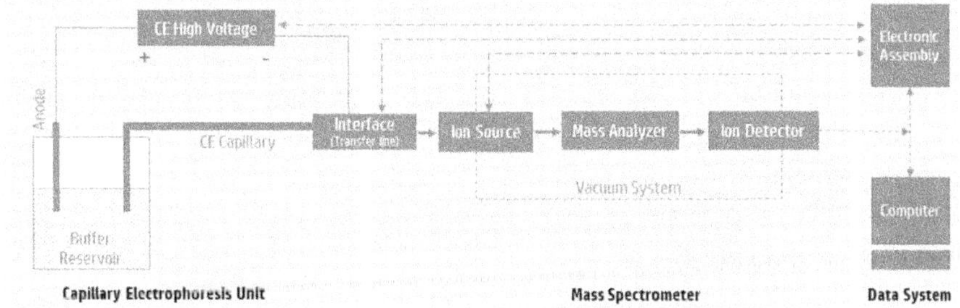

Fig. 9.3. Schematic layout of CE-MS system.

9.6 Preparation and Extraction of Sample

- **Liquid-Liquid Extraction (LLE):**
  This technique proves valuable in segregating analytes from interfering substances through a process that involves distributing the sample between two non-mixing liquids or phases. This is achieved through a partitioning mechanism: one phase is aqueous (hydrophilic), while the other is organic (hydrophobic).
  When an analyte is extracted into the organic phase, it can be effortlessly recovered by evaporating the solvent. Conversely, analytes extracted into the aqueous phase can often be directly injected onto a reversed-phase column. The extracted solution containing the drug can be subjected to evaporation, resulting in the residue being transformed into a dry state. This residue can then be dissolved again in a smaller volume of a suitable solvent, preferably the mobile phase used in chromatography.

  Advantages: This technique is very rapid and efficient as well as less cost required when compared to the other methods Near quantitative recoveries (90%) of most drugs can be obtained through multiple continuous extractions.
- **Solid Phase Extraction (SPE):**
  This partitioning process takes place between a liquid and a solid phase, offering the advantage of achieving higher analyte recoveries. Solid-Phase Extraction (SPE) presents several advantages, including the capacity for multiple samplings, the use of minute solvent quantities, and the incorporation of automation for efficiency.
  SPE involves employing a medical syringe loaded with 0.1 to 0.5 grams of sorbent, often C18 silica. The process includes introducing liquid samples into the cartridge and employing a wash solvent to either strongly retain or not retain the analyte. To mitigate interference presence, the analyte is subsequently eluted using an elution solvent. This eluate can be directly injected into analysis or subjected to evaporation, followed by reconstitution with the HPLC mobile phase.
  Advantages: It increases the method sensitivity by removing the impurities present in the analyte (biological sample). it is more efficient than LLE.
- **Protein Precipitation:**
  This technique serves as a means to eliminate interference from the sample matrix, achieved through denaturation and precipitation

processes. Denaturation and precipitation can be effectively executed using precipitating agents, commonly Trichloroacetic acid and perchloric acid. Various organic solvents, such as methanol, acetonitrile, acetone, and ethanol, are utilized to eliminate plasma proteins.

The process involves mixing one part of the sample matrix with three to four parts of the precipitating agent, followed by thorough mixing, centrifugation, and filtration to remove the protein content. The resulting supernatant or filtrate contains the analyte of interest and can be directly subjected to analysis. For quantitative assessment, the supernatant can be isolated, evaporated to dryness, and subsequently reconstituted using an appropriate solvent prior to analysis.

- **Solid Phase Micro extraction (SPME):**

  This technique offers a straightforward and solvent-free approach to extraction. Solid-Phase Microextraction (SPME) involves utilizing a fused silica fiber that is coated with materials such as polyacrylate, polydimethylsiloxane, carbowax, or other modified bonded phases. This coated fiber is brought into contact with the sample, either by exposing it to the vapor or positioning it within the flow of a gaseous sample. The objective is to extract and concentrate the analyte onto the coating material.

  Subsequently, the coated fibers are moved to analytical instruments, such as Gas Chromatography (GC) and Gas Chromatography/Mass Spectrometry (GC/MS), where the analyte is separated and quantified. This is typically achieved by employing a syringe to introduce the fiber-coated with analyte into the instrument for analysis.

  Advantages: Exposed fiber has the ability to extract and sample delivery is a key aspect of this method. The SPME apparatus is a very simple device. It looks like modified syringe consisting of a fiber holder and a fiber assembly, the latter containing a 1-2 cm long retractable SPME fiber. analyte in the sample is directly extracted and concentrated to the extraction fiber. it saves the preparation time and disposal costs and can improve detection limits. SPME was also introduced for direct coupling with HPLC and HPLC-MS in order to analyse weakly volatile analytes.

- **Matrix Solid-Phase Dispersion (MSPD):**

  This method involves the utilization of solid matrices for sample preparation, making it a microscale extraction technique as it requires a minimal amount of sample and solvent. This leads to a significant reduction of about 98% in solvent use and shortens the sample turnaround time by approximately 90%.

In conventional extraction of an organic analyte from tissue, the process necessitates homogenizing the sample analyte using bulk bonded silica-based sorbents, often conducted using a mortar and pestle. This mechanical shearing can disrupt the tissue's structure. The sample gets evenly distributed onto the surface of the supporting sorbent, driven by hydrophilic and hydrophobic interactions. This results in a semi-dry, homogenous blend of the sample that is free-flowing. Interferences and the analyte can then be eluted by transferring the mixture into a pre-fitted Solid-Phase Extraction (SPE) cartridge. Acid alumina is commonly used as the sorbent to extract the organic analyte in this technique.

- **Supercritical Fluid Extraction:**
  This method finds typical application in extracting nonpolar to moderately polar analytes from a given matrix. Supercritical fluids exhibit properties resembling both liquids (in terms of density) and gases or liquids (in terms of viscosity and diffusivity). By lowering the pressure and enabling evaporation, the recovery of the supercritical solvent can be achieved. Carbon dioxide, in particular, proves effective as a supercritical solvent, having the capacity to dissolve numerous volatile polar compounds. This can be further enhanced in the presence of minute quantities of polar co-solvents like water and short-chain alcohols. The concept of supercritical fluids extends to extracting analytes from various sample types.

9.7 Classical Approach for LC-MS Method Development

LC-MS/MS stands as an extremely sensitive and specific analytical method, proficient in accurately identifying and quantifying compounds within a sample. The journey of bioanalytical method development encompasses the creation of an incredibly sensitive assay, capable of detecting analytes within the low nanogram to picogram per milliliter range. The process involves exacting requirements for developing an LC method tailored to detect and quantify a precise compound along with its associated components in a biological matrix. Several criteria guide the development process, encompassing accuracy, precision, specificity, detection limit, quantitation limit, linearity, range, and robustness. These criteria collectively ensure the method's reliability and performance in quantifying the targeted analytes. Quantifying chemical compounds through LC-MS offers advantages such as selectivity, rapidity, and sensitivity. However, this method also presents certain drawbacks, including its inherent complexity, costliness, restricted dynamic range, and occasionally overly pronounced selectivity.

The process of developing a quantitative LC-MS assay can be considerably time-consuming, especially when faced with challenging assay requirements. Typically, the foremost demands involve achieving sufficient sensitivity and selectivity. These critical factors are influenced by every phase of the assay, as depicted in Figure 9.4.

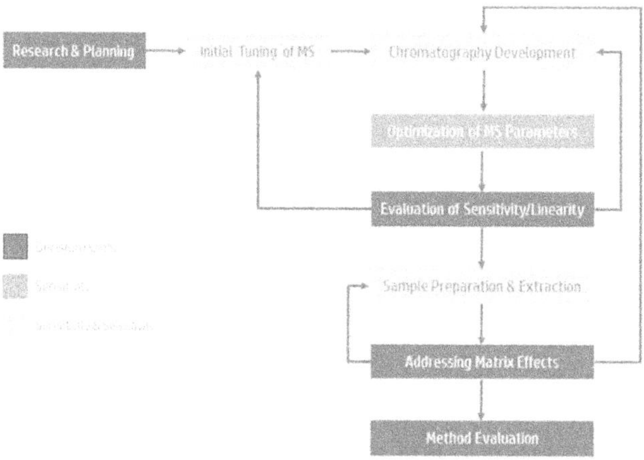

Fig. 9.4. Schematic optimization of LC-MS method.

Moreover, these interdependencies can be balanced against one another to attain the desired outcome. The stages involved in method development and optimization using the LC-MS technique encompass several steps:

1. Research and Planning
2. Initial Tuning of the Mass Spectrometer
3. Chromatography Development
4. Optimization of Mass Spectrometry Parameters
5. Evaluation of Sensitivity
6. Sample Preparation and Extraction
7. Addressing Matrix Effects, including Post-Column Infusion and Post-Extraction Spike
8. Progression of Development
9. Method Evaluation

These stages collectively contribute to the creation of a robust and reliable quantitative LC-MS assay.

Key chromatographic parameters having impact on quantification using LC-MS/MS

The systematic alteration of experimental conditions allows for the deliberate adjustment of the separation between two components. The pivotal parameter influencing quantification is resolution (Rs), which is defined by 3 factors that are closely tied to the experimental conditions: retention factor (k), selectivity (α), and column efficiency (also referred to as column plate number) (N). In numerous LC-MS/MS applications, attaining the highest level of LC selectivity isn't always essential due to the sufficient selectivity often provided by MS/MS. The strategy for LC-MS method development is outlined in Table No. 9.1, providing a structured approach to optimizing the method.

Table 9.1. Scheme for LC-MS method development.

Collection and identification of drug(s)
↓
Literature
↓
Define a Separation goal
↓
Experimental work
↓
Analytical method development
↓
Need for special HPLC procedure, Sample pre-treatment etc
↓
Selection of LC method, Preliminary run, estimate best separation conditions
↓
Optimization of separation Conditions
↓
MS Scanning & Optimisation
↓
Check for problems or requirements for special procedures
↓
Recovery of purified material, qualitative and quantitative estimation
↓
Optimizations of results
↓
Method development report
↓
Validation of developed method
↓
Use of developed method for regular analysis

9.8 AQbD Elements for Bio-analytical Method Development

Creation of Knowledge Space

The initial step involves collecting and comprehensively reviewing all pertinent historical data associated with the analytical method being developed. This includes examining previously established methods that are closely related, as well as delving into existing literature and scientific insights relevant to the subject matter.

Analytical Target Profile

An Analytical Target Profile (ATP) encompasses a set of criteria outlining the specific aspects to be measured (such as the level of a defined impurity or percentage degradation in the sample) and the desired performance benchmarks for these measurements (accuracy, precision, and range, for instance). Employing the ATP, different analytical methods or techniques are initially assessed to align with the method's objectives. The primary aim is often to achieve optimal selectivity coupled with acceptable efficiency, ultimately enhancing measurement reproducibility and repeatability.

This process involves determining the quantity of a drug in an Active Pharmaceutical Ingredient (API) or formulation, with precision and accuracy, through a simple, sensitive, and cost-effective analytical method. Additionally, it can be utilized for quantifying drugs in the presence of impurities (Stability Indicating Assay Method, SIAM) or for gauging the amount of drug released in in-vitro dissolution studies.

Analytical Method Performance Characteristics

Method validation involves assessing several key parameters or characteristics known as Analytical Method Performance Characteristics (AMPCs). These AMPCs are routinely evaluated to ensure the validity and reliability of the method.

Parameters including accuracy, precision, specificity, linearity, range, detection limit, quantitation limit, robustness, and ruggedness are typically determined in accordance with the ICH Q2 R1 guidelines. These evaluations provide a comprehensive understanding of the method's capabilities and establish its suitability for its intended purpose.

Selection of Analytical Techniques

In alignment with the Analytical Target Profile (ATP) outlined in step 2, bioanalytical techniques such as LC-MS, LC-MS/MS, GC-MS, and others are chosen to effectively achieve the established goals. These techniques are selected based on their potential to meet the specific criteria and performance characteristics laid out in the ATP, ensuring that the analytical method is aligned with the desired outcomes and requirements.

Identification of Critical Analytical Attributes (CAAs)

Once a suitable technique is selected, a comprehensive evaluation of the risks associated with various method parameters takes place. This assessment involves factors specific to the chosen technique, such as mobile phase composition, pH, flow rate of the mobile phase, run time, pH of buffer, column type, column temperature, injection volume, detector type, heat block temperature, and more in the case of LC-MS. For GC-MS, parameters like carrier gas type, flow rate, initial and final oven temperatures, injection volume, and column type are considered.

To manage and minimize variability in materials and the method itself, CAAs and CMPs are identified through a risk management process. For bioanalytical techniques like LC-MS and GC-MS, typical CAAs encompass retention time, peak area, resolution, normalized total peak area, and asymmetric factor. This thorough risk assessment and identification of CAAs and CMPs contribute to a deeper understanding of the method and its performance. This, in turn, aids in effective Life Cycle Management (LCM) of the method, ensuring its ongoing reliability and performance over time.

Risk Assessment

These studies serve to elucidate the influence of various factors on the quality profile of the target method. CAAs are employed to establish formal connections between CMPs in the target method's quality profile, prior to conducting risk assessments. This approach aids in categorizing potential causes of issues, enabling the identification of imperfections, variations, defects, or failures.

In risk assessment studies, vital information is extracted based on the likelihood and risk associated with individual factors during analysis. Each individual factor is assigned low, medium, or high-risk scores. According to ICH Q9 guidelines, risk assessment involves three steps: risk identification, risk analysis, and risk evaluation. Prominent risk assessment tools include Failure Mode Effect Analysis (FMEA) and Ishikawa Diagrams (Fishbone Diagrams). This process helps in pinpointing critical method variables that impact the ATP. Commonly utilized risk assessment tools are Ishikawa (Fishbone) diagrams and Failure Mode and Effects Analysis (FMEA). These tools are effective in identifying and classifying primary sources of hazards associated with the method.

Design of Experiments (DoE)

These methodologies offer a potent and efficient strategy for simultaneously assessing the impacts of various factors along with their interactions. They also facilitate the modeling and prediction of the relationships between these factors and Critical Quality Attributes (CQAs) or responses. In HPLC method development, several types of experimental designs are commonly employed.

For screening purposes, techniques such as 2-level full factorial design, fractional factorial design, Taguchi design, and occasionally Plackett-Burman design are frequently utilized. When it comes to optimization, preferences often lean towards Box-Behnken designs (BBD), and Central Composite Designs (CCD). In many instances, CCD and D-optimal designs are notably favored for optimizing HPLC systems when dealing with two critical method parameters (CMPs). Conversely, BBD tends to be preferred when handling three or four CMPs. These designs serve as valuable tools for efficiently navigating the intricate landscape of HPLC method development, aiding in achieving robust and effective analytical methods.

MODR

MODR serves as a tool for creating a multidimensional space, founded on method factors and settings. This approach is pivotal in achieving optimal method performance. Additionally, MODR plays a crucial role in establishing meaningful method controls, such as system suitability, Relative Retention Time (RRT), Relative Response Factor (RRF), etc.

By conducting method verification exercises, MODR assists in ensuring adherence to the Analytical Target Profile (ATP), eventually leading to the definition of the method's Operable Design Region. This region allows for flexibility in adjusting various input method parameters to achieve the anticipated method performance criteria and response, all without necessitating resubmission to regulatory agencies like the FDA.

MODR is rooted in a scientific, risk-based, and multivariate approach, which enables the thorough evaluation of the effects of various factors on method performance. This approach not only supports efficient method development but also aids in ensuring method robustness and compliance with regulatory expectations.

Control strategy

Develop a comprehensive control strategy that covers every aspect of the procedure. This strategy may encompass various elements, including input material controls, process controls, monitoring mechanisms, and the establishment of design spaces around individual or multiple steps in the method development. Final product tests are also integral to this strategy.

The control strategy should be adaptable, factoring in anticipated changes in scale. It is prudent to guide this strategy through a risk assessment, ensuring that potential risks are effectively mitigated. Consistent quality can be assured by continuously monitoring and regularly updating the process, keeping it aligned with the highest standards of quality and performance. This iterative approach ensures that the procedure remains robust, compliant, and responsive to any shifts in conditions or requirements.

Continuous Method Monitoring

Life cycle management serves as a control strategy employed during the commercial stage to implement the design space established. This approach involves the Continuous Method Monitoring (CMM) phase, which represents the final step in the AQbD life cycle. CMM is an ongoing process that revolves around sharing the knowledge acquired during the development and implementation of the design space.

This sharing encompasses multiple aspects, including the outcomes of risk assessments, assumptions based on prior knowledge, statistical design considerations, and the establishment of connections between the design space, Multivariate Optimization Design of Experiments (MODR), control strategy, Critical Quality Attributes (CQA), and Analytical Target Profile (ATP).

Upon successful completion of method validation, the developed method can be applied for routine purposes. Continuous monitoring of method performance becomes crucial at this stage. Monitoring can be facilitated through the utilization of control charts, tracking system suitability data, method-related investigations, and other relevant tools. The essence of CMM lies in its ability to proactively identify and address any deviations from expected performance, enabling timely corrective actions to maintain the integrity and reliability of the analytical method throughout its lifecycle.

***

Practical Examples of AQbD Applied to Bio-Analytical Method Development

Quantitation of Fluoxetine in Human Plasma

Drug Profile

Fluoxetine, chemically known as (±)-N-methyl-3-phenyl-3-[(α,α,α-trifluoro-ρ-tolyl)oxy]propylamine, functions as a selective serotonin reuptake inhibitor (SSRI) and is widely prescribed for the treatment of depression. It is freely soluble in methanol and ethanol; soluble in acetonitrile, chloroform, and acetone; slightly soluble in ethyl acetate, dichloromethane, and water. pKa value is 9.8 (strongly basic).

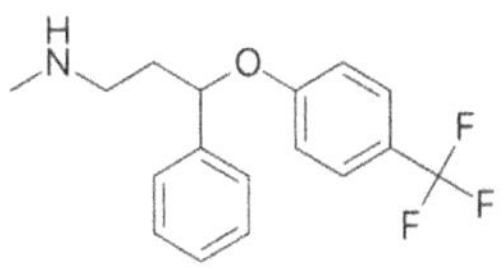

Fig. 9.5. Fluoxetine Structure.

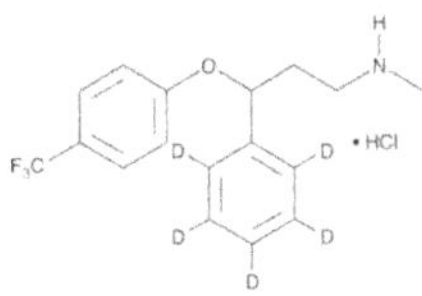

Fig. 9.6. Fluoxetine-D5 Structure.

Literature

Numerous analytical techniques have been devised to quantify fluoxetine in human plasma, encompassing HPLC-UV, GC-MS, and LC-MS/MS. Yet, these methods necessitate the extraction of the analyte from biological samples before chromatographic separation. In these scenarios, the preparation of samples is of paramount importance for accurate analysis of such compounds within biological samples. However, this process can be intricate and time-intensive, potentially resulting in compromised accuracy and precision of the analyte measurement. Consequently, an endeavor was undertaken to establish a Quality by Design (QbD) oriented LC-MS method for the estimation of fluoxetine. This approach aims to overcome the challenges posed by traditional methods by systematically incorporating design principles to optimize the method. Through this approach, it is anticipated that the method's efficiency and accuracy can be enhanced, thus streamlining the analysis process and improving the overall reliability of the results.

ATP

The Analytical Target Profile (ATP) encompasses the creation of a straightforward, highly specific, and linear LC–MS method. This method's primary objective is to achieve precise quantification of Fluoxetine in human plasma, employing Fluoxetine-D5 as the designated internal standard. The focus lies on ensuring accuracy and reliability throughout the analysis process.

CAAs & CMPs

Systematic optimization of the method was carried out by employing Box-Behnken design with flow rate (X_1), pH (X_2) and mobile phase composition (X_3) as the method variables, followed by evaluating retention time (Rt) (Y_1) and peak area (Y_2) as the responses.

DoE

A Box-Behnken design (BBD) was employed to assess the robustness of the method across three independent variables: flow rate (X_1) in mL/min, pH (X_2), and the mobile phase composition (% v/v ammonium formate buffer: acetonitrile (ACN)) (X_3).

Table. 9.2. Design Matrix as per the BBD.

Run	X_1	X_2	X_3	Y_1	Y_2
1	0.6	6.7	0	301,547	3.4
2	1	6.6	5	296,427	3.5
3	0.8	6.7	5	418,865	1.54
4	0.8	6.7	5	418,865	1.54
5	0.8	6.7	5	418,865	1.54
6	1	6.7	10	334,678	5.2
7	0.6	6.7	10	283,573	4.6
8	0.8	6.6	10	382,341	5.4
9	0.6	6.8	5	321,378	4.3
10	0.8	6.8	0	321,378	5.9
11	1	6.7	0	301,463	5.9
12	1	6.8	5	393,542	5.4
13	0.8	6.7	5	418,865	1.54
14	0.6	6.6	5	301,243	3.6
15	0.8	6.6	0	281,438	3.1
16	0.8	6.7	5	418,865	1.54
17	0.8	6.8	10	273,256	4.2

X_1: Flow rate, (mL/min); X_1:: pH; X_1:: MP Composition (%) Y_1: peak area, cm^2; Y_2: retention time, min

From the experimental runs proposed by the BBD, the second-order model with a quadratic experimental domain was chosen for both response variables. The selected model exhibited favorable coefficients of determination (r^2) of 0.9842 for response Y_1 and 0.9145 for response Y_2. This choice was made after comparing the model's performance against other models recommended by the design, which was validated through a lack-of-fit test. The outcomes of this analysis established the superior predictive capability and goodness of fit of the selected quadratic model for the responses in question.

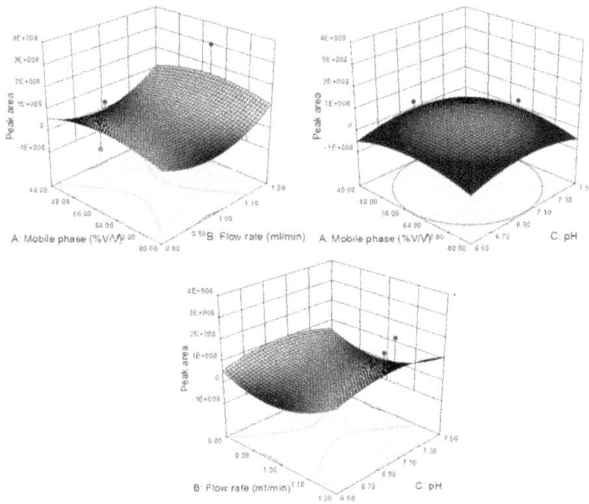

Fig. 9.7. 3D-response surface plots depicting the influence of X_1, X_2, & X_3 on Y_1.

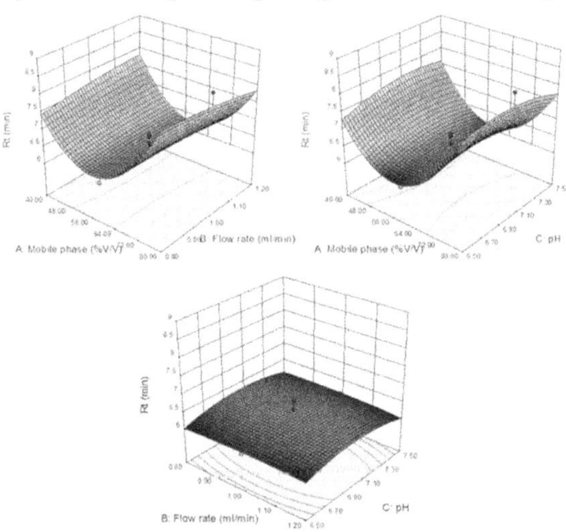

Fig. 9.8. 3D-response surface plots depicting the influence of X_1, X_2, & X_3 on Y_2.

Through the evaluation of the model's individual factors, their impact on the responses was visualized using contour plots that illustrate response surfaces for both Y1 and Y2. These contour plots are presented in Figures 9.7 and 9.8. The analysis revealed that the effects of both responses are contingent upon factor X1 (flow rate) and factor X3 (mobile phase composition percentage), while factor X2 (pH) did not exert any discernible influence on the observed responses. This observation underscores the significant roles of flow rate and mobile phase composition in shaping the outcomes, while pH appears to have a negligible impact within the defined experimental domain.

MODR

A systematic approach to method development was executed through the utilization of the Box-Behnken design (BBD). This approach aimed at evaluating the robustness of the method by investigating the effects of method variables: mobile phase composition, buffer pH, and flow rate. Subsequently, the optimization of these variables' impacts on peak area and retention time (Rt) was undertaken, yielding the responses. Table 9.3 encapsulates the outcomes of this systematic exploration, presenting a comprehensive overview of the method development process, the variables studied, and the resulting responses. This strategic approach ensures a well-structured method development process that encompasses robustness evaluation and optimization, contributing to the method's effectiveness and reliability in achieving accurate and consistent results.

Table 9.3. Numerical Optimization.

Constraints						
Name	**Goal**	**Lower limit**	**Upper limit**	**Lower weight**	**Upper weight**	**Importance**
X_1: Flow rate	is in range	0.6	1.0	1	1	3
X_2: pH	is in range	6.6	6.8	1	1	3
X_3: AF:ACN	is in range	0	10	1	1	3
Solutions						
Number	**Flow rate**	**pH**	**AF Compo-sition**	**Desirab ility**		
1	0.80	6.70	5.00	1	Selected	
2	1.00	6.70	10.00	1		
3	0.80	6.60	10.00	1		

Sample extraction

Thawed CC and QC samples were vortexed after being allowed to thaw at room temperature. Then, 50 µL of IS (~50 ng/mL of Fluoxetine-D5) was added to labeled polypropylene tubes (except blank). Next, 200 µL of plasma was combined with each sample, followed by centrifugation and vortexing. To undergo solid-phase extraction, two rounds of 1 mL methanol and 1 mL elution solution were passed through Oasis MCX 30 mg/cc cartridges under pressure. Cartridges were preconditioned with 1 mL methanol and 1 mL water using positive pressure. The loaded samples were washed twice with 1 mL of washing solution, dried under a nitrogen stream (20 psi, 50 ± 2°C), and reconstituted in 0.5 mL mobile phase. The reconstituted samples were transferred to vials for analysis. The entire sample processing was performed under dark conditions during the study.

LC–MS-MS conditions

HPLC instrument - Shimadzu LC10A connected with an AB SCIEX API-4000 triple quadruple mass spectrometer.

SP : Ascentis express C18 column (75 x 4.6 mm, 2.7 µm)
MP : Ammonium formate and acetonitrile (5:95) ratio
Flow rate : 0.8 mL/min
Injection volume : 10 µL
Run time : 3.5 min.
Mode : +ve ion mode having a turbo ion spray ionization pattern.

Mass spectrometer parameters

Curtain gas : 35
Nebuliser : 50
Heater gas : 50
Focusing potential : 12; Collision cell exit potential: 12
Ion spray voltage : 5,000 V
Temperature : 500°C
Collision gas : 9
Entrance potential : 8 V
Dwell time : 200 ms.

Tandem mass spectrometry

In positive ion mode, product ion mass spectra and scans were acquired for both fluoxetine and fluoxetine-D5. Fluoxetine exhibited protonated molecular ions at m/z = 310.0, while fluoxetine-D5 showed a signal at m/z

= 315.0. Notably, both compounds yielded a signal at m/z = 44.0 in their product ion mass spectra. For quantification, the transition from m/z 310 to m/z 44 and from m/z 315 to m/z 44 were monitored in Multiple Reaction Monitoring (MRM) mode. This precise mode enhances selectivity and sensitivity, facilitating accurate measurement of fluoxetine and fluoxetine-D5 in the samples.

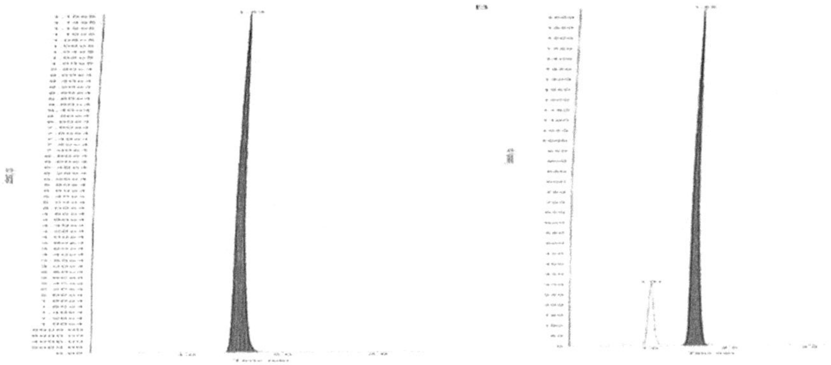

Fig. 9.9. Chromatogram of fluoxetine alone, and Internal Standard i.e., Fluoxetine-D5.

Method validation

Table 9.4. Summary of Validation parameters.

Parameter	Value			
Concentration (ng/mL)	**2.0**	**5.89**	**12**	**25**
Precision (%) - Within batch	5.1	3.2	1.3	0.6
Precision (%) - Between batch	4.9	3.8	1.5	0.8
Accuracy (%) - Within batch	94.3	109.6	100.2	100.1
Accuracy (%) - Between batch	94.3	109.0	99.8	99.9
Concentration (ng/mL)	**5**		**25**	
Stability of Fluoxetine in Human Plasma				
Bench-top stability (13.5 h)	98.1		100.2	
Bench-top extraction stability	96.4		100.0	
Long-term stability (5 days)	101.8		102.6	
Freeze–thaw stability (after 3 cycles)	102.8		99.3	
In injector stability (50.15 h)	96.3		99.5	
LLOQ	2 ng/mL			
r^2	>0.998			
Recovery (extraction) %	Low		Medium	High
	89.4		75.6	73.8

***

Practical Examples of AQbD Applied to Bio-Analytical Method Development

Quantification of Paracetamol & Diclofenac in Human Plasma

Drug Profile

Paracetamol, chemically known as N-(4-hydroxyphenyl) acetamide, is a commonly utilized over-the-counter analgesic and antipyretic medication. It is employed for alleviating mild-to-moderate pain and reducing fever. Diclofenac, chemically referred to as 2-[2-(2,6-dichlorophenyl amino)phenyl]acetic acid, belongs to the class of classical nonsteroidal anti-inflammatory agents (NSAIDs).

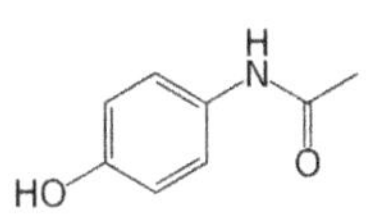

Fig. 9.10. Paracetamol Structure.

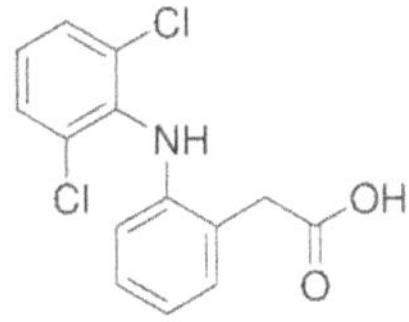

Fig. 9.11. Diclofenac Structure.

Literature

Various analytical techniques such as TLC, liquid chromatography, LC-MS/MS, spectrofluorometry, electrochemical methods, and capillary zone electrophoresis have been documented for the determination of these two drugs. These methods are often employed individually or in conjunction with other analgesics. However, each of these existing methods possesses its own set of advantages and limitations from a method development perspective.

ATP

Analytical Target Profile (ATP) is centered around the Quality by Design (QbD) approach for the creation and validation of an LC-MS/MS method tailored for quantifying paracetamol and diclofenac in human plasma. This method ingeniously incorporates gabapentin as the internal standard (IS).

The sample preparation and extraction phase were executed using the protein precipitation technique.

CAAs & CMPs

Method optimization was meticulously carried out using the BBD. Critical factors, namely mobile phase composition, flow rate, and pH, were systematically explored through this approach. The method's performance was evaluated based on peak area and retention time, which were adopted as the key responses in this optimization process. By integrating QbD principles into the development process, this LC-MS/MS method offers a systematic and reliable approach to accurately quantify paracetamol and diclofenac in human plasma, with gabapentin as an internal standard.

DoE

The robustness study is a valuable tool for detecting any substantial variations in the critical quality attributes of the developed analytical method due to minor alterations in method variables such as mobile phase composition, flow rate, and column oven temperature. Following the chosen Box-Behnken Design (BBD) experimental plan, the trials were executed, and the design was scrutinized based on the resulting experimental data. Table 9.5. presents the list of experimental trials generated by the BBD, which was selected to facilitate response surface methodology-driven optimization. To enhance the optimization process, a mathematical model was constructed using a quadratic model and Design Expert software. The polynomial equation thus generated was subjected to analysis to decipher the nature of the effects. The equations derived for both response variables, namely peak area and retention time for paracetamol and diclofenac (Y_1, Y_2, Y_3, and Y_4), offer insights into the relationship between method variables and the corresponding responses. This systematic approach aids in refining the analytical method and ensuring its robustness under varying conditions.

Table 9.5. Summary of trial runs suggested as per BBD.

Run	X_1	X_2	X_3	Y_1	Y_2	Y_3	Y_4
1	0.5	30	6.7	345864	1.8	335664	2.6
2	0.4	30	6.8	378869	1.5	368863	2.3
3	0.3	20	6.8	329849	1.8	319859	2.6
4	0.5	20	6.8	368892	1.6	358852	2.4
5	0.3	30	6.7	329841	1.7	319843	2.5
6	0.3	20	6.6	339848	1.7	309849	3.1
7	0.5	20	6.6	378894	1.6	368794	2.4
8	0.4	10	6.8	367867	1.5	367866	2.3

Contd...

9	0.4	20	6.7	428868	1.2	445863	2
10	0.3	10	6.7	339549	1.6	329548	2.4
11	0.4	30	6.6	400898	1.5	390888	2.3
12	0.4	20	6.7	428868	1.2	445863	2
13	0.5	10	6.7	358899	1.4	348889	2.2
14	0.4	20	6.7	428868	1.2	445863	2
15	0.4	20	6.7	428868	1.2	445863	2
16	0.4	10	6.6	388765	1.3	378769	2.3
17	0.4	20	6.7	428868	1.2	445863	2

Factors X_1: Flow rate, ml/min; X_2: Composition of MP A; X_3: pH
Responses: Y_1: Peak area (Para); Y_2: Rt (Para) min; Y_3: Peak area (Diclo); Y_4: Rt (Diclo) min

$$\mathbf{Y_1 = +4.289E{+}005+14182.75*A+49.00*B-7866.00*C-831.75*A*B-0.75*A*C-282.75*B*C-57529.38*A^2-27800.38*B^2-16967.87*C^2}$$

$$\mathbf{Y_2 = +1.20-0.050*A+0.087*B+0.038*C+0.075*A*B-0.025*A*C-0.050*B*C+0.33*A^2+0.10*B^2+0.15*C^2}$$

$$\mathbf{Y_3 = +4.459E{+}005+16637.50*A-1226.75*B-4107.50*C-880.00*A*B-4988.00*A*C-2780.50*B*C-74817.50*A^2-37559.50*B^2-31707.00*C^2}$$

$$\mathbf{Y_4 = +2.00-0.12*A+0.063*B-0.063*C+0.075*A*B+0.13*A*C+0.000*B*C+0.37*A^2+0.050*B^2+0.25*C^2}$$

The examination of all the polynomial equations demonstrated a strong alignment of the data with the chosen model. The analysis of ANOVA parameters underscored the statistically significant nature of the model while revealing an insignificant lack of fit. Additionally, other statistical metrics employed to assess the model's appropriateness showcased elevated correlation coefficients nearing 0.999, minimal residual errors, and low coefficients of variance. These findings collectively indicate the high degree of reliability and accuracy in the established model, affirming its suitability for predicting and interpreting the behavior of the analytical method under investigation.

The response surface analysis unveiled intricate interactions among the factors, evident from the pronounced curvature evident in the response surface plots depicted in Fig. 9.12. These figures vividly showcase the intricate relationships and dependencies that exist between the different variables, indicating the complex nature of the interplay between factors and their impact on the responses.

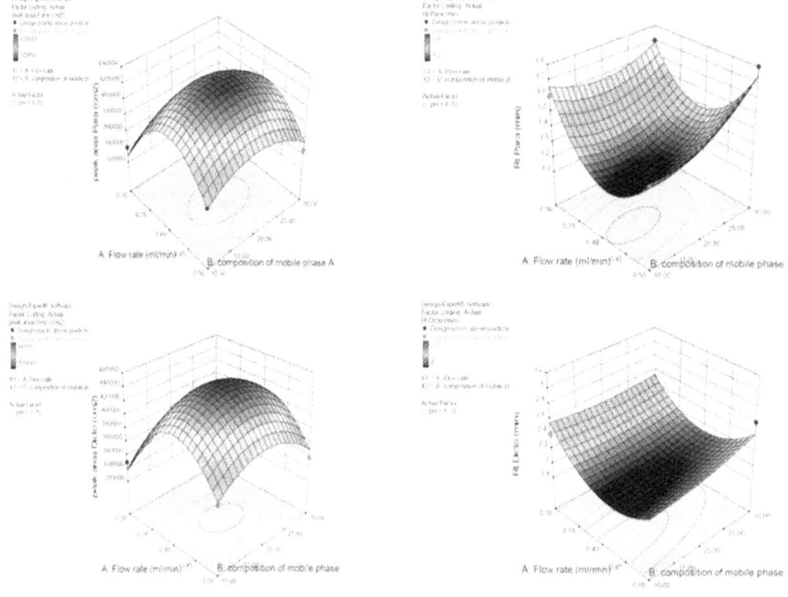

Fig. 9.12. 3D response surface plots depicting the influence of mobile phase ratio, flow rate and Ph on peak area as Y_1, Y_2, Y_3 and Y_4.

MODR

The numerical optimization analysis aimed to identify the ideal chromatographic conditions yielded highly favorable desirability function values, all equal to 1. Target ranges for the response surface variables were established and listed in Table 9.6.

Table 9.6. Numerical Optimization.

Constraints						
Name	**Goal**	**Lower limit**	**Upper limit**	**Lower weight**	**Upper weight**	**Importance**
X_1: Flow rate	is in range	0.3	0.5	1	1	3
X_2: % M.P. - A		10	30	1	1	3
X_3: pH		6.6	6.8	1	1	3
Solutions						
Number	**Flow rate**	**pH**	**AF Composition**	**Desirability**		
1	0.40	6.70	20.00	1	Selected	
2	0.50	6.70	10.00	1		
3	0.50	6.70	30.00	1		

Three optimal solutions were achieved via numerical optimization, each with a desirability function of 1. Furthermore, these optimal solutions indicated a robust chromatographic solution for all response variables. To further analyze the results from the design space, a graphical search technique was employed. The overlay plot in Fig. 9.13 illustrates the optimal area.

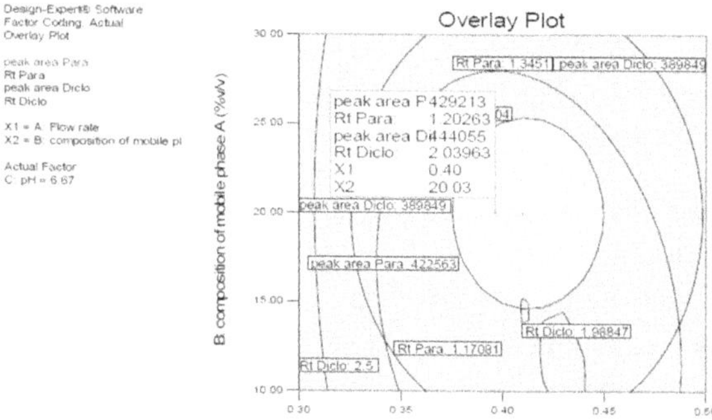

Fig. 9.13. Overlay plot depicting area as the optimal region.

Sample extraction

Calibration curve standards, quality control samples, and plasma samples were retrieved from the deep freezer and allowed to thaw at room temperature. To ensure complete mixing, the thawed samples were vortexed. Then, 0.1 ml of the sample was taken and placed in Eppendorf tubes. Subsequently, 0.05 ml of internal standard (5000 ng/ml) was added to the sample, followed by vortexing for 30 sec.

The samples were eluted with 0.75 ml of 0.1% formic acid in methanol under constant pressure. After elution, the samples were dried using a nitrogen evaporator at a temperature of 50°C and a pressure of 20 psi until complete drying was achieved. The dried contents were reconstituted with 500μL of the mobile phase and transferred to microcentrifuge tubes. Centrifugation was carried out at 14000 rpm for 10 min at 4°C. The resulting sample solution was then transferred to injector vials and subsequently injected into the LC/MS/MS system for analysis.

LC-MS/MS conditions

Instrument : Triple Quadrupole Mass & Shimadzu HPLC

Column : Agilent Zorbax Eclipse XDB-C8, 50 x 4.6 mm (5μm).

Mobile phase : A mixture of solution A and B in the ratio of 20:80

Flow rate : 0.4 ml/min.

Injection volume : 7μl

Run time : 4 min
Mode : Positive ion mode
Ionization : Turbo ion spray ionization.
Gas flow : 10
Ion spray voltage: 3500 V
Temperature : 350°C
Nebulizer : 60 psi
Collision energy : 15 (Paracetamol), 15 (Diclofenac) and 10 (Gabapentin)
Dwell time : 200 msec.

The MRM conditions were carefully monitored for both the analytes and the internal standard. Specifically, the monitored MRM conditions was 151.8/109.9 for paracetamol; 296.1/215.0 for diclofenac, and 172.1/154.1for gabapentin. In terms of retention time, paracetamol exhibited a retention time of 1.2 minutes, diclofenac displayed a retention time of 2.0 minutes, and gabapentin was observed at a retention time of 1.1 min. These retention times are key indicators in chromatographic separation and play a crucial role in the accurate identification and quantification of the target compounds within the analytical method.

Table 9.7. Summary of Validation parameters.

Parameter	Value	
	Paracetamol	**Diclofenac**
Minimum quantifiable (ng/ml)	205	40
Precision (%) - Within batch	3.7	5.2
Precision (%) - Between batch	5.6	7.8
Accuracy (%) - Within batch	93.3	101.4
Accuracy (%) - Between batch	92.2	102.2
Stability in Human Plasma		
Freeze thaw (after 3 cycles) below -15°C	100.4	101.9
Bench-top (6 h)	101.9	98.9
Bench top extraction stability	99.1	101.4
In-injector (50.15 h)	98.4	99.9
Long term stability (7days)	100.75	98.0
r^2	>0.998	
Recovery (extraction) %	101.6	86.9

***

Practical Examples of AQbD Applied to Bio-Analytical Method Development

Quantitation of Enzalutamide in Plasma Sample

Drug Profile

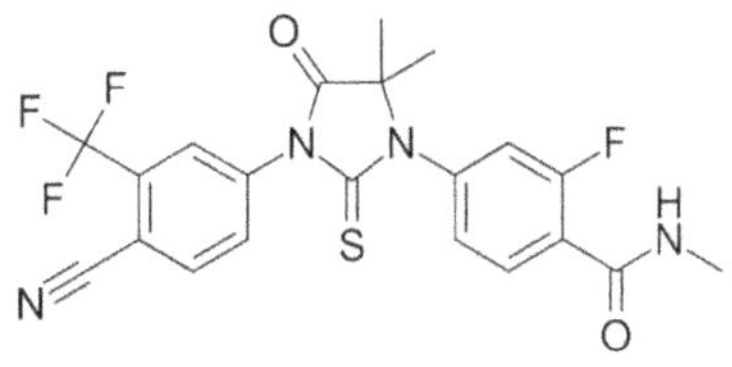

Fig. 9.14. Enzalutamide Structure.

Enzalutamide, marketed as 'Xtandi,' is an anti-prostate cancer drug. It blocks the androgen receptor, inhibiting nuclear translocation and DNA interaction. Its chemical name is 4-[3-[4 – cyano – 3 - (trifluoromethyl) phenyl]-5,5-dimethyl-4-oxo-2-sulfanylidene imidazolidin-1-yl]-2-fluoro-N-methyl benzamide, with a molecular weight of 464.44 and formula $C_{21}H_{16}F_4N_4OS$. Enzalutamide is a white crystalline solid, sparingly soluble in water, methanol, and soluble in acetonitrile, dimethyl sulfoxide.

Literature

Numerous techniques for quantifying Enzalutamide in plasma samples from dogs, humans, and tissue homogenates have been documented. This method under discussion focuses on the optimization of liquid chromatography-tandem mass spectrometry (LC-MS/MS) parameters through simultaneous application of Taguchi orthogonal array and central composite design (CCD) approaches.

ATP

The Analytical Target Profile (ATP) for the titled study is focused on employing the Quality by Design (QbD) approach to develop a liquid chromatography-tandem mass spectrometry (LC-MS/MS) method for quantifying Enzalutamide, an anti-prostate cancer therapy drug, in spiked plasma samples. The goal is to achieve accurate and precise determination of Enzalutamide using a systematic and optimized analytical method.

CAAs & CMPs

In the context of ultrahigh-performance liquid chromatography-electrospray ionization-tandem mass spectrometry (UHPLC-ESIMS/MS), essential factors influencing separation, identification, and quantification processes are referred to as Critical method attributes (CMAs). These encompass parameters such as organic content, buffer strength, pH modifier, flow rate, spray voltage, sheath gas, and auxiliary gas, which impact critical analytical attributes, retention time (R_1) and area (R_2). These variables underwent evaluation initially through a factorial design (utilizing a Taguchi orthogonal array design), followed by a comprehensive assessment using a CCD.

This approach aimed to determine the optimal mobile phase composition for quantifying the standard drug Enzalutamide, alongside its internal standard (deuterated Enzalutamide), in both spiked plasma samples and formulations.

DoE

7 influential factors were identified to impact responses and their influence on Critical Analytical Attributes (CAA) was examined. These factors encompassed spray voltage, sheath gas pressure, auxiliary gas pressure, organic solvent content, buffer strength of ammonium acetate, pH modifier, and flow rate. The chosen CAA for analysis were retention time (R_1) and area (R_2). Utilizing DoE, factors and responses were inputted. Experiments were conducted based on the generated Taguchi orthogonal array design and their respective levels.

Table 9.8. Taguchi Design to screen the parameters of LC-MS/MS.

Factor 1	Factor 2	Factor 3	Factor 4	Factor 5	Factor 6	Factor 7	Response 1	Response 2
-1	-1	1	1	1	-1	1	1.508	312846
-1	1	-1	1	-1	1	-1	1.478	490436
-1	-1	-1	-1	1	1	1	1.487	316092
-1	1	1	-1	-1	-1	-1	1.513	492282
1	-1	1	-1	1	1	-1	1.208	320762
1	-1	-1	-1	-1	-1	-1	1.182	318786
1	1	-1	1	-1	1	1	1.175	490474
1	1	1	1	1	-1	1	1.171	485628

Taguchi -Orthogonal Array Design - Actual levels used		
Factor	**Low (−1)**	**High (1)**
1. Acetonitrile, %	70	90
2. Spray voltage, V	4000	5000

Contd...

3.	Buffer strength, mM	2	10
4.	Formic acid, %	0.1	0.3
5.	Flow rate, mL/min	0.3	0.6
6.	Sheath gas, bar	20	50
7.	Auxiliary gas, bar	10	2

The Pareto charts derived from the factorial design indicated that acetonitrile content has a negative impact on retention time (Rt), as shown in Fig. 9.15 and 9.16, while buffer strength requires further optimization to assess its effect on Rt (R^1). On the other hand, spray voltage was found to positively influence the area, as demonstrated by the Pareto chart and perturbation plot (Fig. 9.17 and 9.18) (R^2). Conversely, auxiliary gas and sheath gas pressure, flow rate, and formic acid concentration did not exhibit significant influence on both responses, as revealed by the perturbation plots for Rt and area (Figures 9.16 and 9.18). Notably, spray voltage emerged as a significant MS/MS parameter affecting peak area and was subsequently investigated more comprehensively through central composite design (CCD). Although the flow rate of LC parameters does affect Rt, it was deemed statistically insignificant for CCD exploration, as evidenced in Fig. 9.18. Similarly, the formic acid concentration was also excluded from CCD investigation, akin to the flow rate.

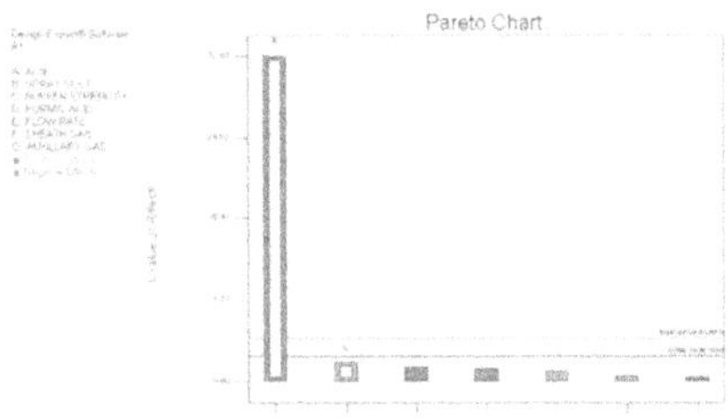

Fig. 9.15. Pareto chart showing effects of CMAs on R_1.

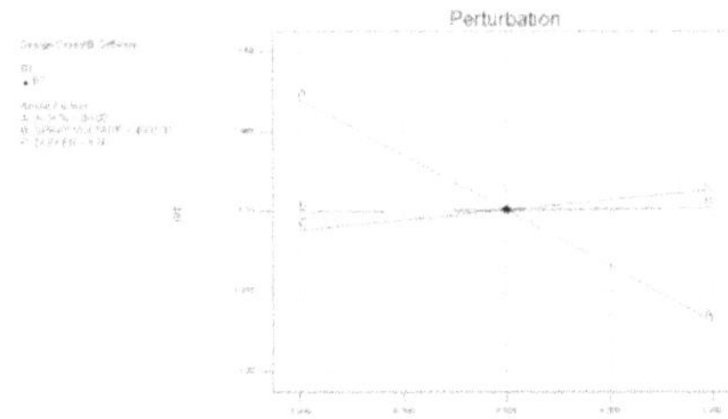

Fig. 9.16. Perturbation plot-the factors effect on R_1.

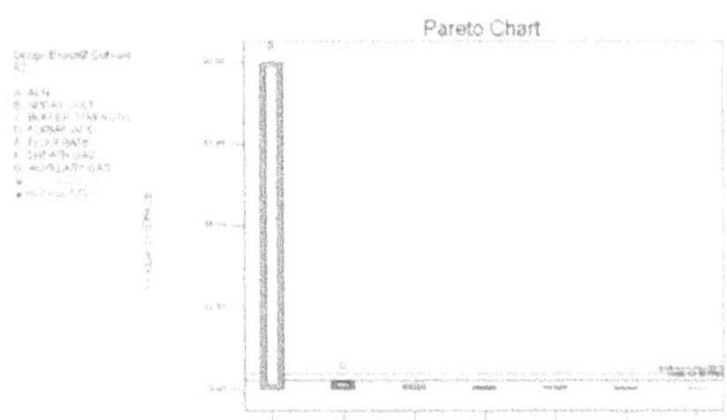

Fig. 9.17. Pareto chart showing effects of CMAs on R_2.

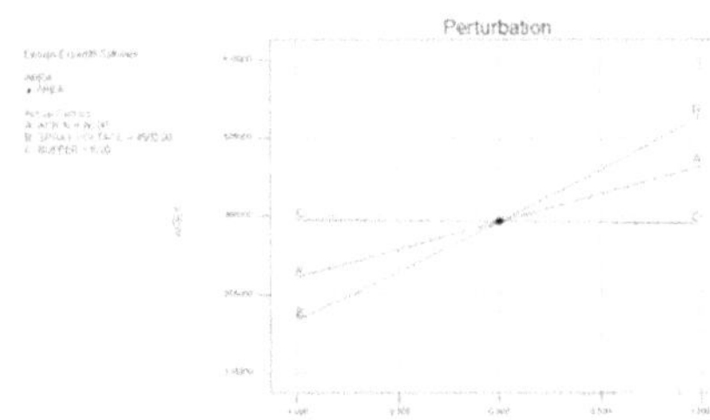

Fig. 9.18. Perturbation plot-the factors effect on R_2.

The content of the organic solvent (Factor 1), spray voltage (Factor 2), and buffer strength (Factor 3), identified as three pivotal factors, are slated for in-depth investigation through CCD. This response surface design aims to enhance both retention time (Response 1) and peak area (Response 2). The design details can be observed in Table 9.9.

Table 9.9. Details of central composite design to finalise the parameters of LC-MS/MS.

Factor 1	Factor 2	Factor 3	Response 1	Response 2
-1.414	0	0	1.582	378920
-1	1	1	1.510	503094
-1	-1	-1	1.489	314734
0	-1.414	0	1.343	323476
0	1.414	0	1.365	600346
0	0	-1.414	1.299	460340
0	0	1.414	1.388	456744
0	0	0	1.338	458762
0	0	0	1.340	452348
0	0	0	1.341	454982
0	0	0	1.335	456992
0	0	0	1.329	448902
1	1	-1	1.179	603456
1	-1	1	1.201	404800
1.414	0	0	1.092	528004

Actual levels of factors used in CCD

Factor	Low (-1)	Center (0)	High (+1)
Acetonitrile, %	70	80	90
Spray voltage, V	4000	4500	5000
Buffer strength	2	6	10

The generated models indicated interaction terms involving spray voltage, acetonitrile, and buffer strength for retention time (R_1) and area responses (R_2). Derringer's desirability function was crucial in identifying optimal response levels due to opposing influences of acetonitrile on both responses. Optimization aimed to maximize area and minimize retention time, considering factors like organic modifier content and spray voltage's significant influence on sensitivity. Buffer strength had a comparatively lesser effect on area. Interaction terms of main factors contributed to models for both retention time and area, linked to changes in mobile phase behavior. Optimizing buffer strength at 2 mM reduced capillary electrode salt deposition, enhancing instrument lifespan.

MODR

Achieving a desirability of 0.937 (Fig. 9.19), the optimized conditions were determined by analyzing the response surface plots (Fig. 9.20 and 9.21). These conditions consisted of 80% acetonitrile and 20% 2 mM ammonium acetate buffer with 0.1% formic acid, and a flow rate of 0.6 mL/min. The MS/MS parameters were set as follows: spray voltage at 4750 V, sheath gas pressure at 50 bar, and auxiliary gas pressure at 10 bar. With these settings, the predicted retention time (Rt) was 1.33, closely matching the obtained value of 1.34 (Fig. 9.22).

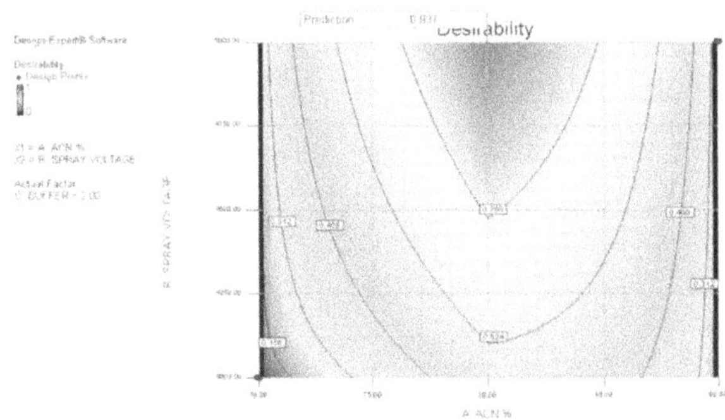

Fig. 9.19. Desirability plot for the selected factors.

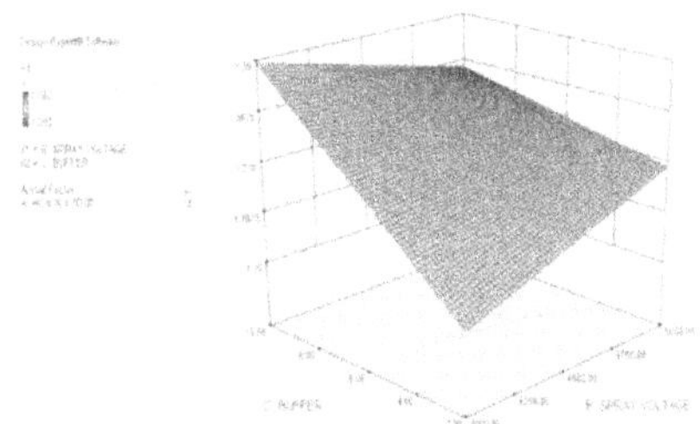

Fig. 9.20. Response surface plot showing the effects of factors on R_1.

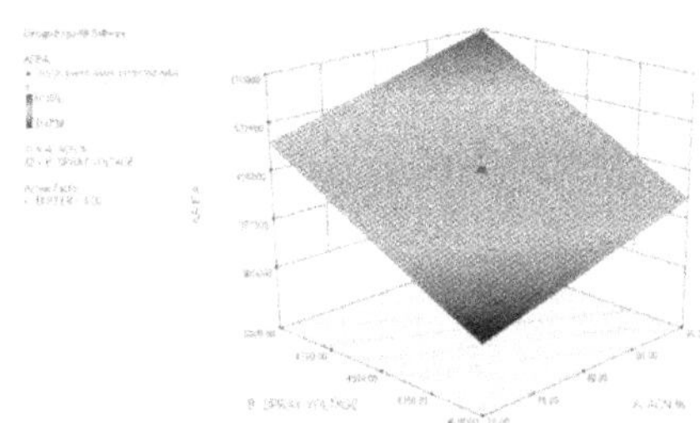

Fig. 9.21. Response surface plot showing the effects of factors on R_2.

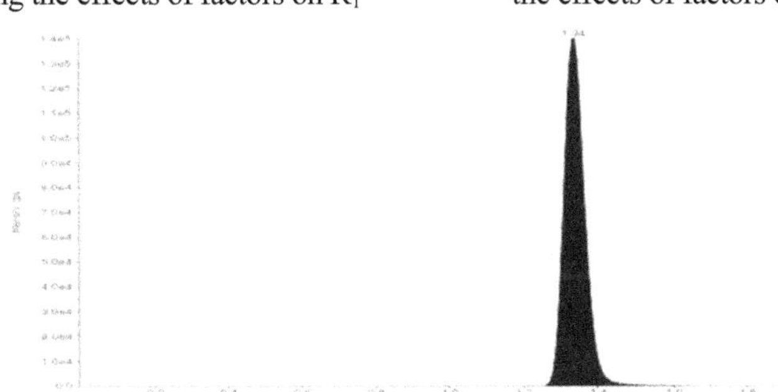

Fig. 9.22. Representative chromatogram of the enzalutamide.

Sample extraction

Approximately 100 μL of human plasma samples were augmented with 50 μL of both enzalutamide and enzalutamide internal standard (100 ng/mL). Subsequently, 1.8 mL of an extraction mixture, comprising 80% acetonitrile (a protein precipitant) and 20% 2-mM ammonium acetate buffer (pH adjusted to 3.0 with 0.1% formic acid), was introduced. The sample was then thoroughly mixed using vortexing and subjected to centrifugation at 13,000g. Following centrifugation, 10 μL of the resulting solution was directly injected into the triple quadrupole LC-MS/MS system.

Method validation

Table 9.10. Summary of Validation parameters.

Precision and accuracy studies			
Amount present, ng/mL	Amount recovered ng/mL	Accuracy % Recovery	Precision % RSD
0.685	0.651	95.04	1.953
22.75	20.013	87.97	2.634
39.35	36.788	93.49	3.626
% Level added to 22.75 ng/mL	Amount recovered ng/mL	Accuracy % Recovery	Precision % RSD
40	27.78	88.19	2.703
80	36.053	89.02	1.963
120	44.867	90.64	2.571
Stability of Fluoxetine in Human Plasma	0.62 ng/mL	21.5 ng/mL	35.5 ng/mL
Bench-top stability (11 h), %	91.78	92.96	90.12
Freeze–thaw stability (after 3 cycles), %	92.31	92.35	94.22
Short-term stability (2days), %	90.1	87.2	93.93
Long-term stability (5 days), %	91.51	90.1	90.25
Autosampler stability (30 h)	90.66	94.19	91.71
Parameter	**Value**		
LLOQ, ng/mL	0.078		
r^2	0.9984		
Regression equation	$y = 0.0615\ x + 0.000474$		

***

Practical Examples of AQbD Applied to Bio-Analytical Method Development

Quantitation of Sildenafil in Human Plasma

Drug Profile

Sildenafil is a medication commonly prescribed to male patients for erectile dysfunction. Its chemical composition is 1-[4-ethoxy-3-(6,7-dihydro-1-methyl-7-oxo-3-propyl -1H-pyrazolo [4,3-d] pyrimidin-5-yl) phenyl sulfonyl]-4-methyl piperazine, as depicted in Fig.9.24.

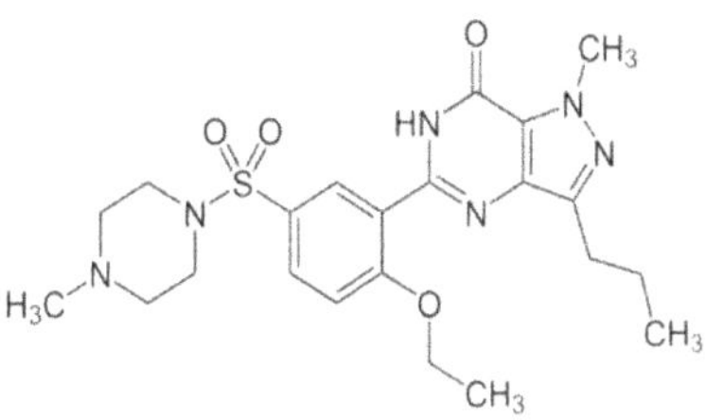

Fig. 9.23. Sildenafil Structure.

This drug acts as a powerful and selective inhibitor of the phosphodiesterase type 5 enzyme. It has a water solubility of 0.46 mg/mL. Its pKa values are 7.63 (Strongest Acidic) and 5.98 (Strongest Basic).

Literature

Numerous analytical methods have been established to quantify sildenafil in human plasma and other samples. These methods encompass techniques such as HPLC with UV or electrochemical detection, GC–MS, LC–MS, and LC–MS-MS. Typically, these approaches involve extraction processes prior to chromatographic separation, as outlined in various literature sources.

ATP

The current developed method focuses on the analysis of sildenafil using lorazepam as an internal standard. This method outlines its applicability for quantification in diverse biological samples such as human plasma, urine, and serum. The approach emphasizes the utilization of cost-effective solvents and careful control of column temperature to enhance chromatographic separation. The optimization of method variables is achieved through Box–Behnken design (BBD).

CMAs & CAAs

Through the systematic utilization of Box–Behnken design, the method was meticulously optimized. Key parameters such as mobile phase flow rate, pH, and mobile phase composition were considered as critical factors. The optimization process focused on evaluating these factors with regards to their impact on retention time and peak area, both serving as essential responses.

DoE

To optimize and assess robustness, the BBD was employed. This design incorporated three dependent variables: flow rate, mL/min, pH, and composition (% v/v) of the mobile phase (ammonium acetate buffer:acetonitrile). These variables were chosen as they impact the method's robustness. Additionally, two responses, namely retention time (Y_1) in minutes and peak area (Y_2) in cm², were selected as indicators of robustness. A total of 17 experimental runs were conducted. (Table 9.11.)

Table 9.11. Summary of trial runs suggested as per BBD.

Run	X_1	X_2	X_3	Y_1	Y_2
1	0.8	6.7	30	1.4	273256
2	1	6.7	15	0.7	418865
3	1	6.8	30	1.4	263216
4	1	6.7	15	0.7	418865
5	0.8	6.7	0	1.3	173256
6	0.8	6.8	15	0.9	323252
7	1	6.6	30	1.2	213256
8	1	6.8	0	1.4	183453
9	1.2	6.8	15	1.2	343256
10	1	6.7	15	0.7	418865
11	1.2	6.6	15	1.2	373256
12	1	6.6	0	1.3	158956
13	0.8	6.6	15	1.1	243759
14	1.2	6.7	30	1	173454
15	1	6.7	15	0.7	418865
16	1.2	6.7	0	1.4	203256
17	1	6.7	15	0.7	418865
Factors X_1: Flow rate, ml/min; X_2: pH; X_3: Composition of MP Responses: Y_1: Rt, min; Y_2: Peak area					

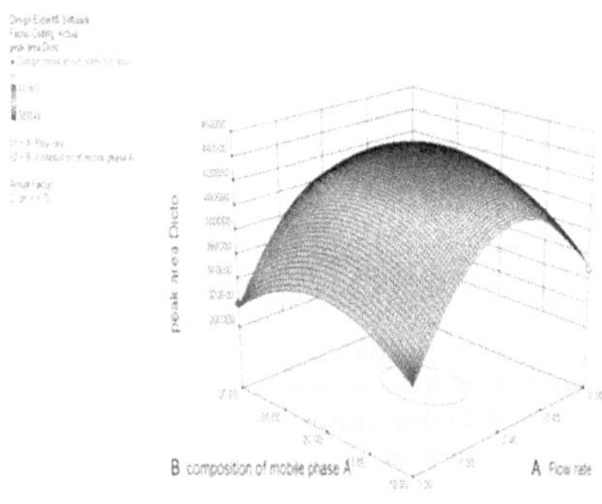

Fig. 9.24. 3D-response surface plot depicting the influence of factors on Y_1.

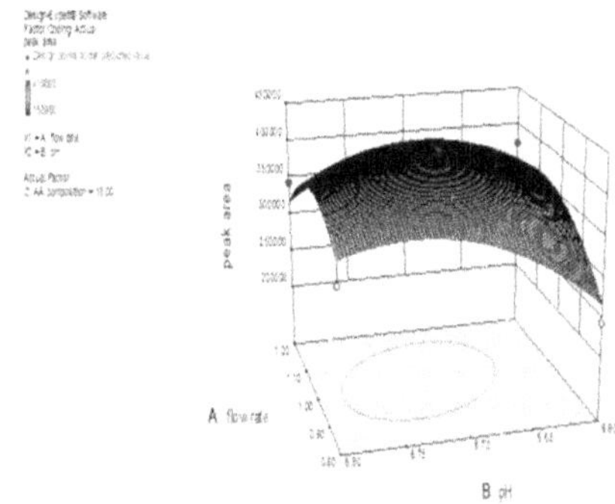

Fig. 9.25. 3D-response surface plot depicting the influence of factors on Y_2.

The impact of individual factors on the model was evaluated through contour plots illustrating the responses Y_1 and Y_2, as presented in Fig. 9.24 and 9.25. These plots indicate that the influence of both responses is linked to factors X_1 (flow rate) and X_3 (mobile phase composition % age), while factor X_2 (pH) has no discernible effect on the obtained responses.

The validation of this model was further confirmed by investigating interactions among different factors and their effects on the responses.

The equations representing the two responses, namely retention time and peak area, are as follows:

$$\mathbf{Y_1 = +0.70 + 0.013X_1 + 0.013X_2 - 0.050X_3 + 0.050X_1X_2 - 0.13X_1X_3 + 0.025X_2X_3 + 0.18X_1^2 + 0.22X_2^2 + 0.40X_3^2}$$

$$\mathbf{Y_2 = +418900 + 9{,}962.38\ X_1 + 15{,}493.75\ X_2 + 25{,}532.63X_3 - 27{,}373.25\ X_1 X_2 - 32{,}450.50\ X_1\ X_3 + 63{,}65.75\ X_2\ X_3 - 48{,}449.50\ X_1^2 - 49{,}534.75\ X_2^2 - 164600\ X_3^2}$$

The model proposed by BBD was subsequently implemented on the system, and the parameters for numerical optimization are outlined in Table 9.12.

Table 9.12. Numerical Optimization Parameters

Constraints						
Name	**Goal**	**Lower limit**	**Upper limit**	**Lower weight**	**Upper weight**	**Importance**
X_1: Flow rate	is in range	0.8	1.2	1	1	3
X_2: pH	is in range	6.6	6.8	1	1	3
X_3: % M.P.	is in range	0	30	1	1	3

Contd...

Solutions						
Number	Flow rate	AA Compo-sition	pH	Desira bility		
1	1	15	6.7	1	Selected	
2	1.2	15	6.8	1		
3	1	30	6.6	1		

Sample extraction (solid phase extraction)

Thawed calibration curve standards and QC samples were vortexed and mixed. Lorazepam internal standard (ISTD) at a concentration of ~50.0 ng/mL was added to labeled tubes. Plasma samples (500 μL) were combined with 200 μL of 5% formic acid and vortexed. HLB cartridges were used for solid phase extraction, with cartridge conditioning using methanol and water. Sample loading and elution were performed under positive pressure. Cartridges were washed with water and eluted with methanol solution (1 mL) twice under pressure. After drying under nitrogen, the eluate was reconstituted in 0.500 mL of mobile phase and transferred to vials for analysis, all procedures conducted under low-light conditions.

LC–MS-MS conditions

Triple quadruple mass spectrometer and Shimadzu HPLC

Column : A Zorbax SB C18, (50 x 4.6 mm, 5 μm

M.P. : Acetonitrile : ammonium acetate (% v/v 85:15)

Flow rate : 1 mL/min

Injection volume :10 μL

Run time : 3.0 min

Rt of sildenafil : 0.7 min

Rt of lorazepam : 0.6 min

MS parameters

Mode : Positive ion mode (turbo ion spray ionization

Curtain gas : 35

Nebulizer : 50

Heater gas : 50

Focusing potential : 10

Collision cell exit potential :12

Ion spray voltage :5,500 V

Temperature : 500°C

Dwell time : 100 ms

The MRM conditions were monitored for the analytes, 475.1/100.1, and IS, 321.0/274.9.

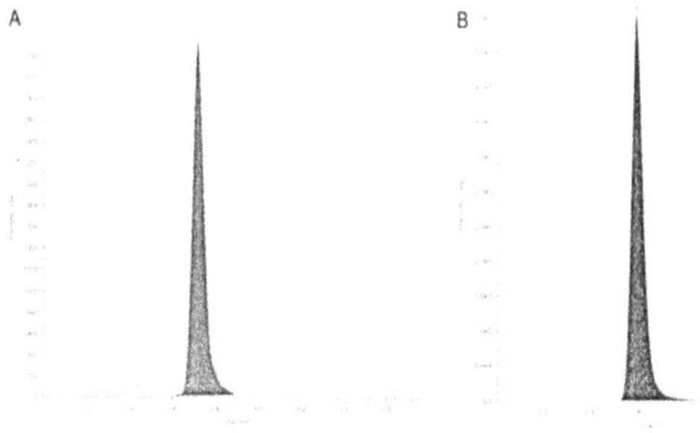

Fig. 9.26. Chromatogram of (A) analyte at LLOQ level. (B) Internal Standard at LLOQ level.

Method validation

Table 9.13. Summary of Validation parameters.

Parameter	Value			
Concentration (ng/mL)	**3.5**	**10.2**	**682.9**	**1360**
Precision (%) - Within batch	5.5	2.4	2.7	1.6
Precision (%) - Between batch	4.7	3.3	1.2	0.9
Accuracy (%) - Within batch	100.1	100.7	100.3	99.9
Accuracy (%) - Between batch	100.1	100.0	99.7	99.7
Concentration (ng/mL)	**10.2**		**1360**	
Stability of Sildenafil in Human Plasma				
Bench-top stability (24 h)	97.6		98.2	
Bench-top extraction stability	95.3		98.9	
Long-term stability (43 days)	99.8		99.3	
Freeze–thaw stability (after 5 cycles)	98.3		97.5	
In injector stability (186 h)	95.4		97.7	
LLOQ	3.47 ng/mL			
r^2	>0.997			
Recovery (extraction) %	Low	Medium	High	
	93.4	85.6	83.8	

***

REFERENCES

1. **UV-Visible Spectrophotometric method development**
    - Monika L. Jadhav, Santosh R. Tambe, Manoj V. Girase, Analytical Quality by Design Approach for development of UV Spectrophotometric Methods in the Estimation of Trospium Chloride from Capsule Dosage Form, *International Journal of Pharmacy and Pharmaceutical Sciences*, 2014, Vol 6, Issue 10, 530-533.
    - Rita B. Prajapati, Priya B. Patel, Rajvi Mahida, Spectrophotometric Determination of Chlorpheniramine Maleate in its Pharmaceutical Dosage form using Quality by Design Approach, *Journal of Pharmaceutical Science and Bioscientific Research*, 2019, 9(6), 260-267.
    - Shanta K. Adiki, Prashanti M, Baishakhi Dey, Prakash Katakam, Fathi H. Assaleh, Nagiat T. Hwisa, Rajeev K. Singla, Babu R. Chandu, Design of Experiment Assisted UV-Visible Spectrophotometric and RP-HPLC method development for Ambrisentan Estimation in Bulk and Formulations, *World Journal of Analytical Chemistry*, 2014, Vol. 2, No. 2, 23-30.
    - Yogita B. Wani, Dipak D. Patil, An experimental design approach for optimization of spectrophotometric method for estimation of cefixime trihydrate using ninhydrin as derivatizing reagent in bulk and pharmaceutical formulation, *Journal of Saudi Chemical Society*, 2017, 21, S101–S111.
2. **HPLC method development**
    - Atul Jain, Teenu Sharma, Gajanand Sharma, Rajneet Kaur Khurana, Om Prakash Katare & Bhupinder Singh, QbD-Driven Analytical Method Development and Validation for Raloxifene Hydrochloride in Pure Drug and Solid Oral Dosage Form, *Analytical Chemistry Letters*, 2019, 9:4, 463-477.
    - Shantanu Bandopadhyay, Sarwar Beg, O.P. Katare, Teenu Sharma, and Bhupinder Singh, Integrated Analytical Quality by Design (AQbD) Approach for the Development and Validation of Bioanalytical Liquid Chromatography Method for Estimation of Valsartan, *Journal of Chromatographic Science*, 2020, Vol. 58, No. 7, 606–621.
    - Surendran Vijayaraj, Narahari N Palei and Thummala Katyayani, Quality by Design (Qbd) Approach to Develop HPLC Method for Estimation of Gliclazide and its Impurity (Gliclazide Impurity A) in Bulk Drug, *Current Pharmaceutical Analysis*, 2019, Volume 15, Issue 7, 716 - 723.
    - Aruna Gundala, KVSRG Prasad, Bharathi Koganti, Application of quality by design approach in RP-HPLC method development for simultaneous estimation of saxagliptin and dapagliflozin in tablet dosage form, *Brazilian Journal of Pharmaceutical Sciences*, 2019;55:e18129, 1-10.

3. **GC method development**
   - Joydeep Mazumder, Devender Pathak, Rachna Kumria, Analytical Method Validation of an Herbal Formulation by Headspace Gas Chromatography Using QbD, *International Journal of Pharmaceutical Sciences and Drug Research*, 2014; 6(4): 291-302.
   - Kyoungmin Lee, Wokchul Yoo and Jin Hyun Jeong, Determination of Three Alkyl Camphorsulfonates as Potential Genotoxic Impurities Using GC-FID and GC-MS by Analytical QbD, *Separations* 2022, 9, 246.
   - Silvia Robu, Aurelia Romila, Olimpia Dumitriu Buzia, Adrian Florin Spac, Camelia Diaconu, Dana Tutunaru, Elena Lisa, Aurel Nechita, Contribution to the Optimization of a Gas Chromatographic Method by QbD Approach used for Analysis of Essential Oils from Salvia officinalis, *Revista de Chimie (Bucharest)*, 2019, Vol. 70, No. 6, 2015-2020
   - Kyoungmin Lee, Wokchul Yoo and Jin Hyun Jeong, Analytical Method Development for 19 Alkyl Halides as Potential Genotoxic Impurities by Analytical Quality by Design, *Molecules* 2022, 27, 4437.
4. **HPTLC method development**
   - Rajneet Kaur Khurana, Satish Rao, Sarwar Beg, O.P. Katare, and Bhupinder Singh, Systematic Development and Validation of a Thin-Layer Densitometric Bioanalytical Method for Estimation of Mangiferin Employing Analytical Quality by Design (AQbD) Approach, *Journal of Chromatographic Science*, 2016; 54(5): 829–841.
   - Amod Shivaji Patil, Atul Arun Shirkhedkar, Application of Quality by Design in the Development of HPTLC Method for Estimation of Anagliptin in Bulk and in-house Tablets, *Eurasian Journal of Analytical Chemistry*, 2017, 12(5):443-458.
   - Pintu Prajapati, Hitika B. Patel, Shailesh Shah, DoE based failure mode effect analysis (FMEA) to development of stability indicating HPTLC method for estimation of apremilast, *SN Applied Sciences* (2020) 2:1371.
   - Pintu Prajapati, Vipul Radadiya, Shailesh Shah, Failure Mode Critical Effect Analysis and Design of Experiment-Based Robust Chromatographic Method for Simultaneous Estimation Lornoxicam and Eperisone Hydrochloride, *Journal of Chromatographic Science*, 2020, Volume 58, Issue 10, 929–939.
5. **Bioanalytical method development**
   - Mohammad Saquib Hasnain, Salman Siddiqui, Shireen Rao, Priyadarsan Mohanty, Tahseen Jahan Ara, and Sarwar Beg, QbD-Driven Development and Validation of a Bioanalytical LC–MS Method for Quantification of Fluoxetine in Human Plasma, *Journal of Chromatographic Science*, 2016, Volume 54, Issue 5, 736–743.

- Preeti Bhatt, M Saquib Hasnain, Amit Kumar Nayak, Bushra Hassan & Sarwar Beg, Development and Validation of QbD-Driven Bioanalytical LC-MS/MS Method for the Quantification of Paracetamol and Diclofenac in Human Plasma, *Analytical Chemistry Letters*, 2018, 8:5, 677-691.
- ASK Sankar, Shanmugasundaram Palani, and Ravichandiran Velayudham, Quality by Design–Applied Liquid Chromatography-Tandem Mass Spectrometry Determination of Enzalutamide Anti-Prostate Cancer Therapy Drug in Spiked Plasma Samples, *Analytical Chemistry Insights*, 2017;12, 1-11.
- M. Saquib Hasnain, Shaukat Ali Ansari, Shireen Rao, Mohammad Tabish, Mukul Singh, Mohammad Syafiq Abdullah, Mohammed Tahir Ansari, QbD-Driven Development and Validation of Liquid Chromatography Tandem Mass Spectrometric Method for the Quantitation of Sildenafil in Human Plasma, *Journal of Chromatographic Science*, 2017, Volume 55, Issue 6, 587–594.

***

INDEX

Note: Page numbers followed by *"f"* and *"t"* refer to figures and tables, respectively.

***

www.ingramcontent.com/pod-product-compliance
Lightning Source LLC
Chambersburg PA
CBHW031352230926
51848CB00002B/492
9789349488427

മാറി മറിഞ്ഞുപോയ്
ഓർമ്മകൾ തിങ്ങിയൊരു
നെടുവീർപ്പിൽ പോയ കാലം
ചിത്രങ്ങൾ നെയ്തു
ഇനിയെല്ലാം നിശ്ചലം
അങ്ങോട്ടോയിങ്ങോട്ടോയില്ല
മറിക്കാനായി താളുകൾ
മായ്ക്കുവാനാവാത്ത ഇന്നത്തെ അക്കം
ചുവന്നനിറത്തിൽ അടയാളമാവും
അപ്പോഴും മിടിക്കുന്ന ഹൃദയങ്ങൾ
നാളെകൾക്കായുള്ള നെട്ടോട്ടത്തിൽ
മറിയുന്നു കലണ്ടറിൻ
താളുകൾ നിലയ്ക്കാതെ

അക്കം തീർന്ന കലണ്ടർ

നഷറ സി.എച്ച്.
ആലത്തൂർ

കലണ്ടറിന്റെ താളുകൾ
കാറ്റിൽ കലമ്പിയാടി
താഴെ നിശ്ചല ശരീരവുമായി
അവൾ നീണ്ടു നിവർന്നു കിടന്നു
അടുത്ത 25 ന് മകളുടെ
വിവാഹമാണ്.
അതിന്റെ ഒരുക്കങ്ങളുടെ
തകൃതിക്കിടയിലാണ്
അവളുടെ യാത്ര
അവളെ സംബന്ധിച്ച്
കാലഹരണപ്പെട്ട
അക്കങ്ങൾ അവസാനിച്ച
കാലക്രമീകരണം
അപ്രസക്തമാണ്
എന്നാൽ
ജീവിച്ചിരിക്കുന്നവർക്ക്
തീർച്ചയായും
മറ്റൊരു കലണ്ടർ അക്കം
അനിവാര്യമാണ്
വേനലും, വർഷവും
നിറഞ്ഞു പൂത്ത വസന്തവും
താളുകളിൽ അക്കങ്ങളായെത്ര

വാത്സല്യം നിറഞ്ഞ അമ്മ

നിജിൻ യു.ആർ.

താരാട്ട് പാട്ടിന്റെ ഈണം
അമ്മ നൽകുന്ന വാത്സല്യപ്പൂക്കൾ
ഓർക്കുവാനെന്തു ചേല്
ബാല്യം സുന്ദര മഞ്ജുതലോകം
പിഞ്ചു പാദങ്ങളിലങ്ങ് ഓട്ടും
വീഴും പുഴയിൽ കണ്ണീരാലാകും
വാരിപ്പുണർന്നമ്മ ഉമ്മ
കളേകും
തലോടിയാ വേദന തീർക്കും
കുസൃതികൾ കണ്ടു ജ്വലിക്കുമ്മ
കോപഠതല്ലായി മാറുന്ന നേരത്ത്
പൈതലിൻ പുഞ്ചിരിക്കൊഞ്ചൽ
കണ്ടമ്മ സ്നേഹത്തിൻ
പാൽക്കടലാകും